# MISTAKING AFRICA

17-41

# MISTAKING AFRICA

*Curiosities and Inventions*
*of the American Mind*

THIRD EDITION

## Curtis Keim

MORAVIAN COLLEGE

WESTVIEW
PRESS

A MEMBER OF THE PERSEUS BOOKS GROUP

Westview Press was founded in 1975 in Boulder, Colorado, by notable publisher and intellectual Fred Praeger. Westview Press continues to publish scholarly titles and high-quality undergraduate- and graduate-level textbooks in core social science disciplines. With books developed, written, and edited with the needs of serious nonfiction readers, professors, and students in mind, Westview Press honors its long history of publishing books that matter.

Find us on the World Wide Web at www.westviewpress.com.

Every effort has been made to secure required permissions for all text, images, maps, and other art reprinted in this volume.

Westview Press books are available at special discounts for bulk purchases in the United States by corporations, institutions, and other organizations. For more information, please contact the Special Markets Department at the Perseus Books Group, 2300 Chestnut Street, Suite 200, Philadelphia, PA 19103, or call (800) 810-4145, ext. 5000, or e-mail special.markets@perseusbooks.com.

Designed by Timm Bryson

Library of Congress Cataloging-in-Publication Data
Keim, Curtis A.
    Mistaking Africa : curiosities and inventions of the American mind /
Curtis Keim.—3rd ed.

        p. cm.

    Includes bibliographical references and index.
    ISBN 978-0-8133-4894-0 (paperback)—ISBN 978-0-8133-4895-7 (e-book)
1. Africa—Foreign public opinion, American.    2. Africa—In mass media—United States.    3. Public opinion—United States.    I. Title.
DT38.7.K45 2013
960—dc23

                                        2013005324


10  9  8  7  6  5  4  3  2  1

*To George Brooks,*
*Phyllis Martin, and David Waas*

# Contents

## PART TWO
# EVOLUTIONISM

### PART THREE
# FURTHER MISPERCEPTIONS

**PART FOUR**
# NEW DIRECTIONS

# Preface

Over the years that I have been teaching Africa survey courses, I have found that students' ability to approach the continent is deeply influenced by American stereotypes about Africa. Many students filter accurate information through their inaccurate stereotypes, thus making learning less effective than it could be. Therefore, I have written this book for students and others who are just beginning to think about Africa and need to consider how we commonly misperceive and misrepresent Africa. At the beginning of every course, I take time to discuss our heritage of ideas about Africa. I ask students to explore what our stereotypes are, how we have acquired them, where they appear in our culture, and why they persist. As each course proceeds, I find moments when students can pause to think about how our stereotypes relate to the topics at hand.

Africanist scholars have extensively described and criticized American stereotypes about modern Africa. They have had the most obvious successes in improving K–12 textbooks, children's literature, and news reporting, but their studies apply to numerous areas of American culture. Thus, I have been able to rely on experts in many fields for both ideas and examples. My own contributions lie in having gathered and organized many ideas, located further examples, and written accessibly, primarily for undergraduate college and university students.

As in the other editions, the chapters in this volume are brief, and each chapter can more or less stand on its own. Teachers thus have many options for how they use the book, ranging from assigning one or two chapters to basing an entire course on the book's ideas. In the latter case, students may examine some of the sources referred to in this book and find many new examples. They may also interview Africans or people who have traveled to Africa as tourists or missionaries, on business, or otherwise.

The first and second editions both found their way to many readers other than college and university students. I have received mail from many Africans who have thanked me for putting into words what they have often felt about American perceptions of Africa. I am frequently amazed by the good grace with which Africans observe our misunderstanding of their homelands. I am also pleased that the first two editions helped diplomats, travelers, church groups, international student advisers, reporters, K–12 teachers, and others to think about how we treat Africa. I hope this third edition will be equally useful to those who are not students.

This book is mostly about what Africa is *not*. For those readers who want to learn more about what Africa *is* and who do not have access to an Africanist specialist as a guide, I have added a brief section at the end of the book on how to learn more about Africa and how to find teaching resources.

# Acknowledgments

In the acknowledgments for the first and second editions, I listed friends and colleagues who helped me research, write, and edit those works. Their help also shaped this edition, and I thank them again. Thank you especially to Hwa Yol Jung and other colleagues at Moravian College for their scholarly encouragement and support.

During the summer and fall of 2012, Kyle Davies, a history major at Moravian College, was my assistant and colleague as we searched for up-to-date ideas and examples for this edition. I also thank Sarah Soden, a graduate, who continues to send examples of advertisements and articles that treat Africa as exotic, natural, or primitive.

At Westview Press, I especially thank Priscilla McGeehon, executive editor; Annie Lenth, project editor; and Deborah Heimann, copyeditor. Thanks also to the following reviewers who offered valuable suggestions for making the third edition more helpful in their classrooms: Esperanza Brizuela-Garcia, Montclair State University; Trevor Getz, San Francisco State University; J. Akuma-Kalu Njoku, Western Kentucky University; and Jonathan Reynolds, Northern Kentucky University.

My greatest appreciation goes to my family—Karen Keim, Nathan Keim and Stephanie Wissel, Ann West, and Steve Keim—who continually share acts of kindness and support.

— *C. A. K.*

## PART ONE

# INTRODUCTION

# 1

# CHANGING OUR MIND ABOUT AFRICA

Most of us who are Americans know little about Africa. We might have studied Africa for a few weeks in school or glanced occasionally at newspaper headlines about genocide, AIDS, malaria, or civil war, but rarely have we actually thought seriously about Africa. If we do want to learn about Africa, it is difficult to find ample and accurate information in our popular media such as television and newspapers. Africa and its people are simply a marginal part of American consciousness.

Africa is, however, very much a part of the American subconscious. Ironically, although we know little about Africa, we carry strong mental images of the continent. Once you begin to notice, you find that Africa appears in the American public space quite frequently. Although it may not figure often in the news, it shows up in advertising, movies, amusement parks, cartoons, and many other corners of our society. And although most Americans do not possess many facts about Africa, we do know certain general truths about the continent. We know, for example, that Africans live in tribes. And we know that Africa is a place of famine, disease, poverty, coups, and large wild animals.

General images are useful and perhaps necessary for our collective consciousness. We can't know everything about the world, so we have to lump some things into big categories that are convenient if lacking detail. Life is too short for most of us to become experts on more than a couple of subjects. Thus, these images help us to organize Africa's place in our collective mind. A war in Congo? Ah, yes, that's more of the "African trouble" category. Elephants being used in a commercial? Yes, wouldn't it be fun to have an elephant wash your car. There are lots of large animals living in the wilds of Africa, aren't there?

If our general categories are reasonably accurate, they help us navigate our complex world. If, however, they are inaccurate, these categories can be both dangerous and exploitative. If, for example, we are wrong about Africa's supposed insignificance, we will be blindsided by political, environmental, or even medical events that affect how we survive. Or, if we think of Africa only as a place of trouble, a large zoo, or a storehouse of strategic minerals rather than as a place where real people live real lives, we will likely be willing to exploit the continent for our own purposes. France's former president François Mitterrand demonstrated this possibility graphically when, speaking to his staff in the early 1990s about Rwanda, he noted that "in some countries, genocide is not really important."[1] Although in the short term the exploitation of Africa might help France or us, in the long term the planet's society and environment will pay dearly for our failure to care.

## Speaking "African"

Anyone who wants to study Africa in depth needs to learn African languages, because language is the major key to understanding how people mentally organize the world around them. Likewise, anyone who wants to understand Americans must examine the words Americans know and use. You can begin to discover American ideas about Africa by trying some free association with the word *Africa*. Ask yourself what words come to mind when you hear *Africa*. Be aware that this is not the time to "clean up your act" and impress yourself with your political correctness. Rather, search for the words your society has given you to describe Africa, some of which will seem positive, some negative, and some neutral.

My students have helped me create lists of words that come to mind during such an exercise. Within a few minutes, a class frequently generates thirty or forty words that Americans associate with Africa. *Native, hut, warrior, shield, tribe, savage, cannibals, jungle, pygmy, pagan, voodoo,* and *witch doctor* are commonly associated with "traditional" Africa. "Tourism words" include *safari, wild animals, elephant, lion,* and *pyramid.* There are also "news words," including *coup, poverty, ignorance, drought, famine, tragedy,* and *tribalism.* And then there is a group of "change words" (indicating Western-induced change), such as *development, foreign aid, peacekeeping,* and *missionary.* Occasionally, a really honest person will come up with "racist words" he or she has heard, like *spear chucker* or *jungle bunny.*

Although some American words might be positive—*kinship, wisdom,* or *homeland*—the overwhelming impression gained from studying American language about Africa is that Africa is a primitive place, full of trouble and wild animals, and in need of our help. A survey by a major American museum on popular perceptions of Africa found a number of widely held misconceptions, including the following: Africa is just one large country; Africa is all jungle; Africans share a single culture, language, and religion; Africans live in "grass huts"; Africans mainly hunt animals for their subsistence; and Africa has no significant history.

If you think you have escaped these concepts, you are either extraordinarily lucky or you fool yourself easily. The messages that perpetuate such impressions pervade American culture. They are ideas that have deep roots in American history as well as strong branches that entwine our daily lives. At one time in our history, most of white America did not even consider Africans to be equal as humans! By comparison, today's understanding is positively enlightened. Yet historical misperception, ignorance, stereotype, and myth still cast shadows upon our thinking. Once you begin to look for them, you see inaccurate portrayals of Africa that reproduce the blatant old images in subtler, modernized versions. In fact, a worthwhile exercise is to ask yourself where the words listed above have come from. Home? School? Church? Friends? Television? Newspapers? Magazines? Movies? Books? Amusement parks? It is difficult to get complete and balanced views of Africa in everyday American life. This topic will be discussed further in Chapter 2.

This book investigates the histories of our inaccurate and stereotypical words and ideas and suggests alternatives. For example, Africans are sometimes referred to in everyday America as "natives." You may or may not think that *native* is a negative word, but its use is a legacy of the colonial period in Africa, when words were weapons employed by outsiders to keep Africans in their places. In the first part of the twentieth century, most Americans believed that Africans could be (indeed, *should* be) subjugated because they were primitives, natives. The problem is not the term itself, however. The first dictionary definition of *native* is someone who belongs originally to a place. Thus, "He is a native of Boston" is a neutral and acceptable use of the word. We also use *native* in a positive political way in the term *Native American,* which implies that an "American Indian" has rights and connections that go beyond those belonging to the rest of us who are more recent immigrants. But the term *African native* evokes a negative connotation, whether intended or not, that is a holdover from its colonial meanings of primitive, savage, or unenlightened. Why can we think of Africans as natives, but never the Chinese? The answer is that we have long thought of Africans as primitive and Chinese as civilized. Today, even when we intend no insult to Africans, we have these leftover phrases and connotations that get in the way of conceiving of Africans as real people like ourselves.

You can get around the "African native" and "native African" problem in a number of ways. For example, if you are referring to an African living in a rural area, you can say "a rural African." If you mean someone who is an inhabitant of Africa, just say "an African." If you mean someone who belongs to the Kikuyu ethnic group, use the words "a Kikuyu." These phrases are more precise and therefore less likely to create images that evoke stereotypes. And, to avoid even a hint of insult, you might steer clear of phrases like "He is a native of Kenya," which in most other contexts would be neutral but in the African context might elicit musings on whether you are referring to the stereotype.

## The Use and Misuse of Stereotypes

In an ideal world, we would abandon our stereotypes about Africa and learn to deal with Africans as they really are. Human cognition does not allow this, however. Everybody stereotypes. And we do it about practically everything. The reason for this is, first of all, that we are biologically wired to try to make sense of reality, even when it makes no particular sense. Whether through science, history, literature, religion, or whatever, humans strive to understand and categorize what is in front of them. We also stereotype because it is virtually impossible to know everything that is going on in reality, and therefore we are bound to base our judgments on partial information. Moreover, we often use ideas provided by our culture instead of investigating things for ourselves. If our culture has a pre-made picture of reality for us, we are likely to accept it. One way to think about this is to invert the notion "seeing is believing," making it "believing is seeing." Once we "know" something through our culture, we tend to fit new information into the old categories rather than change the system of categorization.

To say that we inevitably use stereotypes is really to say that we use mental models to think about reality. But the word *stereotype* also implies that some models are so limiting that they deform reality in ways that are offensive, dangerous, or ridiculous. Thus we need to strive to make our mental models as accurate as possible. We should, for example, study African art, history, literature, philosophy, politics, culture, and the like so we can differentiate between Africans. We should also ask ourselves whether we cling to inaccurate models of Africa because they shore up our self-image or allow us to do things otherwise unthinkable.

Following are brief discussions that explore different reasons for the persistence of our misconceptions about Africa. Later in the book I offer extended discussions of many of these topics.

## *Leftover Racism and Exploitation*

During much of American history, a large majority of Americans considered racism and exploitation of Africa acceptable. Although the United States never ruled colonies in Africa, Americans did enslave Africans and maintain both a slavery system and segregation. Moreover, we profited from our businesses in Africa, sent missionaries to change African culture, and did not protest the colonization undertaken by Europeans. This exploitation of Africa, whether direct or indirect, required thinking about Africans as inferiors. In other words, our culture has had a lot of practice, hundreds of years of it, in constructing Africa as inferior. The legacy is obvious in the words and ideas we call to mind when we hear the word *Africa*.

Our legacy of negativity poses a question: Can we attribute a major portion of our modern stereotypes about Africa to our just not having gotten around to changing the myths we inherited from our racist and imperialist past? Perhaps we no longer need most of these myths, but they persist because only a few decades have passed since the end of the colonial period and it has been a similarly brief amount of time since the passage of the US Civil Rights Act of 1964.

Support for this view comes from the fact that African independence and the civil rights movement have made it increasingly unacceptable for news reporters and commentators to use the most blatantly negative of the words we once associated with race and with Africa. Likewise, schoolbooks are vastly improved in their treatment of Africa. One could argue that with greater sensitivity to the issue and more time, Americans will change. To put this idea another way, shouldn't we give Americans the benefit of the doubt and assume that most people do not consciously intend to exploit or misrepresent Africa? I believe that we should.

## Current Racism

I am assuming that most readers are not intentionally racist, because people who are probably wouldn't read this kind of book. While the most derogatory images of Africa can no longer appear in public spaces, they persist because we learn them in the more private aspects of our lives, from family and friends, and often through jokes or offhand comments. Unfortunately, such private racism is difficult to eradicate, because continuing efforts like this book can do little for those who would not seriously consider them. Others of us, perhaps most of us, are a different kind of racist, for although we truly want to believe that all humans are equal, we entertain undercurrents of racist doubt in our minds that make us susceptible to more subtle myths about Africa. It is this real but unintentional racism that concerns us here, because a deeper consideration of the issues can help us see Africans more clearly.

It would be incorrect, however, to say that all or even most of the public stereotypes about Africa come from unintentional racism. First, each of us has negative, nonracist stereotypes about others. Second, not all of our stereotypes about Africa are negative. Inaccuracy and insensitivity are not necessarily racist, even when they have racist roots and produce racist results. This is a fine distinction to make, especially if you are a victim of racism, and it seems a useful distinction if we are to help decent, willing people to see Africa in new ways.

## Current Exploitation

We also perpetuate negative myths about Africa because they help us maintain dominance over Africans. From our perspective in the United States, it is difficult for us to see how globally influential our country actually is. In simple terms, we are a superpower. To wield this kind of might and still think of ourselves as good people, we need powerful myths. Whereas in the past the myth of the racial inferiority of Africans was the major justification for Western control of Africans, now cultural inferiority is a more likely reason. Our news media, for example, are much more likely to inform us about African failures than about African successes. And the successes we do hear about tend to demonstrate that our own perspectives on reality are correct. It doesn't take much imagination to figure out that modern Americans who deal with Africa—bureaucrats, aid workers, businesspeople, missionaries, and others—might have an interest in describing Africa in ways that justify the importance of their own work.

## Entertainment

If Africa were portrayed as being "just like us," it would be quite uninteresting. "Man bites dog" sells more newspapers than "Dog bites man." The word *exotic* describes the point; *exotic* portrays African culture as excitingly different. Usually this is at the expense of African culture, which is removed from its everyday context in a way that allows us to believe that the culture is exceptional rather than common like ours. Movies and novels thrive on this sort of thing. America, too, is often portrayed overseas as exotic, and we are thus frequently mistaken. In his book *American Ways*, for example, Gary Althen describes an international student who was misled by myths about exotic America. Coming to the United States having watched American movies, the student expected to find a lot of women ready for sexual activity with him. Actually, he found them, but it took him nearly two years to figure out that such easy women were also marginal and often disturbed and that more desirable women were not so readily available.[2]

I provide African examples in later chapters, but give a first illustration here. One *National Geographic* issue includes a short article on the gold of the Asantehene, the traditional ruler of the Asante people in Ghana.[3] Ten beautiful photographs show the gold clothing and ornaments of the Asantehene, his court, and his relatives. But the authors make almost no effort to tell us how all of this fits into the life of the Asante or of the modern country of Ghana. Presumably, *National Geographic* does not intend to portray Africans in stereotypical ways. Without (con)text, however, the reader might think almost anything.

This is exoticism. Exoticism portrays only a portion of a culture and allows the imagination to use stereotypes to fill in the missing pieces. Most frequently, when we supply the missing pieces, we extrapolate that other people are more different from us than they are similar. Thus we can too easily sustain our myths about Africans and believe that words such as *mysterious* and *the Dark Continent* actually apply to Africa.

## Self-Definition

Sometimes we use other people, including Africans, as a mirror. We want to know about them so we can know about ourselves. This very human activity accounts at least partially for our interest in people-watching in parks and the appeal of television sitcoms, movies, literature, history, and many other cultural phenomena. In the case of Africa, we might say that many of us want Africans to be a bit savage so we can feel more satisfied with our own lot in life. The *Looney Toons* announcer on the Cartoon Network puts it well: "Without nuts like these, the rest of us look crazy." Perhaps you have never thought of Bugs Bunny, Daffy Duck, and Elmer Fudd as therapists, but doesn't Africa often serve the same function? If we focus on ourselves without comparison to others, don't we look pretty messed up? But if we can see that others are poorer, less educated, or more chaotic, then it is easier to believe that we are fine despite our problems. To put it differently, we can't be rich without the poor, developed without the underdeveloped, saved without the sinner, normal without the abnormal, civilized without the uncivilized, and so forth.

Our culture is especially susceptible to this kind of thinking because of the way we conceive of time. Our idea of time as a continuum from the past to the future—rather than, for example, as a circle returning to a golden age of the past—is embodied in our concept of progress. For us, progress generally means going forward, moving on, getting over it, improving ourselves, growing up, and a whole collection of other ideas implying that the past is negative and the future is positive. Of course, if we believe this to be true, we will expect reality to substantiate the belief.

Indeed, one way we perceive African reality reveals this way of thinking. We see African community life as basic, but impossible to *return to* in our own communities. And tribalism is something we have *gotten beyond*. It wouldn't help to find much that is of use to us in Africa, because that would contradict our understanding of progress.

Positive myths about Africa also serve Western self-definition. Those who are dissatisfied with modern American life might construct Africa to present viable alternatives. Some might search African customs for a more natural way to live. Some might look to Africa for a less racist culture. Some, specifically African Americans, might be looking for their idealized personal and cultural roots.

## Stereotypes over Time

As Europeans spread across the world from the 1400s onward, they had to make sense of the new peoples and places they encountered. Over time, and for reasons explained later in this book, Africans and Africa became representative of extreme "otherness." They were not the only representatives of difference, of course: there were also Aborigines, Native Americans, and so forth. But Africa certainly became a primary symbol that Europeans and white Americans used to express difference. Even black Americans found Africa's difference useful at times.

Fortunately, with each passing decade, Americans have been treating Africans with less prejudice. Perhaps we are in the midst of a real withdrawal, however slow, from the myths of primitive Africa. Indeed, we cannot afford such myths. Africa, because of its sheer size, population, resources, and modernization, will play an increasingly important role in the world, whether for good or ill, and will have to be taken seriously. Our long-term interest in our shrinking world is to understand Africa with as little bias as possible.

The point is not that an accurate and whole picture of Africa has to be totally positive. Indeed, such a claim would be a continuation of our stereotyping. What we should strive for is a view of Africa as a continent full of real people, both like us and not like us. On the surface this seems easy: "It's a small world after all!" "Why can't we just get along?" "All we need is love!" "Just leave them alone." But these stereotypical, facile solutions don't automatically work in the real world. As you will find in the pages that follow, seeing others as fully human without desiring to change them into ourselves is exceedingly difficult. It may be, however, the only thing that will make our home—the planet—a safe place to live.

# A Word About Words

Before we go any further, a warning is in order. As I wrote this text, I realized that some of the words I use regularly are problematic. For example, the word *Africa* is used incorrectly throughout the book, because I mean "Africa south of the Sahara." This is a problem that might be helped by replacing all occurrences of *Africa* with *sub-Saharan Africa*. However, that would make reading difficult, and the change would not solve the problem entirely. For example, not all sub-Saharan Africans are the subjects of the stereotypes discussed in this book, assuming we consider the millions of European Africans in South Africa, Zimbabwe, Kenya, and elsewhere to be Africans. Following the example of other scholars, I have opted to use the convenient expression *Africa* instead of a more accurate term. I assume that readers understand what is meant and will fill in missing qualifiers where needed.

Likewise, terms such as *Westerners* and *Americans*, and the pronouns *we* and *our*, are frequently distortions of the truth. There is, you will agree, no such thing as an average American, just as there is no such thing as an average African. As I wrote this book, I found myself generalizing and perhaps overgeneralizing about Americans for the sake of calling attention to "our" stereotyping of Africans. We need to remember, however, that in every era there have been Americans who did not accept the general view and who spoke out on behalf of Africans.

One of the biggest difficulties with generalizing about American views of Africa concerns the inclusion of African American views. The problem is complex because American culture is complex. Until at least the 1960s, for example, it was quite common for African Americans to think of Africans as having primitive cultures. This should not be too surprising, considering the dominance of European culture and the fact that most information about Africa was filtered through European American eyes. Thus when I say that "we Americans" believed Africa to be primitive, it can be taken as somewhat accurate for black as well as white Americans.

On the other hand, African Americans since well before the American Revolution have resisted white efforts to define black reality, and therefore they cannot be said to have invented the idea of African primitiveness, even if they believed in portions of it. They were victims in much the same way that Africans have been victims. Moreover, African Americans have largely rejected white American interpretations of race, and many have attempted to teach America about African achievements. Until the mid-twentieth century such teachers were largely ignored, but their efforts make it more difficult to generalize about "Americans."

In this book, I have usually focused on white American myths about Africa—because they have been the most dominant, the most negative, and the most in need of change. Although I include a brief summary of African American perspectives in Chapter 5, the subject deserves a fuller treatment. What seems most strikingly similar about white and black American perspectives on Africa is that all of us have generally "used Africa to think with." Whether Africa has been constructed in a negative or positive manner, we have used the continent to reflect upon who *we* are in relation to each other and in relation to Africa. Much of this thinking, negative and positive, has stereotyped Africa in ways explained in this book.

# 2

# HOW WE LEARN

In the 1970s, scholars of Africa realized that American high school textbooks were filled with stereotypes about Africa. With the coming of independence for African countries in the 1960s and with the American civil rights movement, the most glaring myths had disappeared, but less obvious myths persisted. In a 1978 study, *Africa in Social Studies Textbooks*, Astair Zekiros and Marylee Wiley detailed the extent to which our public schools were perpetuating myths and inaccuracies about Africa. They noted that most textbooks were written by "'armchair' authors who rely on weak sources for their own information." Thus, no matter what the textbook authors were discussing, they tended to make Africa look like the place they imagined rather than the one that existed.[1]

While several decades later our textbooks are much better, today's most common experiences for high school students are either not to study Africa at all or to acquire more Dark Continent myths. By the time students get to college, most still have outdated ideas about the continent. A 2007 survey asked American college students studying in several African countries to describe their attitudes toward Africa before and during their time there. When asked what they had *expected* to find in Africa, they provided words much like the ones described in Chapter 1, especially *poor, dangerous, hot, underdeveloped, violent, tribal,* and *spiritual.* When they described how they felt *after* spending time in Africa, they emphasized words such as *beautiful, diverse, friendly, culture misunderstood, developing, changing,* and *vibrant,* and overall the students' perceptions were significantly more positive.[2] My own experience with students mirrors this study.

Both teachers and students are bombarded with mistaken images of Africa in our everyday culture, so it is not surprising that they often mistake Africa for what it is not. Correcting these errors is not a losing battle, but it *is* an uphill one. If readers of textbooks and teachers of classes are wearing tinted glasses, even the most accurate texts will appear to be the same color as the glasses. What is the tint of these glasses? "Americana," the hue of our cultural heritage. Thus, to know how Americans learn about Africa, we must look at the more general culture in which our glasses get manufactured.

## Television Culture

One way to study how we learn about Africa is to examine *popular culture,* the ordinary information we get from television, magazines, movies, novels, and other common sources. This approach leads us first to television. In sheer numbers of programs, Africa is actually better represented on American television than are many other areas of the world. Regrettably, however, the shows do not provide a very accurate view of Africa, in part because of the large number of nature programs. Today's nature shows still tend to portray Africa as a place filled with wild animals, park rangers, and naturalists who battle against poachers and encroaching agriculture. By featuring carnivores, the programs also use Africa to emphasize "survival of the fittest" motifs. Yet most Africans never see many wild animals because they live in towns or in parts of the continent where the human population is dense. Furthermore, relationships in nature are vastly more complex than those symbolized by the few large animals that nature programs favor.

As stations on cable and satellite television have multiplied, so have programs on African *people.* The number of programs is not great, but from time to time the Learning Channel, the Discovery Channel, the History Channel, Black Entertainment Television, the Travel Channel, and other stations show Africa-related ethnographies and documentaries. What is still lacking, despite the growing number of programs, is a serious understanding of how Africans currently live. Today, 40 percent of

Africans live in cities, and most rural Africans are deeply connected to cities in one way or another. Why, then, do shows about African culture rarely show a city scene, middle-class Africans, a paved road, or a farmer producing a crop that will be sold in a town or eventually reach us? One reason is that urban documentaries are more difficult to film than those about life in rural areas. Most African elites live in cities and don't like reporters and filmmakers prying into their affairs.

Perhaps a more significant reason for television's preference for rural over urban Africa is our ongoing romance with the exotic. We consider nature and the life of people with less contact with modern cultures more interesting and more enlightening than studies of everyday modern African life. An African shopping mall or television studio isn't as interesting to us as life in an African village. Thus, greater television access to Africa as a result of the cable revolution has rarely led to a more complete image of African life. A 2011 episode of *Bizarre Foods*, for example, visited a rural Madagascar village and, despite its respectful treatment of individual villagers, described the village as an example of what life was like in the Middle Ages.[3] The host's Travel Channel web page adds, "Most people still live the way they did 100s of years ago—hunting and gathering for food."[4]

But this is not true for Madagascar or for the village visited in the program. It is true that Madagascar is largely rural, quite poor, and badly governed. But most people are farmers and herders, not hunter-gatherers, and UNICEF reports that in 2010 life expectancy was a strong sixty-six years, most children were immunized against childhood diseases, the incidence of HIV was low, 40 percent of people had mobile phones, 80 percent of children finished primary school, two-thirds of those under twenty-five years old were literate, and girls were as literate as boys.[5] This is hardly the Middle Ages.

If we can only rarely find a whole picture of Africa on television shows, we should be able to turn to television news to find out about contemporary Africa. Yet here the picture is even bleaker. What usually prompts the infrequent appearances of Africa in the news or in news documentaries is a war, coup, drought, famine, flood, epidemic, or accident. Such events certainly occur, but they are not the essence of Africa or of any other part of the world. To be fair, despite the problems, our reporters are providing more context for such news events than ever before. Cable News Network (CNN), for example, occasionally runs stories produced by African reporters. And television coverage of the transition to majority rule in South Africa included a great deal about the history and life of South Africans. Since that time, however, South Africa has almost disappeared from the news except for occasional reports of trouble.

Of course, charges that news reportage is biased are common for all areas of the world, including American cities. Defenders of television news say that reporters have too little time to provide background and that Americans don't want to watch it anyway. Increasingly, news programs border on entertainment. We want our emotions aroused, but not so much that we actually might feel compelled to think deeply or take some kind of action. Moreover, news from Africa is expensive. If all this is true, it is clear that we learn what we want to learn and that we like our picture of Africans the way it is now.

## Newspapers

Newspapers provide about the same coverage of Africa as television news does and for the same reasons. Unless you subscribe to a world-class paper such as the *New York Times*, the *Christian Science Monitor*, or the *Washington Post*, you are likely to find no more than a couple of column inches of space devoted to Africa per week. And the stories tend to be of two kinds: "trouble in Africa" and "curiosities from Africa." The "trouble in Africa" reporting usually follows a pattern. At any given time, only a handful of American reporters cover Africa south of the Sahara, a region containing a population more than twice as large as that of the United States. These reporters either are based in one of the big cities, such as Johannesburg (South Africa), Nairobi (Kenya), or perhaps Abidjan (Côte d'Ivoire), or are visiting these cities. They report on local events, and if trouble arises in a neighboring country, they fly in, get the story, and fly out, or they collect what information they can from where they are. News about Gabon, Nigeria, or Zimbabwe might be broadcast from Abidjan. It sounds authentic because it comes from Africa, but it might as well be from the United States, which has equally good or better communications with most African cities. When there is a big story, reporters flock to it, stay for a while, then leave. And because reporters rarely speak local languages or have well-developed local contacts, the result is shallow reporting. In many cases, we hear nothing from a country for months or years, and then it appears in the news once or even every day for a couple of weeks before disappearing until trouble occurs again.

Charlayne Hunter-Gault—a longtime observer of Africa, reporter for the *New York Times*, correspondent for PBS and National Public Radio, and CNN South Africa bureau chief—makes the point well in her book *New News Out of Africa*. She writes that

> the perception throughout Africa is that foreign media are only interested in stories that fit the old journalistic maxim "If it bleeds, it leads." Much of the shallow coverage of death, disaster, disease, and despair for which foreign media treatments of Africa are criticized derives from what is called "parachute journalism"—dropping in for a brief look at a situation, then flying back out without taking the time to delve deeply into the background or put a story in context.[6]

If we try to put a positive spin on reporting about "trouble in Africa," we might concede that our reporting is about the best we can hope for, considering the difficult conditions under which reporters must work. We are badly served, however, because our news is superficial, sensationalist, and infrequent.

Moreover, because journalists usually do not know local situations well, they often rely on Western-based aid groups for information and perspectives. Karen Rothmyer, who studies Africa news sources, says that Western-based aid groups have an interest in exaggerating both African troubles and the Western role in solving Africa's problems. If Africa has big problems that only outsiders can solve, then the NGOs (nongovernmental organizations) can look good and raise more money.[7]

Ironically, bias in media coverage can also be found in the desire of some reporters to treat Africa well. Ugandan journalist Charles Onyango-Obbo observes that in the 1990s younger liberal Western journalists began reporting on what they termed a "new breed" of African rulers who they supposed would bring democracy, honesty, and development to African governments and economies. In producing such reports, the journalists glossed over the undemocratic and dishonest features of the new regimes, thus allowing the new rulers to believe that the West would look the other way if they acted badly. "Africa, the continent," Onyango-Obbo concludes, is a collection of nations that are pretty much like others elsewhere in the world, struggling with successes and with failures, and there should be no special type of journalism reserved for its coverage. The patronizing reporting one witnesses today is as bad as the condescending work of the past. What the African continent needs is good journalism, one that tells the stories as they are reported and observed. What has happened to coverage of Africa in the Western media today offers the latest proof that there is no alternative to this proven approach.[8]

Stories that can be characterized as "curiosities from Africa" also appear regularly in newspapers. Witchcraft accusations in South Africa, killing of albino persons in Tanzania, crocodile attacks in Zimbabwe, lion killing by young Maasai pastoralists—all these are reported without context, so Africans are made to seem irrational rather than normal. And why isn't there news about normal everyday life in Africa? Weeks go by in my local paper without any substantial news from Africa, and then the paper includes a front-page story about "newest version of Nigeria-based rip-off targets dog lovers," a scam luring people to send money to buy or rescue purebred puppies that don't exist.[9] Is this news about Africa? Yes. Is it interesting? Kind of. Does it give us perspective on what is happening in Africa? Not much. Is it useful? Somewhat. Is it the most important news from Africa? Not at all. Once again, however, we should remind ourselves that there has been progress. In this case, the story about puppies was not about curiosities of African village life, but about Africans living in cities with everyday access to modern tools such as the Internet.

## Magazines

We should do better in our magazines if only because they offer fewer urgent deadlines and more space to provide context. Indeed, journals such as the *New Yorker*, *Atlantic Monthly*, *Current History*, *Discover*, and *Vanity Fair* have published thoughtful, largely unbiased articles about Africa in the last few years. Once again, progress. Yet the number of "trouble in Africa" articles outweighs the number of articles that help us to see Africans as real people attempting to solve their problems in rational ways, even if the solutions might be different from the ones we would choose.

Most Americans read less sophisticated fare as a daily diet. In more popular magazines, most articles about Africa are of the "African safari" genre. A few wild animals, a few natives, a camp, a curio market, a little art, a gourmet meal, and you're home. Other themes include "celebrity goes to Africa," "curious customs," and "African agony." These views of Africa not only evoke stereotypes we already hold but reinforce them as well.

One very popular magazine, *National Geographic*—with an astounding global circulation of over eight million—is America's picture window on the world. What are we likely to see through this window? The editorial policy of the magazine since its early days has been to avoid controversy and print "only what is of a kindly nature . . . about any country or people."[10] That policy, still followed more than a century later, directs the organization toward wild animals and ethnography and away from the social, political, and economic conditions in which Africans live. Countries such as Congo (Kinshasa) and Malawi were featured in the 1970s and 1980s, but in the 1990s most African countries became unsuitable for *National Geographic*. As conditions worsened in Africa, it was increasingly difficult to be kind to modern Africa, at least from the American perspective, and the frequency of *National Geographic* articles dealing with individual African countries declined correspondingly.

In the 1990s and after, *National Geographic* continued to run articles on Africa, but they tended to feature animals. The exceptions are most frequently "trouble in Africa" articles that, for example, warn against environmental deterioration, describe problems with oil extraction, and decry violence. Although often useful, these articles, even taken as a whole, offer a distorted picture of Africa. "Curse of the Black Gold," a 2007 piece, deals with the problems of the oil industry in the Niger Delta (Nigeria) and appropriately points to the failure of aid programs and the neglect of international companies such as Shell. However, the article ends on a pessimistic note, giving no suggestions for action and claiming that there are "no answers in sight."[11] This statement effectively tells the reader not to look for answers and not to act, reaffirming the stereotype of Africa as a hopeless place.

A 2004 article on modern Johannesburg would have been a good place to discuss both the positives and negatives of African urban life. But the article, "City of Hope and Fear," focuses on fear and violence rather than hope in this South African city.[12] The article stands out because only a year later the magazine's sister publication, *National Geographic Traveler*, also included an article on Johannesburg, "Brash and Brilliant," that celebrates "Jo'burg" as a tourist destination.[13] Although portions of South Africa do have high rates of violent crime, as do portions of the United States, journalist Charlayne Hunter-Gault, quoted earlier, chastises the media for focusing on the violence of Johannesburg:

> Many people say that they want to visit Africa for the adventure, for some of the world's greatest natural wonders, and because it is the last best place to see animals not in a zoo. Many tell me they are making plans to go there, especially to South Africa, whose struggle against apartheid engaged so many of them. Then, in the next breath, they express concern about the reports of crime they've heard. One caller shared with me the report his son came back with that "everyone" in South Africa carries a gun, which was news to me, a Johannesburg resident of almost ten years.[14]

While recent *National Geographic* articles treat Africa less stereotypically than in the past, the Dark Continent bias is still there. A 2010 article, for example, considers the issues facing people living in the Omo Valley of Ethiopia. The sympathetic article shows that the people of the area are increasingly in contact with outside forces such as the Ethiopian government, NGOs, Christianity, guns, Western education, cellphones, water pumps, and the damming of their river. But there are disturbing problems with the article. The title, "Africa's Last Frontier," is followed by this statement: "Ethiopia's Omo Valley is still a place ruled by ritual and revenge," implying with the word "still" that all of premodern Africa was once ruled by "ritual and revenge."[15] The article also implies that ritual and revenge are ending only now because of the arrival of Western education, Christianity, and modern values spread by the Ethiopian state. This would seem to indicate that the rest of Africa got rid of the irrationality of "ritual and revenge" only by adopting Western values. Indeed, the author says that because Europeans never colonized Ethiopia, the Omo Valley and its people were left in their premodern state longer than other peoples in Africa. The author seems to know little about African history or about the ritual and revenge that takes place in modern Western politics.

The author has essentially left the Omo peoples without history or culture. To him, they are what they are because that is the *nature* of people before the arrival of modern civilization. We learn nothing about the human circumstances in which revenge killing is used as a way to settle disputes. We learn little about how prevalent revenge killing is among the Omo peoples or about other ways they settle disputes. We learn almost nothing about the last hundred years of Omo history that led to today's situation. And we also don't learn why the author chose to focus on revenge killings rather than the many other aspects of Omo life that are important.

Moreover, while the article at least makes an attempt to situate the local people in an encroaching modern world, the photographs try to tell a much different story. The text says that rich European tourists come to the Valley "hoping for something of the Africa that exists in the Western imagination, all wild animals and face paint and dancing. Tourists say they have come to see the Omo before it becomes like everywhere else."[16] There is a striking photograph of such tourists with their cameras, but most of the article's photos show exactly what the Western imagination would expect of traditional Africa, including wild animals, lip plugs, face paint, and dancing. With bare breasts and naked men, it's like looking at a *National Geographic* from the 1940s or 1950s. The point is not that these things do not exist, but that the bulk of the images conflict so clearly with the theme of the article and with pictures taken by others in the region. The article says, with some difficulty, that these people are not so primitive as Westerners would like to think, while the photographs present a mostly contradictory message. For most readers, which message do you suppose is more powerful?

Finally, the article does not take a position on the new dam on the Omo River, which surely will destroy the lives of the 200,000 people living in the Omo Valley. To the author, the dam is merely part of modernization and globalization, and while it might be regrettable and controversial, it is inevitable. Obviously, were *National Geographic* to oppose the dam and its consequences on behalf of the voiceless people of the Valley, they would be unable to photograph again in Ethiopia, and they would also be shunned by governments in other parts of the world for fear of similar negative comments about what they are doing. Other organizations, like Survival for Tribal Peoples, have been more outspoken about the damage this will cause to the Omo peoples.[17]

*National Geographic*, our window on the world, is rarely a place to get a balanced picture of Africa. This magazine calls itself scientific, yet avoids controversy, thriving on beautiful photography, entertainment, and safe topics. It would have to take such an approach to be so widely accepted in the United States and indeed in the world. Is this publication then useless? No, beauty and safety have their places, and, like our other media, *National Geographic* is improving. Forty years ago *National Geographic* would not have published on topics such as environmental degradation and oil extraction, as it does today. But even if the magazine doesn't actively exploit, it does reinforce our stereotypes by focusing on "natural" and "traditional" Africa, and it confuses us by asserting that beauty, safety, and bland analysis are somehow equal to science and geography.

## Movies

Movies, too, teach us our African stereotypes. Whether oldies such as *The African Queen*, *Mogambo*, and *Tarzan the Ape Man*, or newer pictures such as *The Constant Gardener* and *The Last King of Scotland*, there are dozens of such "African" feature films, and each tells a story that seems to be about Africa but in which Africa only provides an exotic background. One funny movie, *The Gods Must Be Crazy*, a South African shoestring production that has become popular as a video and DVD release, is an exception because of its many scenes featuring African actors. However, it is full of South African white stereotypes of hunter-gatherers, villagers, Cuban revolutionaries, African dictators, and white damsels in distress—pure entertainment. There is nothing wrong with entertainment, of course, except that this is where we pick up our ideas about Africa. Africa has appeared more recently in such feature films as *Tears of the Sun*, *Lord of War*, and *Blood Diamond*. However, as their titles suggest, these movies perpetuate myths of Africa as remote, exotic, and full of violence and disease. All three films echo Leonardo DiCaprio's line in *Blood Diamond*: "God left this place a long time ago."

*Tears of the Sun*, an action film, is an example of how difficult it is to portray Africa as savage while portraying Africans as civilized. The premise of the film is that the Navy SEAL commando played by Bruce Willis delves into war-torn Nigeria to extract an American doctor from the cross fire—the war being flippantly explained in terms of "tribal hatred," as if that phrase is enough to encompass the whole array of causes for war and to silence any hopes of remediation. However, despite its stereotypical basis, the film treats its African characters with relative dignity. African refugees in *Tears of the Sun* arm and defend themselves, and two of them have personalities that are as well developed as those of the white characters. Thus the film's image of Africans as rational, functional human beings conflicts with its overall message that African wars are caused by ancient, "tribal" rivalries and cannot be ended by rational means.

*Lord of War* tells the story of an international arms dealer and features Africa in only its second half. The movie represents Africa as a heart of darkness, the geographic equivalent of the Nicholas Cage character's descent into human depravity in the arms trade. Dialogue from the movie reinforces this idea: the main (white) character refers to the outskirts of Monrovia as "the edge of hell." Individual characters are also shallow: African men are all members of a corrupt and licentious governing elite, and the women are hypersexual and mute. The film gives the sense that Africa is a place even a hardened international arms dealer finds unsettling. Gratuitous images of violence, such as a dead man lying unattended in the street beside a hotel, reinforce this image.

*Lord of War* also evokes African remoteness. In one scene the central character is forced to make an emergency landing and unload his cargo of AK-47s before an Interpol agent catches him. He does so by offering the contents of his plane to a crowd of poor villagers, who strip the plane not only of its contents but of its structure as well, dismantling it for scrap materials.

*Blood Diamond*, the most offensive of the three films, damages the image both of the continent and of the individual African. Solomon, the film's only significant African character, is hollow, unintelligent, and aggressively instinctual. During a scene in which he and the character played by Leonardo DiCaprio are hiding from passing trucks of militants, Solomon thinks he spots his missing son and cries out, alerting the enemy to their presence. He does not seem to realize his mistake even the following day, after a sharp rebuke from DiCaprio. Later, in another chaotic fighting scene (instigated once again by an act of stupidity), in which everyone is using firearms, Solomon picks up a shovel to bash in the head of the man who kidnapped his son.

In *Blood Diamond*, the whites are always the ones scheming, plotting, dealing, and above all, *thinking*. The film's Africans never so much as protest at the injustices of their society, let alone fight back. Solomon, apparently motivated by little more than animal instinct to protect his son, is unable to think through his actions. Dialogue also makes ample use of the abbreviation TIA (for "This is Africa") to dismiss anything violent or distressing that occurs, implying that in Africa, misery is the only way of life.

While it is no longer acceptable to create a film set in Africa that does not feature Africans or that makes overtly racist statements without encasing them in the dialogue of unsavory characters, Hollywood stereotyping of Africa has become veiled rather than less prevalent. Fortunately, several contemporary films from international producers offer more enlightened perspectives. *The Constant Gardener*, *The Last King of Scotland*, *Tsotsi*, *Shake Hands with the Devil*, *Hotel Rwanda*, and *Doctor Bello* are particularly good, though each has its problems. These problems are small, however, compared to those of films produced entirely by Americans.

## Amusement Parks

Busch Gardens Africa in Tampa, Florida, is another prime example of how we learn about Africa and also how this learning process is changing. In the 1970s the park was called Busch Gardens: The Dark Continent. As a result of protests, Busch Gardens Africa has tried to change its "Dark Continent" image. Now the park focuses instead on neutral images: the large animal park, replicas of African houses, African-made tourist art, and rides that have mildly African themes. Nostalgia for nineteenth-century stereotypes persists, however, and thus there are endless inconsistencies. The idea of Ubanga Banga Bumper Cars in the section called The Congo would be hilarious except for the underlying message this stereotypical "African" name sends about Africa. It is strange to think of the Dolphin Theater and Festhaus restaurant being in Timbuktu, a town on the southern edge of the Sahara Desert. The park's Stanleyville area is named after the violent white conqueror of the Congo River, Henry Morton Stanley, and the colonial town that bore his name. Modern Congolese found the name odious enough to change it to Kisangani. And the real Kisangani doesn't have warthogs, orangutans, or a barbecue smokehouse. The conflicts with reality go on and on, but to anyone who knows little about Africa, these inconsistencies aren't readily apparent.

Busch Gardens claims to offer a chance to "immerse yourself in the culture of the African continent as you experience its majestic wildlife."[18] How is observing wildlife equal to participation in anyone's culture? Moreover, how does Busch Gardens' silly version of African culture represent the complexity of African realities? Instead, Busch Gardens Africa teaches Americans damaging stereotypes about Africa.

Another amusement park, Disney World in Orlando, has become a global pilgrimage destination. When I visited, I was reminded of Africa at several turns (literally) as I took the Jungle River Cruise in boats named after real rivers and places in the Congo rain forest (not jungle): Bomokandi Bertha, Wamba Wanda, and so on. It was all fun and a bit hokey, of course, and the site's designers included elephants and a pygmy war camp. But pygmies don't have war camps—they are more like conservationists than soldiers—and Africa is certainly more than elephants, jungles, and riverboats.

The boat trip guides have a rollicking time telling jokes during the trip. For example:

> On the left, a friendly group of native traders. Ukka Mucka Lucka . . . Ubonga Swahili Ungawa . . . Wagga Kuna Nui Ka. . . . It's a good thing I speak their language. [*Turns to guest*] They want to trade their coconuts for your [*wife/child/husband*]. . . . I think we should hold out for at least four.
>
> This is my good friend Sam, who runs the Cannibal Cafe. The last time I talked to Sam was at his cafe. I told him that I didn't like his brother very much. He told me, "Next time, have the salad."[19]

These couldn't be funny if our culture hadn't put Dark Continent images in our heads before the trip.

In 1998 Disney expanded its treatment of Africa with Animal Kingdom, an animal theme park located near Disney World. The African Savanna section of the park is set up to give visitors the sense that they are in a genuinely natural environment. Participants in the Kilimanjaro Safari, which visits the savanna, buy tickets from a window in a building that looks like a decayed colonial-era outpost. Conquest nostalgia is sold here.

And visitors are escorted in buses outfitted to give the feeling of a "real" safari. Further, as visitors pass certain points, underground sensors trigger events in the fashion of similar tours at Disney World and Disneyland. This is wild nature on demand. And there is a story line: you are hot on the trail of a group of poachers. You can save Africa.

Disney also evokes nostalgia for an imagined Africa in the Animal Kingdom Lodge. Here elephant tusks and other trophies give the feeling of a hunting lodge. And, "thatched ceilings, large beams, hand-carved golden-tone furnishings, real African artifacts and a vast mud fireplace in the main lobby surround you in the inimitable spirit of Africa."[20] That inimitable spirit, the supposedly unique essence of Africa, is clearly uninfluenced by the last one hundred years of history.

In Disney's topsy-turvy world, fictional animals compete with real ones, entertainment competes with understanding, an imagined past competes with history, and corporate profits compete with what is termed scientific research. Captivity promotes wildness, we're told, while African complexity is further reduced to stereotypes. And the hunt for poachers models Disney's other enterprises, which from their founding in the 1950s have epitomized the Western dream of the conquest and management of nature through science and technology.

## Other Sources

The other places where we learn our ideas about Africa are too numerous to discuss here. How about children's books, place mats in restaurants, and Africa-themed resorts, billboards, and computer games? I've seen Africa used in exotic, inaccurate, and sometimes offensive ways in each of these examples.

My impression is that children's book authors are ahead of many others in our culture in trying to portray Africa accurately. Nonetheless, there are matters to pay attention to. Yulisa Amadu Maddy, a Sierra Leonean theater artist and director and novelist, has taken an interest in American children's literature related to Africa. He notes that although children's books today intend to capture the positive spirit of Africa, they still contain mistakes that confuse readers and insult Africans. In *The Market Lady and the Mango Tree*, for example, a greedy market lady claims a mango tree that grows in the marketplace as her personal property and refuses to give mangoes to children unless they pay. She buys a Mercedes-Benz with her profits and then begins selling her mangoes to a jelly factory at such a high price that the villagers cannot afford them. In the end, the market lady's guilty conscience makes her sell the car and give the mangoes to children free of charge. It is a well-intentioned story, meant to reinforce community values and favor children, except that it portrays the market lady as a stereotypical rich, power-hungry African elite and the village as responding in helpless, un-African ways. There are no doubt greedy people in Africa, but this short book—despite its positive intentions and excellent illustrations—gives a distorted picture of African reality. Says Maddy, "No one in his or her right mind, no matter how greedy, would claim a mango tree in the marketplace as private property."[21]

Maddy also notes that in Ann Grifalconi's *Flyaway Girl*, east and west are confused: a mask and a food item from West Africa are associated with the Maasai of East Africa. In Paul Geraughty's *The Hunter*, African ivory poachers are blamed for killing elephants when, in fact, Western demand for ivory should also be blamed. Frequently, adds Maddy, stories based on African folktales rely on biased colonial sources that modified the folktales to make Western moral points, not African ones.[22] While most authors of children's books profess universalism, say Maddy and coauthor Donnarae MacCann, there are still many Darkest Africa and neocolonial myths in children's literature about Africa.[23]

Churches and missionaries also play a role in reinforcing the idea of Africans as primitives. Missionaries returning from Africa often communicate to churches in the West that non-Christian Africans need fundamental change because they are culturally, if not biologically, primitive. Ironically, missionaries themselves are often more respectful of African cultures than parishioners in the United States. Those parishioners who give money for African causes frequently want to feel that they are converting or helping poor, unenlightened savages in the old-fashioned missionary mode. The refrain of a 1998 Christian song entitled "Please Don't Send Me to Africa" encapsulates such an attitude toward the continent:

> *Please don't send me to Africa*
> *I don't think I've got what it takes*
> *I'm just a man, I'm not a Tarzan*
> *Don't like lions, gorillas, or snakes*

*I'll serve you here in suburbia*
*In my comfortable, middle-class life*
*But please don't send me out into the bush*
*Where the natives are restless at night*[24]

This sentiment, "Please don't send me to Africa," appears also in sermons, blogs, and other church literature to represent a significant sacrifice.[25] But while intended to satirize the faintness of Christian hearts, it does a severe disservice to Africa. Africa is mistaken as a wild, distant place where animals and restless natives abound and discomfort is standard.

And museums? It's remarkable that we continue the nineteenth-century practice of putting animals and "native" peoples in the same museum, the "natural history" museum. In the American Museum of Natural History in New York, the Field Museum in Chicago, the National Museum of Natural History in Washington, D.C., and many others, the implication is that premodern African cultures belonged to the history of nature rather than the history of civilization. Moreover, such treatment implies that animals and Africans can be considered separately from ourselves in our understanding of the world. Aware of these problems, natural history museum curators do what they can to overcome them.

Art museums pose a somewhat different problem. Art curators must help us understand that what we consider art is not a universal category appreciated in the same way by all humans. When we see a display of African art—in which masks and statues are usually overrepresented—we see something entirely different from what most Africans themselves do. I might add that curators in both art and natural history museums are frequently ahead of their advertising departments in teaching us about Africa. Curators are often trained as specialists in African studies. Publicists, by contrast, are trained to attract an audience, so they often play on exotic and stereotypical aspects that reflect public interest in Africa. They are correct in assuming that the public is interested in the exotic. But because museums are also committed to accuracy, exhibits since the 1990s and their advertising have displayed much less stereotyping.

Corporate advertising also uses Africa to sell products. ExxonMobil, Dow, Snapple, Coca-Cola, Honda, Microsoft, and IBM, among others, have recently produced ads depicting their products in association with Africa. Advertisers easily pick up on our stereotypes and use them to convince us to buy. Moreover, they educate us about what our culture already "knows" about Africa.

These are only some of the ways Africa is misrepresented in our popular culture. Once you are aware of the ways we commonly treat Africa, you will soon (and perhaps frequently) see Africa treated stereotypically in everyday life. I hope you will also begin to think about why our stereotypes persist. Few such treatments are conscious attempts to make Africa look bad. Far from it. Despite American racism, or perhaps because of it, we are probably more sensitive to this question than most other people in the world. At least in the public sphere, we make explicit efforts to avoid derogatory allusions to Africa or Africans. Therefore, such unintended stereotypical references are all the more indicative of how we see the world. Clearly, they indicate that our belief in an Africa full of animals, "the bush," and desperate people is so embraced by Americans that we do not even see it as derogatory. The problem, of course, is that such views become self-perpetuating. Even if we want to avoid portraying Africa in stereotypical terms, we are bound to do so because we have few other models of Africa to which we can compare these images.

## PART TWO

# EVOLUTIONISM

# 3

# THE ORIGINS OF "DARKEST AFRICA"

Across the grasslands of West Africa, the epic of Sundiata continues to be told almost eight hundred years after this hero united the kingdoms of the upper Niger River and founded the massive Mali empire. In the best-known prose translation of the epic, the singer-storyteller Mamoudou Kouyaté begins by relating his qualifications as speaker: "My word is pure and free of all untruth." For him, "the art of eloquence has no secrets." He then commands his audience to pay attention: "Listen then, sons of Mali, children of the black people, listen to my word, for I am going to tell you of Sundiata, the father of the Bright Country, of the savanna land, the ancestor of those who draw the bow, the master of a hundred vanquished kings."[1] In any of its many versions, the ensuing story is full of confidence, adventure, and wisdom. It is the story of "the Bright Country."

How different the Sundiata epic is from the stereotypical Western view of Africa as the Dark Continent. In the Western view, Africa has been a land of primitives who practice the "darkest" of customs, including cannibalism, ritual murder, incest, witchcraft, and incessant warfare. Everywhere Westerners looked in Africa they found depravity. Or they found peoples who had never advanced beyond the stage achieved by European children. They had only rudimentary languages, forms of government, and art—even a rudimentary ability to think.

This dark view of Africa has been so predominant that we must ask where it came from. Scholars have investigated this question by going back to the origins of Western civilization to see whether Africans have always fared so badly. They have concluded that the image of the Dark Continent is a recent fabrication, developed in the nineteenth century as Europeans became increasingly interested in both science and African conquest.

## Africans in Antiquity

In ancient Greece and Rome, race does not seem to have been a significant issue. Frank M. Snowden Jr., who has prepared what is perhaps the most complete study of race in the ancient Mediterranean, states that these civilizations regarded "yellow hair or blue eyes a mere geographical accident, and developed no special racial theory about the inferiority of darker peoples."[2] Indeed, Mediterranean peoples referred to exceptional physical traits to assert the fundamental unity of humanity. Thus, the extraordinary fairness of the Scythians and the darkness of the Ethiopians became lessons in how physical difference should make no difference in judging a person's worth.[3] Cultural conflicts did arise in these times, of course. The various city-states and empires frequently displayed ethnocentrism toward other cultures, and they certainly engaged in war. Nonetheless, at most times a certain cultural equality prevailed that allowed interaction and relatively free traffic in goods and ideas. It was not considered strange to find Ethiopians residing and thriving in Greece, Rome, and elsewhere in the ancient Mediterranean.

We also know that Africa contributed to the other cultures of the Mediterranean. Pre-Arab Egypt and even the Upper Nile kingdoms such as Meroë were relatively well known to Greeks by the fifth century BCE.[4] What we do not know is *how much* the Greeks and others borrowed from Africa. Some historians claim that Greek civilization actually emerged from African ideas and that nineteenth-century European scholarship tried to hide the debt for racist reasons. It will take some time to sort out the evidence, but this debate is largely a modern one over racial bias. In the ancient world, the debate would not have made much sense, because the people of that time didn't think in such racial terms.

The question of race has also been raised with respect to ancient Hebrews and Christians because they are the progenitors of modern Western religions. No evidence, however, points to Jewish or Christian racism toward Africans or anyone else. One does find an effort in Judaism to exclude those who were not Jews, but this exclusion was based on religion and culture, not race. In modern times, Christian racists have insisted that the Hebrew Bible supports the view that God believes blacks to be inferior. Their primary evidence comes from their understanding of Genesis 9:18–29, in which Noah curses his youngest son Ham and Ham's descendants, the Canaanites: "Cursed be Canaan; a slave of slaves shall he be to his brothers." Ham is supposed by some to have been black, and the curse is believed to indicate God's approval of slavery, American segregation, the colonization of Africa, and apartheid. But there is no evidence that the Hebrews saw it this way or that they were anti-African or racist. Today's mainstream biblical scholars agree unanimously that the passage in Genesis was not a condemnation of the black race but an attempt to explain the rift between Israel and Canaan (the name of a people in the eastern Mediterranean and of one of Ham's sons) and to denounce Canaan for its immoral culture. There is no indication in the Bible that the inhabitants of Canaan were black.[5] Nor is there any indication that blacks were considered inferior.[6]

The most frequently studied case in which race might be a factor in the Christian testament comes from the story of Philip, a Christian who baptized the black eunuch treasurer of the queen of Nubia (not Ethiopia, as is often asserted). Superficially, this tale from the Acts of the Apostles might be understood as a comment on race and used as an endorsement of either missions to Africa or racial equality. But modern scholars assert that it was neither and that the issues of Africa and race were not important in the story. Rather, the point was that Christians should accept even eunuchs, whom Jews had refused to receive as converts.[7] Moreover, Snowden writes, the early Christians adopted the Greek view of the unity of humanity and used both Ethiopians and Scythians to illustrate how Christianity was for all. For example, both Origen and Augustine, early Christian commentators, employed the metaphor of blackness to describe the souls of sinners. But in a play on words and ideas, they contrasted the blackness of the Ethiopians' skin, which was natural, with the blackness of a sinner's soul, which was acquired by neglect. All sinners were black, whereas Ethiopians who followed Christ were white. Although blackness was employed as a metaphor for sin, it was specifically dissociated from the blackness of the Ethiopians' skin.[8]

The Arab conquest of North Africa after 639 CE made direct contact between Europeans and black Africans difficult. Thus, black Africa was of minor concern to Europeans for the next eight hundred years. Black Africans did appear in Europe, however, in various roles. One of their most interesting occupations was as "black knights," important characters in some medieval epics. In these epics, African difference was treated in several ways and served as a device to construct medieval ideas about chivalry. In light of modern European racism, it is striking that in the medieval epics, black knights were considered fully human and often exceptionally competent.[9] We also know that Europeans traded regularly with Africans south of the Sahara through Arab intermediaries. Evidence even suggests that the Renaissance in Europe was fueled by the importation of large quantities of West African gold. In addition, the works of a few Arab geographers who traveled to sub-Saharan Africa became available in medieval Europe. Indeed, until the late 1700s, the best knowledge on the interior of sub-Saharan Africa came from Arab sources.

Europeans in ancient and medieval civilizations were, it should be emphasized, ethnocentric, but not particularly racist. They all believed that their civilizations were superior and that others' civilizations were inferior. In general, the less they knew about a civilization the worse they thought about it and its inhabitants. But there is considerable evidence that Europeans considered the Africans who lived in Europe to be fully human.

## Western Views of Africans, ca. 1400–1830

With the opening of Europe's Age of Exploration in the mid-1400s, Africans and other non-Europeans fared increasingly badly in European consciousness. This time, the relationship between Europe and Africa and, indeed, between Europe and the rest of the world was quite different. The Portuguese, Spanish, British, Dutch, and French explorers, and others who followed them, were a pugnacious lot out to profit from non-Europeans, and eventually they conquered most of the world. And yet the Europeans were not mere predators. They felt a need to justify their actions in moral terms, and they frequently wondered about the meaning of their relations with other peoples.

Historian Michael Adas argues that until the mid-eighteenth century, Europeans' perspectives on their relationships with non-Europeans tended to be formulated by and confined to missionaries and philosophers. Less educated Europeans who traveled would have found it difficult to originate such broader views, because they were largely ignorant of the achievements of their *own* civilization. They could not have made comparisons, for example, between Europe and Africa or between Europe and China. This was fortunate for Africa in the sense that ordinary travelers who wrote accounts of African societies did not filter what they observed through any strong ideological biases.[10]

In his book *The Image of Africa: British Ideas and Action, 1780–1850*, Philip D. Curtin makes the point more forcefully. Curtin says that in the eighteenth century, when at least six million slaves were taken from Africa, Europeans in general "knew more and cared more about Africa than they did at any later period up to the 1950s."[11] This remarkable statement is based on two factors that were prevalent during this time: Europeans could obtain information about Africa from relatively unbiased traders and travelers, and Europeans *had not yet completely connected race and culture* in ways that prevented them from seeing Africa fairly.

And yet European attitudes toward Africa were becoming more negative and more racist. According to A. Bulunda Itandala, European artists—painters, sculptors, playwrights, and poets—increasingly portrayed Africans stereotypically and unfavorably. He emphasizes that during the Renaissance, Europe still relied heavily on the medieval worldview, which divided the world into Christian and non-Christian spheres or, more starkly, into a struggle between Christianity and the devil. Thus the story of Ham, mentioned above, was used widely to justify the slave trade. As Europe's knowledge of Africa grew through exploration and trade, including the slave trade, Europeans increasingly painted Africa and Africans in negative terms. And those negative terms were increasingly associated with physical features such as color and not just culture.[12]

In sum, eighteenth-century Westerners preferred their own culture to all others and were not without racist ideas, but, unlike nineteenth-century Europeans, they did not presume that everything Africans did was inferior simply because of their race. Eighteenth-century links between race and culture were still largely unconscious and imprecise. Curtin calls this a form of "moderate racism," which "condemned individual Africans as bad men—or all Africans as savage men—but . . . left the clear impression that Africans *were* men."[13]

One way to illustrate this attitude is to point out the efforts that Europeans made to help Africans who had been forcibly removed from Africa to return to the continent. In Britain, the example of Sierra Leone is foremost. Conceived in the 1780s by philanthropists who wanted to give free blacks residing in Britain and non-African parts of the British Empire the opportunity to repatriate, this colony on the west coast of Africa was organized on utopian principles supposedly applicable to all human societies.

The effort was clearly racist in the sense that it rid European territories of many blacks. However, such plans show that in the eighteenth and early nineteenth centuries, Britons still believed that blacks could not only rule themselves in Africa but also establish utopian communities if they were provided the proper tools and legal framework. Unfortunately, planners of such resettlement experiments rarely took into account the actual physical conditions in Africa, the training and skills of the settlers, or previous failed attempts to establish utopian communities. In 1808 the British government took over Sierra Leone as a naval base and as a colony in which to resettle the thousands of Africans freed during the effort to end the slave trade.[14]

An American example also illustrates the ambiguous Western attitudes toward race. Beginning in the 1820s, the American Colonization Society supported a Back-to-Africa movement that attempted to colonize Liberia, on the coast of West Africa, with groups of freed American slaves. As in Sierra Leone, the organizers had mixed motives. Helping African Americans to live in Africa was in one sense a vote of confidence for blacks' ability to rule themselves. However, most society members were northern whites troubled by the growing number of freed slaves in northern cities, and many saw the enterprise as an opportunity to establish Christian missions in Africa. The US government contributed funds for colonization, and one settlement was named Monrovia after President James Monroe, a member of the society.[15] Like Sierra Leone, however, Liberia was never prosperous.[16]

The antislavery movement provides another illustration of the "moderate racism" that existed in the minds of early-nineteenth-century Europeans and Americans. From our perspective it seems logical that abolitionists would attempt to eliminate racism in their efforts to end slavery. But the abolitionists' arguments were primarily about the immorality of slavery and the slave trade rather than the immorality of racism. Proslavery and antislavery activists alike were racist, but both assumed that cultural factors were at the heart of the slavery question. For proponents of slavery, the Africans' inferior culture justified the institution. Antislavery activists argued that Christian charity required abolition and that Africans had the *potential* to acquire civilized culture.[17]

## Birth of the Dark Continent

Sometime in the mid-eighteenth century a new trend in the way Europeans viewed the rest of the world began to develop. It did not reach its peak for a century or more, but in hindsight it is clear that the old models were already being challenged. The reason for this transition was the series of revolutions under way in Europe: the Enlightenment, the scientific and industrial revolutions, and the resulting global revolutions in trade and conquest. These new conditions lent increased prestige and power to those concerned with the material world and with domination of other cultures. The revolutions also helped to undermine views of the world that promoted the essential equality of humanity. Europeans had a growing sense that theirs was a superior and powerful civilization.

Michael Adas argues that as the modern global revolutions began, the interpreters of the non-West were increasingly traders, scientists, technicians, soldiers, and bureaucrats. They, not missionaries or philosophers, subsequently determined what Europeans thought of the world. These new interpreters had pragmatic interests—domination rather than conversion or understanding—and they aggressively shaped European thinking to serve their goals.[18]

We can see this shift in perspective in Western attitudes and actions toward China, which had been celebrated in the late seventeenth and early eighteenth centuries as an example of a gifted civilization. A popular artistic style, chinoiserie, imitated Chinese motifs in furniture, architecture, art, fabrics, porcelain, gardens, and the like. In the same way, Chinese laws, administration, commercial practices, and ethics were considered solid, if not perfect. By the late eighteenth century, however, China's image in Europe was in severe decline. European traders complained about excessive bureaucracy, corruption, and trade restrictions. Protestant missionaries complained about superstitions. And many observers derided the Chinese for not achieving more in science and technology. By the time of the First Opium War (1839–1842), when Europe demonstrated its brutality as well as its new technological superiority, Western assessments of China had turned overwhelmingly negative.[19] In the United States, meanwhile, the use and abuse of Chinese laborers in the American West contributed to this image.

For Africa the shift was equally significant but less noticeable, because Africans had never been held in high esteem among Europeans. In the last half of the eighteenth century, portrayals of Africans became increasingly negative, and they increasingly linked African race and African culture. This growing race consciousness was frequently expressed in the new language of science. One of the questions addressed was whether science supported the biblical account of the origin of the different races. Until the scientific revolution, the Hebrew Bible provided the most common explanation of human diversity: God created humans and they were dispersed after the fall of the Tower of Babel. Those who thought more deeply about the question, however, found problems with the biblical stories. How, for example, was it possible for Adam and Eve's sons to find wives (Genesis 4)? And if all humans descended from Adam, how could they have achieved such physical diversity?

By the beginning of the nineteenth century, the principal contending explanations for human diversity were either that all humans descended from Adam—the monogenist position—or that separate creations accounted for separate races—the polygenist position. Slavers and slaveholders tended to be polygenists because the belief in separate races implied that God could approve of inferior treatment for blacks. Reformers tended to be monogenists, but they nonetheless believed that Africans had degenerated and needed a great deal of help to return to the level of Europeans, if such a return was possible at all.

The Bible could not settle the debate, but scientists in the United States believed they might. They began to ask whether nature, by itself, could have produced the immense diversity of plants and animals on Earth. They made two basic assumptions: that nature could bring about diversity through the influence of climate and that the biblical account of creation was correct in dating the age of Earth at between 4,000 and 5,000 years. The scientists then concluded that nature could *not* have produced

Earth's biological diversity in such a short time. Therefore, by the 1840s most American scientists believed that science supported the polygenist, multiple-creation position, a view consistent with racism.[20]

⌈Nineteenth-century science was, of course, heading for a collision with the biblical view of creation⌉ The monogenists and polygenists both assumed that the biblical account of creation was fact and that science needed only to fill in the details. Meanwhile, new archaeological discoveries in Egypt near the turn of the nineteenth century began to cast doubt on biblical chronology by demonstrating that human life on Earth was far older than the Bible indicated. And the study of fossils began to show that Earth itself might be vastly older than the Bible allowed. If these findings were accurate, neither the polygenist nor the monogenist theory could explain human origins or human interrelationships.

As the long chronology of evolution became more apparent, scientists began to work toward understanding the actual biological mechanism by which diversity could occur. For example, among the theories proposed early in the century was Jean-Baptiste Lamarck's inheritability of learned traits. Then, in 1859, Charles Darwin described the theory of natural selection in *The Origin of Species* and showed how species could evolve through interplay between biology and the environment. Darwin's natural selection theory prevailed, of course, but it caught on very slowly. Moreover, it still lacked an adequate explanation of the biological mechanism by which individuals came to vary from each other.

Darwin himself remained a Lamarckian, believing that learned traits were inherited. He thought that biological variation arose because parents learned traits they passed to their offspring at conception. Interestingly, the Lamarckian understanding of variation seems at least partially responsible for the fear some European colonists had of "going native" (taking on African customs) while in Africa. Many believed that by dressing up formally for dinner while in the African "bush," they were more likely to give birth to civilized children. It was only in 1902 that Gregor Mendel's work with plant variation was rediscovered after being lost for a century in an obscure journal, and the genetic theory of variation began to spread. Not until the 1920s and 1930s did American scientists commonly accept the genetic theory of evolution; American cultural acceptance took decades longer. In fact, belief in these theories still has not permeated all corners of our society.

Well before Darwin, the new scientific theories of evolution began to add fuel to Western racism. Race logic in America and Europe concluded that if humans had evolved, presumably from apes, some humans had evolved more than others. Such logic naturally kept the creators of the new myths—white, upper-class, northern European males—at the top of the evolutionary hierarchy. Below them came women, other races, and other classes. Among the inferior races, Asians were most advanced, then Africans, Native Americans, and Australian Aborigines. These scientific theories, unlike the older race theories, inextricably linked race and culture. Curtin notes that "whereas race had been *an* important influence on human culture, the new generation saw race as *the* crucial determinant, not only of culture but of human character and of all history. Hundreds of variant theories were to appear in the mood of this new emphasis."[21] The scientific proof seemed to be everywhere—in the shape and size of heads, in skin color, in differences between males and females, in comportment, in the complexity of societies, and in the nature of art and religion. The greater the perceived physical and cultural difference from European culture, the less developed the race.

While Europeans developed these pseudoscientific ways of linking race and culture, they also became convinced that they had to conquer Africa. What is striking here is that they waited so long to begin. By the time Europeans invaded sub-Saharan Africa in the 1880s and 1890s, Africa had long remained the only continent unsubdued by European power. Reasons for the delay included the difficulty of the environment, the danger of violence, the slave trade, and the lack of easily tapped mineral wealth. But the second half of the nineteenth century brought the end of the slave trade; improvements in guns, boats, and medicine; an intensified search for industrial raw materials and markets; and heightened nationalist competition among the European states. Explorers set out to "discover" the African interior, traders staked out regions, and missionaries founded stations as far inland as they could while still maintaining their supply lines. As the century progressed, interest in Africa grew until it finally became impossible for European governments *not* to colonize the continent.

This shift toward imperialist thinking was already apparent by midcentury. In theoretical terms, the shift was marked by fewer arguments for the *conversion* of Africans than for European *trusteeship* over Africans. Conversion had been an attempt to make Africans more like Europeans, implying that Africans were just as human as Europeans. In Senegal, for example, the French allowed some educated Africans to become French citizens. Trusteeship, however, implied that Africans were biologically inferior and needed to be taken care of, a perfect justification for conquest. Europeans in Africa naturally began to look for evidence that Africa needed European help.[22] Educated Africans, who had formerly been entrusted with responsibilities, were moved aside and labeled incompetent. African customs were increasingly described as savage. Cannibalism was imagined in practically every corner of the continent. Childhood became the universal metaphor for the African state of mental and cultural development.

## A Myth for Conquest

Thus the myth of the Dark Continent was born. It originated in mid-nineteenth-century Europe when scientific race theory was developed, without reference to the actual cultures of Africans in Africa. Then it was transferred to Africa by Europeans who had both a theoretical and a practical interest in seeing Africa as primitive. And when scientific race theory combined with imperialist urges to conquer, there was no end to the primitiveness that could be found.

The Dark Continent myth is still with us a century and a half later, at least in diluted form. Its legacy leads us to many of the "African" words listed in Chapter 1. Anyone who reads the literature of late-eighteenth-century European travelers in Africa—who describe Africans as human—and then reads the literature of late-nineteenth-century travelers—who criticize Africans as depraved—will wonder if this is the same continent. In the eighteenth century, Europeans on the whole were genuinely interested in discovering what Africans were doing, even if they disapproved of what they found. For example, Mungo Park—considered by some to be the first modern European explorer of Africa—traveled to the upper Niger River in 1796; although he underwent many difficulties, he evaluated individuals and experiences on their own merits and did not generally condemn whole groups or cultures.[23] By the late nineteenth century, however, Europeans could see only a primitive continent full of tribes of savages and barbarians.

Of course, a great deal of hypocrisy was involved in this attempt to reduce Africans to the lowest forms of humanity. European violence eradicated African violence. Christian love justified missionary control. And the white race, which had only recently stamped out its own slave-trading and slaveholding practices, called Arabs and Africans inferior because they traded and held slaves. When European slave trading in Africa came to an end in the 1870s and 1880s, Europeans engaged in an antislavery campaign against Arab slave traders on the Nile and in East Africa, and then against African traders. As discussed above, in the antislavery campaign in Europe in the early part of the century, the arguments made by both sides were more cultural than racial. Now, however, Europeans demanded that racially inferior Arabs and even more racially inferior Africans allow themselves to be saved from their depravity by racially superior Europeans. Patrick Brantlinger, a scholar of Victorian literature, writes:

> The myth of the Dark Continent defined slavery as the offspring of tribal savagery and portrayed white explorers and missionaries as the leaders of a Christian crusade that would vanquish the forces of darkness. . . . When the taint of slavery fused with sensational reports about cannibalism, witchcraft, and apparently shameless sexual customs, Victorian Africa emerged draped in that pall of darkness that the Victorians themselves accepted as reality.[24]

Actually, several versions of the Dark Continent myth were available, the choice depending on whether the source was Christian or secular evolutionist. In the Christian version, God becomes the sponsor of the colonial effort. Christian missionaries, who were mostly whites, were called upon to save God's pagan children in Africa. This version can be seen clearly in the mission movement that grew dramatically during the nineteenth century. More secular versions of the myth ranged from a crass survival-of-the-fittest conquest to a more sophisticated "trusteeship on behalf of civilization." Official government policies tended toward the latter definition, and twentieth-century colonial bureaucrats spoke in terms of the care they were providing: colonialism was, they claimed, a generous gift to Africans.

At the popular level, Rudyard Kipling's famous poem "The White Man's Burden" illustrates the secular trend. Although not specifically about Africa, Kipling's verses summarized the secular justification for domination of Africa and other parts of the world at the turn of the century. "White man's burden" is now a common phrase used to capture the essence of the colonial mentality. Kipling's poem was sent to President Theodore Roosevelt just after the American annexation of the Philippines in 1898. It urged Americans to embrace colonialism as Britons had done:

> *Take up the White Man's burden—*
> *Send forth the best ye breed—*
> *Go bind your sons to exile*
> *To serve your captives' need;*
> *To wait in heavy harness,*
> *On fluttered folk and wild—*
> *Your new-caught, sullen peoples,*
> *Half-devil and half-child.*
>
> *Take up the White Man's burden—*
> *Ye dare not stoop to less—*
> *Nor call too loud on Freedom*
> *To cloak your weariness;*
> *By all ye cry or whisper,*
> *By all ye leave or do,*
> *The silent, sullen peoples*
> *Shall weigh your Gods and you.*[25]

For Kipling, race itself is the sponsor of the colonial enterprise. The colonial burden is not a call from God, but from whiteness. Americans are urged to send "the best ye breed"—presumably upper-class white males—to serve people at the bottom of the racial hierarchy who are "half-devil and half-child." One might presume that the "half-devil" reference is a plea to Christians, but the poem's audience has "Gods"—plural—who are surely secular as well as Christian. Kipling is considered a defender of secular colonialism, not of religious missions. And the reference to "half-child" is pure scientific racism: the more racially different, the more childlike other peoples were thought to be. Furthermore, Americans were to serve their captives forever, in "weariness," because the captives were biologically incapable of learning the ways of civilized peoples.

The most public examples of Dark Continent thinking among Americans come from Henry Morton Stanley and Theodore Roosevelt. Stanley, an orphan who left England as a young man, served on both sides during the American Civil War and was a newspaper reporter on the western frontier. He went to Africa in the late 1860s as a reporter for the *New York Herald*. His goal was to find the famous missionary David Livingstone, who had not been heard from in several years, and create one of the biggest news stories of the century. Stanley found Livingstone, of course, but more important, he became attached to Africa and spent the rest of his life involved with the continent. From 1875 to 1877 he crossed the continent from east to west, and he later described the harrowing journey down the Congo River in his book *Through the Dark Continent*.[26] In the late 1870s and throughout the 1880s, Stanley participated in the conquest of the Congo by King Leopold of Belgium.

In both Britain and the United States, Stanley was easily the most influential explorer of nineteenth-century Africa. Stanley's reputation was made as a bold adventurer who conquered every obstacle, both natural and human. Although some believe that he was not a racist because he did not use the racist jargon of the day, he was nonetheless quick to judge Africans as inferior and quick to turn to violence against those Africans who stood in his way.[27] Throughout the white world, red-blooded men and boys read and talked about Stanley well into the twentieth century. Anyone interested in Africa certainly read Stanley, and a direct line of influence extends from his books to nearly every one of the white adventurers who followed him to Africa. Stanley also inspired the stories of Edgar Rice Burroughs (who created Tarzan) and H. Rider Haggard, authors read widely by Americans.

Theodore Roosevelt also read Stanley and developed a remarkably similar outlook on colonialism. Although Roosevelt belonged to the American upper middle class and was not known as a violent man, he was nonetheless a conqueror. He was an enthusiastic proponent of American colonies, including Puerto Rico and the Philippines, and as president he supervised the construction of the Panama Canal. Like Stanley, Roosevelt saw a similar "wildness" in the American West and in Africa. After his presidency, Roosevelt spent a year on safari in Africa (described in Chapter 9). In a 1909 dispatch from Africa to American newspapers, he commented that, "like all savages and most children, [Africans] have their limitations, and in dealing with them firmness is even more necessary than kindness; but the man is a poor creature who does not treat them with kindness also, and I am rather sorry for him if he does not grow to feel for them, and to make them in return feel for him, a real and friendly liking."[28] This is, of course, a restatement of the sentiment of "The White Man's Burden." Roosevelt's paternalistic and racist views, encapsulated in the adventure of his safari, were widely read and appreciated in the United States.

For most Americans—whether missionary, scientist, or ordinary citizen—Roosevelt's Dark Continent perspective was unquestioned in the first part of the twentieth century. Indeed, this view has been so widely and firmly held that it still persists in various forms and will likely survive well into the twenty-first century.

# 4

# "OUR LIVING ANCESTORS"

## *Twentieth-Century Evolutionism*

*Heart of Darkness*, by Joseph Conrad, is widely considered to be one of the finest works of prose fiction in the English language. In the story, the character Marlow describes his 1891 trip up the newly explored Congo River in a small, wheezing steamboat. His mission is to find the ivory in the hands of Kurtz, a white trader who has "gone native" in the deep interior of the vast Congo rain forest. Conrad's story is gripping because it uses entry into Africa as a metaphor for entry into the dark heart of the human subconscious. As Marlow ascends the river, he experiences ever deeper human depravity until he finally reaches Kurtz, who lives among his own tribe of shouting cannibals with his sensuous African mistress. "Going up that river," says Marlow, "was like travelling back to the earliest beginnings of the world, when vegetation rioted on the earth and the big trees were kings." "We were wanderers," he recalls, "on a prehistoric earth."[1]

It is a superbly written story, but many consider it racist. Indeed, the Nigerian novelist Chinua Achebe argues that *Heart of Darkness* cannot be considered great literature, no matter what its aesthetic merits, because it rests on racist premises.[2] One might hope that in a future era the story will not make sense without an extensive introduction to the way people in the nineteenth century connected Africa with the primitive. For the present, however, the story is quite comprehensible because we are still not sure that Africa is not the Dark Continent or that Africans are not primitives.

We can see similar thinking, for example, in a 1990 *National Geographic* article about a trip up the Congo River. The author specifically compares the Congo today with the river as portrayed by Conrad: "As the days passed, the river appeared just as it had to Conrad a hundred years ago: Going up that river was like traveling back to the earliest beginnings of the world."[3]

Knowing little of African languages or African thought, the *National Geographic* author jumps from noting that in the Lingala language the concepts for *yesterday* and *tomorrow* are expressed by the same word, to concluding that for Congolese, "time seemed to stand still. . . . There is now, and there is all other time in both directions."[4] Although this makes for intriguing reading, it is bad science, bad linguistics, and bad reporting. Nonetheless, it represents a common American understanding of Africa as representing a primitive past.

## Biological Evolutionism

The key to our thinking about Africa as primitive is our idea of evolution. Primitive *means* less evolved. Therefore, if we are going to untangle ourselves from Dark Continent myths, we need to deal with evolutionary theory. The problem is not the modern scientific understanding of evolution but an old-fashioned view that still has some currency in American popular culture. This view features three articles of faith relevant to this discussion: evolution takes place along a single line that leads to progress; some species and subspecies are more evolved than others; and species claw their way to the top.

In this older version of evolutionary theory, change occurs along a line that stretches from the simplest living forms to the most complex, from microbes to mammals. As each successive species evolves, a new and higher rung is added to the evolutionary ladder. Humans, who have climbed to the top, are the most advanced of the species. But all humans are not equal. White human males of the upper socioeconomic classes are at the very top of the human segment of the ladder. Others trail in a biological hierarchy constructed according to class, sex, and race.

The mechanism by which evolution worked according to this nineteenth-century theory was "survival of the fittest." Those species and subspecies that could dominate others would rise to the top. The *exact* way this would happen was not clear, because scientists did not have a firm grasp of genetics until well into the twentieth century. What did appear clear was that species were in competition with each other for survival. The "law of the jungle" was eat or be eaten.

When Conrad wrote in *Heart of Darkness* that he was going back in time as he went into Africa, he did not just mean that he was going back in historical time. He meant that he was going back in evolutionary time. Africans were literal biological specimens of what whites had once been. Whites had left these living ancestors in the evolutionary dust. In America, as in Europe, this "truth" was held almost universally. Theodore Roosevelt, writing to Americans from East Africa in 1909 shortly after the end of his presidency, echoed this view: "[In Africa,] nature, both as regards wild man and wild beast, did not and does not differ materially from what it was in Europe in the late Pleistocene."[5]

## Evolutionism

In the second half of the nineteenth century, evolution became one of the primary ideologies by which Westerners organized and perpetuated their world. They applied theories of biological evolution to societies and devised a system that became known as Social Darwinism. Since Darwin's version of evolutionary theory was more accurate than the versions used in Social Darwinism, the association of his name with this social theory is somewhat unfair. Many scholars, therefore, now refer to it as Social Evolutionism, or simply *evolutionism.*

Evolutionism is composed of a variety of nineteenth-century theories about how societies advance from the simple to the more complex and how the degree of advancement in one's society reflects the degree of advancement of one's race. In America, Lewis Henry Morgan (1818–1881), an upstate New York lawyer turned anthropologist, developed a widely used model. He described three categories of peoples: *savage, barbarian,* and *civilized.* Savages were hunters and gatherers, barbarians were agriculturists, and the civilized lived in cities, used writing, and had organized states. For Morgan, progressive human inventions allowed early humans to evolve psychologically, and as a result, societies advanced toward civilization.

William Graham Sumner (1840–1910) proposed a more overtly racist theory, arguing that all men were not created equal and that competition within and among the races would result in the elimination of the ill-adapted and encourage racial and cultural progress.]Sumner, a Yale professor, was widely known in America as an ardent advocate of laissez-faire capitalism, individual liberties, and evolutionism. Culture, he believed, originates in instincts such as the sex drive and hunger. He was against society providing any help to the lower classes, because of their biological inferiority and because it would drain resources from the superior middle class.

Evolutionism eventually filtered into the popular imagination in Europe and America. Gaetano Casati, an Italian explorer, expressed the survival-of-the-fittest model quite graphically as he described what he observed in Central Africa in the mid-1880s:

> The life of primitive nations is an incessant agitation for the attainment of progressive comfort, which leads to higher civilization. Ignorant of the future and careless of the present, the savage tribes instinctively attack and destroy one another. Sooner or later the weaker are reduced to impotence, the stronger fortifies itself, rules, and assimilates with the conquered, and in the end makes the weaker submit to its caprices.[7]

Roosevelt described Africans in evolutionist terms that are both unilinear and racist. In the foreword to his collection of dispatches from East Africa, he noted that "the dark-skinned races that live in the land vary widely. Some are warlike, cattle-owning nomads; some till the soil; . . . some are fisherfolk; some are ape-like naked savages, who dwell in the woods and prey on creatures not much wilder or lower than themselves."[8] Roosevelt also included descriptions of the low state of African culture, such as the following: "Most of the tribes were of pure savages; but here and there were intrusive races of higher type; and in Uganda . . . lived a people which had advanced to the upper stages of barbarism."[9]

According to the logic of evolutionism, race and culture were one; superior races produced superior cultures, and naturally, the white race and white culture were superior. Who would devise such a theory and put themselves anywhere except at the pinnacle? Evolutionist theories also had a self-justifying aspect. Other cultures were defined not just in terms of how they *differed* from Western culture but also in terms of what they *lacked* that Western culture had. With this kind of logic, other cultures and races were always bound to lose out when compared to the West, because Western culture and the white race were the only standards that counted. Africans as well as others with very different cultures were inferior *by definition*.

## The Primitive African

[The logic of evolutionism assumed that Africans were mentally equivalent to children and therefore could not produce art, religion, language, writing, literature, or political structures as advanced as those of the West.] Perhaps in the distant future, in hundreds or even thousands of years, Africans would evolve to become capable of higher forms of culture.

Let me illustrate by describing the Western evaluation of the Mangbetu of northeastern Congo (Kinshasa), the African culture with which I am best acquainted.[10] In the eighteenth century the Mangbetu consisted of many small and separate clans that spoke closely related dialects. Interspersed among them also lived clan groups of peoples speaking several unrelated languages. Toward the end of the century, one particular Mangbetu clan, the Mabiti, began to dominate the others through force and clever marriage alliances. By the mid-nineteenth century the Mabiti leader had carved out a small kingdom, which he organized into chiefdoms ruled by family members. Over time, the king could not maintain the unity of his lands, and some of the subordinate chiefs broke away to found new kingdoms. In 1873 the original kingdom itself was conquered by non-Mangbetu neighbors, leaving the purely Mangbetu kingdoms arrayed in a ring around the usurpers. The usurpers largely adopted the Mangbetu culture of their subjects.

This centralization of the Mangbetu kingdoms led to a courtly lifestyle for the rulers. Georg Schweinfurth, the first European to visit the region (in 1870), was greatly impressed as he described the capital of the central kingdom in his travel account. The large village included a broad central plaza surrounded by the houses of King Mbunza's favorite wives, a meeting hall that measured 150 feet long and 50 feet high, and a large royal enclosure where the king had storehouses of weapons, food, and regalia. Thousands of people were present for public gatherings. Schweinfurth employed words such as *elegant*, *artistic*, and *masterpiece* for the wide range of Mangbetu artistic culture he observed—music, dance, dress, architecture, metallurgy, woodworking, basketry, and pottery.[11]

Although all of the Europeans who visited the Mangbetu were impressed, they did not consider the Mangbetu their biological or cultural equals. Instead, they fit them into the evolutionist hierarchy, proclaiming the Mangbetu to be more evolved than their neighbors, who had not yet developed kingdoms. The Europeans perceived the Mangbetu rulers as having slightly more European physical features such as lighter skin and longer noses, and they deemed this to be the reason for the higher level of Mangbetu culture. But they still considered the Mangbetu less evolved than the lighter-skinned Arabs who came to the region to trade in slaves and ivory.

Schweinfurth qualified his positive evaluation of the Mangbetu so he could fit them into the racial hierarchy. He portrayed the Mangbetu as *advanced savages*, noting, for example, that in Africa it was possible to speak of "culture, art, and industry in but a very limited sense."[12] He also depicted Mbunza as "a truly savage monarch" in whose eyes "gleamed the wild light of animal sensuality."[13] Most important, Schweinfurth created the myth that the Mangbetu were the world's greatest cannibals, with Mbunza dining daily at cannibal feasts (see Chapter 7).

It is astounding today to realize that Schweinfurth evaluated the Mangbetu after spending only a few days in the area and without speaking a local language or even mixing with the Mangbetu more than a few times. He excused his lack of language skills by declaring that the Mangbetu language was rudimentary and that direct observation was a superior way to understand others. Even more astounding, Schweinfurth's 1870 evaluation went unchallenged until after the 1960s. Those who followed him as explorers, conquerors, colonizers, and missionaries largely accepted his perspective. Regarding cannibalism, for example, when others found that the Mangbetu were not as hungry for human flesh as Schweinfurth had reported, they attributed this to the fact that Europeans had outlawed the practice.

The Western evaluation of the Mangbetu and their neighbors is duplicated for African groups everywhere south of the Sahara. The more an African culture resembled a Western culture, the more evolved its creators were supposed to be. The lighter an African people's skin, the more Europeans found advanced features in their culture. In all cases, however, Africans were still deemed primitives.

Virtually every Western academic discipline worked out classifications that connected African culture to biological inferiority. In religious studies, for example, use of magic and witchcraft, worship of multiple gods, and reverence for ancestors were considered not only backward but irrational. Missionaries who labored to convert Africans therefore believed that although many Africans outwardly complied with the forms of Christianity, they would always need missionaries because, like children, they could not understand the religion's deeper meanings and were always in danger of backsliding.

Psychologists, led by such notables as Sigmund Freud and Carl Jung, believed that Africans and other "primitive" peoples could provide clues to the human subconscious because Africans were thought to operate at a more basic mental level than Westerners. Freud wrote: "We can . . . judge the so-called savage and semi-savage races; their psychic life assumes a peculiar interest for us, for we can recognize in their psychic life a well-preserved, early state of our own development."[14] He added that "a comparison of the psychology of the primitive races . . . with the psychology of the neurotic . . . will reveal numerous points of correspondence."[15] Other theorists proposed that Africans actually desired a dependent, colonial relationship with superior Europeans.[16] In popular culture, Africans who began to think and act like Europeans were frequently said to "ape" the Europeans because such Africans' actions were considered imitative rather than fully intelligent and conscious.

Likewise, African artists were regarded as only basic and imitative. Westerners came from an artistic tradition of realism, so the abstractness of much of African art was thought to be an indication of African inability to produce realistic depictions of natural forms such as the human body. Because Westerners value overt displays of creativity in art, they did not recognize that in Africa forms tended to endure, though artists played with variations on those forms. Assuming that Africans did not know how to create, Western observers missed the significance of abstraction, the subtle creativity within similar forms, the importance of individual artists, and the wide variety of African creative arts not linked to religion or leadership.

One of the major ways Westerners evaluated Africans was in terms of science and technology. European culture was strong, of course, in its understanding of the elements of nature and in its ability to combine those elements into practical tools. Whether it was firearms, clocks, trains, boats, medicines, matches, cloth, or axes, Westerners could produce more, higher-quality, and less expensive goods than Africans. We might even say that in the late nineteenth century, Europeans were so far ahead of Africans in the technology of domination (guns, boats, trains, medicines, and so forth) that the gap between the two has never been larger, before or since, thus making conquest easier and cheaper than it would have been at any other moment in history.

This technology impressed Europeans as much as Africans. Indeed, many scholars believe that the whole evolutionist idea of progress became primarily associated in the late nineteenth century with the conquest of nature and the acquisition of wealth. For Westerners, the symbol of progress was machinery, with each new invention symbolizing ever greater progress—the clock, steam engine, locomotive, lightbulb, telephone, automobile, airplane, radio, rocket, television, and computer. Africans in the nineteenth century did not have trains or steamboats. They did not even have wheelbarrows or plows.[17]

What Africans did have was knowledge of overall human dependence on nature and the technology necessary to survive in many different African environments. Dependence on nature was frequently expressed through elaborate rituals that evoked natural powers, spirits, and ancestors. However, Africans also utilized their extensive and accurate knowledge of nature in their methods of hunting, gathering, farming, herding, fishing, house building, pottery making, woodworking, and in their other economic pursuits. Westerners frequently mistook African ritual for African science and therefore made erroneous comparisons with Western science and technology. Yet, despite its degradation of African knowledge, colonialism always depended heavily in practice on African understanding of both society and nature.

## Changing Paradigms

Most of us no longer talk or even think about Africa in the stark evolutionist terms discussed above, because our civilization made significant changes in this regard during the twentieth century. It is important to reflect on how we have changed and how our own views of Africans are still in the process of changing. For the sake of simplicity, we can divide the ways our views have changed into three broad categories: views of ourselves, views of others, and views of nature.

## Changing Views of Ourselves

The Dark Continent portrayals of Africa developed at a time when Westerners envisioned themselves as potential masters of both society and nature. Indeed, there was much to encourage them. The peoples of Africa were subdued and organized into colonies that produced raw materials for the West's growing industries, while the Asian colonies continued to increase their output as well. Scientists made regular and important discoveries, and technological advances poured forth in medicine, transportation, communication, weaponry, electricity, and many other fields.

But even while the West was making such progress, Westerners began to discover that colonialism, science, and technology had limits and drawbacks. World War I serves as an example of certain ambiguities in this progress. The Allies confidently heralded the conflict as the "war to end all wars," yet it was only among the first of many twentieth-century wars. Moreover, using new inventions of modern genius, including airplanes, tanks, machine guns, and chemical weapons, Europeans killed each other by the millions.

The rest of the twentieth century produced similar ambiguous "successes." Despite their progress, Westerners continued to experience massive setbacks: a global economic depression, a second world war even more destructive than the first, the Holocaust, the dropping of the atomic bomb, the Cold War, the decline of colonialism, and threats to the environment. Achieving global empire proved impossible, and science and technology became problematic. The United States experienced the difficulties of a pluralistic, urban, consumer-oriented society in which racial, ethnic, gender, and class relationships were in constant turmoil. Westerners had to take second and third looks at the optimistic assumptions they had made about themselves at the beginning of the century. They could no longer be sure that they had all the answers.

## Changing Views of Others

A second major way in which twentieth-century thinking has changed concerns Western views of other cultures. Two primary influences forced a reinterpretation of non-Western cultures: anthropology and the collapse of colonialism. Anthropologists were among the first to take the so-called primitive cultures seriously. From about 1900 onward, a growing number of them assumed that Africans were humans equal to whites, with complex cultures, significant histories, meaningful philosophies, high art, and so forth. This transformation took a century to complete and, in a sense, is still in progress; however, by mid-century it was well under way and spreading quickly to other disciplines.

There is no one moment or place where this transformation began, but the work of Franz Boas, an American anthropologist, is illustrative. A German-born and German-educated natural scientist, Boas became interested in the 1880s in the cultures of the Native Americans of western Canada and the US Pacific Northwest. Originally convinced that natural laws governed human conduct and social evolution, Boas changed his mind after he had lived with and studied Native American peoples. Once Boas began to accept these peoples on their own terms, he found them to be his equals. He concluded that the differences among human societies are due solely to the various ways by which those societies learn to adapt to their circumstances. In addition, Boas came to understand that all societies had "evolved," but in a multilineal fashion. To Boas, there were no primitive peoples and no primitive cultures. He became a proponent of what is widely known as *cultural relativism*, the idea that each culture should be understood on its own terms rather than in comparison to others.

Boas proposed that to discover how a particular society came to be the way one found it, one had to take into account many different factors including environment, history, cultural practices, nutrition and disease, invention and discovery, and borrowing and trade. The anthropologist therefore had to adopt a holistic perspective on culture, studying practically everything a society did. Boas insisted that professional anthropology had to include *fieldwork*, in which scholars actually lived with the peoples they studied and participated in their daily lives.

In the evolutionist climate of the day, Boas's work was not immediately accepted by scholars or by Americans in general. Over time, however, his influence on anthropology and on the American view of other cultures has become enormous. He taught at Columbia University for forty-three years (until 1942) and trained many of the most famous American anthropologists of the first half of the twentieth century, including Margaret Mead, Ruth Benedict, and Melville Herskovits. Boas is considered the founder of modern anthropology in America. Not surprisingly, the race supremacists of Nazi Germany rescinded his PhD and banned his books in the 1930s.

When anthropologists began to adopt relativist perspectives and undertake serious fieldwork among Africans, they found that they agreed with Boas. The customs the West had considered primitive were found to be both rational and creative efforts to cope with environment and history. Indeed, after about 1960, anthropologists began to look at European and American societies in the same way they looked at nonmodern societies, and they discovered that the West was no more rational or creative than African societies.

Building on the work of Boas and many others, anthropologists of today are reticent to make generalizations about cultures or to trust systems that purport to explain the evolution of societies. Although many anthropologists categorize the world's societies according to different types, virtually none links categories to race or considers one type of society to be superior to another. Some anthropologists have abandoned classification entirely, because they see that all labeling does injustice to the enormous variety of societies and situations.

The discoveries of twentieth-century anthropology spread slowly to other disciplines and then began to filter into American popular consciousness. Scholarship was not, however, the only force pushing us toward new views of other cultures. The West's colonial empires began to crumble after World War II; Europe was simply too exhausted and too preoccupied with rebuilding itself to hold on to them. India and Pakistan gained their independence from Britain in 1947, and other European colonies in Asia followed, by consent or by revolution. The Philippines, Hawaii, and Puerto Rico moved away from US colonial control, either by gaining outright independence or by modifying their relationship with the government in Washington. In the United States, African Americans made headway against racism. And in Africa, Western-educated Africans led the push for independence in the 1940s and 1950s. By the mid-1960s, only a few African territories, including the five white settler colonies of southern Africa, remained under white rule.

The newly independent countries of Asia and Africa were fragile, frequently in need of aid, and vulnerable to pressure both from their former European colonizers and from the two global superpowers—the United States and the Soviet Union. But global realities were nonetheless changing. In the mid-1970s, a news commentator observed that a recent global summit had been the first occasion when world leaders had all sat at one table and each had considered everyone else to be fully human. Essentially, the commentator's observation was correct. The independence of Africa had finally forced the West to consider Africans as real people, even if they were poor or powerless.

## Changing Views of Nature

The third major twentieth-century change that modified our view of Africa is the transformation in the way we view nature. The old evolutionist model of unilineality, separate human races, and survival of the fittest has been deeply undermined by the biological sciences. In fact, we now know that many of the evolutionists' ideas about nature were completely backward. Instead of life evolving along only one pathway, it evolves along many. Instead of humans belonging to many races, they belong to only one (see Chapter 11). And instead of survival of the strongest, there are multiple survival strategies, including the ability to cooperate and fit in.

At first, evolutionists and racists attempted to take the new biological knowledge and turn it to old purposes. They were, for instance, deeply interested in linking discoveries in genetics with human behavior. An example is eugenics, advocated by the English scientist Francis Galton in the second half of the nineteenth century. Galton suggested that marriage partners ought to be selected so that superior men and women would breed and produce a superior race. The American Eugenics Society, founded in 1926, argued that immigration from the "inferior" nations of southern Europe ought to be limited; that insane, retarded, and epileptic persons ought to be sterilized; and that the upper classes attained their positions because of their superior genes. Indeed, the US Congress did limit immigration, and many states passed sterilization laws. Eugenics began to lose followers, however, after the atrocities of Nazi Germany, which called for the elimination of Jews, Gypsies, blacks, homosexuals, and others based on such reasoning.

One of the most important biological lessons of the twentieth century is the realization that we *must* cooperate and fit in with one another if we are to survive. The relatively new biological science of ecology is founded on the model of life as a web, not a line or a ladder. The late Lewis Thomas, a physician, scientist, and author of thoughtful essays, reminds us of the dangers of one-path evolutionism and the belief that only our path represents progress:

A century ago there was a consensus that evolution was a record of open warfare among competing species, the fittest were the strongest aggressors, and so forth. Now it begins to look different. The great successes in evolution, the mutants who have made it, have done so by fitting in with and sustaining the rest of life. Up to now we might be counted among the brilliant successes, but classy and perhaps unstable. We should go warily into the future, looking for ways to be more useful, listening more carefully for signals, watching our step and having an eye out for partners.[19]

## Lingering Evolutionism

Evolutionism is an attractive theory for many Americans because it puts whites (and especially white *men*) at the top of nature's ladder. A theory like this will certainly die a slow death in the minds of those whom it comforts most. Indeed, deep pockets of evolutionism remain despite the twentieth-century lessons of history, anthropology, and biology. The most apparent Dark Continent images of the first half of the twentieth century are thankfully behind us, but more subtle versions remain.

One source of lingering traces of evolutionism is contemporary racist thought. It is difficult, however, to find specific examples of the ways racism affects our current attitudes toward Africa, because since the mid-1900s, most Americans have learned to hide their race prejudices from public view. Perhaps the clearest cases we find are in off-the-record comments made by national leaders. We know, for example, that President Richard Nixon and many prominent members of his staff routinely used racist slurs when talking in private about African affairs.[20] More recently, in 2002, the Senate Majority Leader, Republican Trent Lott of Mississippi, said that had the country voted in 1948 for Strom Thurmond, then the declared racist candidate for the presidency, "we wouldn't have all these problems over all these years, either." As a result of his comments, Lott lost the leadership of the Senate, but his unguarded comment makes us wonder how much covert racism affects our national policies regarding both African Americans and Africans. We also have seen many veiled references to race surrounding the election and presidency of Barack Obama.

Some segments of our society, however, do not hesitate to express openly their race prejudice toward Africans. As just one example, Stanley

Burnham, in *America's Bimodal Crisis: Black Intelligence in White Society*, includes a chapter entitled "Primitive Society in Africa."[21] Repeating practically every Darkest Africa myth in his discussion of precolonial Africa, Burnham concludes that "cognitive deficiency" was the cause of Africa's perceived backwardness. Likewise, his chapter on modern Africa is filled with horror stories; Burnham quotes psychologists of the 1930s and 1950s to document a "real-life personality profile" that characterizes Africans as having "a short attention span, an impatience with abstractions, and a relative inability to empathize with others."[22] In light of what we know today about culture and psychology, it might seem that Burnham himself fits the profile better than any African. But to see such untruths in print serves as a painful reminder that the harshest of American race evaluations of Africa have not completely ended.

Even if Americans were to rid themselves of racism, they might still maintain substantial portions of the evolutionist myth. For example, I frequently hear people say, "Africans are living as we did seventy-five years ago!" or ask, "How far behind us are Africans?" Such statements and questions imply a kind of cultural evolutionism, the idea that African cultures will someday evolve to look like our culture. Cultural evolutionism is plausible because we know that a hundred years ago we, too, lived in a mostly rural society and that Africans are currently moving into cities and adopting modern ideas. Thus, many assume that Africans will inevitably pass through certain historical stages—"like we were in the 1920s" or "like we were in the 1950s"—and then eventually "catch up" to us. But history doesn't work that way. A more complete discussion of the problems with "catching-up thinking" can be found in Chapter 6.

The idea that there are no backward peoples, no primitives, is difficult to grasp. It is not the same as saying that there are no ideas, individuals, or societies that are dysfunctional. And it does not mean that there are no irrational or incompetent individuals. It merely means that, on the whole, other people are about as rational *and* irrational as we ourselves are. If they are different, it is because they have lived in different circumstances and have had different understandings of reality and different problems to solve.

The Pleistocene era is long past, and we find ourselves living together on the planet in the twenty-first century. People most *unlike* us are just as much a part of the present as we are. They should not make a headlong rush to "catch up" to what Lewis Thomas called our "classy and perhaps unstable" Western culture. We have many lessons to teach the world, and we also have much to learn in order to build a society that is able to sustain all of us, as well as the planet itself. Our best partners may be those who are *not* going in exactly the same direction as we are.

# 5

# WHERE IS THE REAL AFRICA?

On a university tour to Zimbabwe, students spent their first few days in the capital, Harare, where they lived with urban families and studied culture, politics, and language. Then they moved to a village where they again lived with families. The village had small, brick houses with concrete floors and corrugated iron roofs. People wore Western-style clothing and went to Christian churches. Village kids attended school, listened to the radio, followed Zimbabwean soccer and politics, and knew about international and American popular music. One of the visiting students was assigned to the house of the village chief where, on the first night, there was a traditional funerary celebration. The next morning the wide-eyed student told the group that he had finally seen "the Real Africa." In the capital and the village, the student had just seen modern and modernizing Africa, connected to the world in hundreds of ways, but for him these were not part of the Real Africa.

The student's reaction is representative. We Americans seem to expect and want the Real Africa to be different, and often the more different the better. To find the aspects of Africa that are similar to us somehow doesn't satisfy us in the way that difference does. In this chapter, we explore what Americans seem to expect the Real Africa to be.

The difference we prefer in our Real Africa seems to focus on the idea that Africa is *natural* while we are *civilized*. Africa, this idea goes, is what we would be if we didn't have our history, science, law, democracy, advanced technology, religion, cities, and so forth. Our Real Africa is what we imagine existed in our own distant past when we lived close to nature and, indeed, were a part of nature. This imagined naturalness of Africa comes in two main versions, negative and positive. In the negative version Africa is a survival-of-the-fittest jungle with poverty, sickness, starvation, warfare, corruption, and an inability to rise above itself. In the positive version Africa has good features that we fear we have lost, such as wisdom, community, hospitality, and joy.

These versions might seem to be opposites, but they aren't. They each portray Africans as being closer to "natural" humans than Americans. Africans represents what all humans would be if they were not influenced by both the positive and negative aspects of history and civilization. This idea of African naturalness gets extra support from the popular stereotype of Africa as full of wild animals (discussed in Chapter 9).

It is tempting to say that the American focus on Africa's "natural" difference is racist. After all, race implies biological difference and biology is natural. However, I don't believe the current impulse of most (but not all) Americans is to think of the people of Real Africa as being biologically more primitive than American whites *or* blacks (or Asians, etc.). Rather, it seems that the idea of the Real Africa as closer to nature is a legacy of our ignorance and our racist past. Today we have transformed many of the ideas expressed in biological, and thus racial, terms into milder cultural terms. Now most Americans would say that it's African culture, not African biology, that is responsible for the Real Africa being close to nature. This is progress, of a sort.

Let's take a look at some of the ways that African difference is evoked in modern American popular culture.

## Troubled Africa

It's relatively easy to find evidence in the American media of Africa's multiple woes. The point here is not that these do not exist. Indeed, Africa does have many woes. Rather, there are two other points to make. First, Africa's woes need to be understood as a result of Africa's history rather than "Africa's nature," and second, sub-Saharan Africa has a population of over 875 million people, and not everyone living there is troubled. In the United States one in seven households has food insecurity, but most of us don't say that the hungry caused their own troubles or that hunger defines our country. Just as we should not define America as hungry, we also should not define Africa primarily as trouble.

To take an example, it is common for news items to imply that a particular conflict is caused by age-old ethnic or religious animosities and that such animosities are natural to people who do not live in modern societies. What is missing, however, is a complex and accurate understanding of both history and culture. Violent conflict is not inevitable in small-scale societies or among devout believers and the causes of such conflict are generally complex and rooted in modern history rather than in the distant past. In Chapter 8, there is a discussion of "tribe" that shows how limited the idea is when discussing today's Africa.

## Helpless Africa

Kathryn Mathers, a South African scholar, recently found that American study-abroad students arrive in Africa with Dark Continent stereotypes and that they have a strong urge to help Africa overcome its troubles. She believes that the students want to help others so they can feel confident and superior in a post-9/11 world in which Americans fear they are losing control of the world and their own country.[1] While I'd date the strong desire of Americans to help Africa much earlier (think about missionaries, for example), it is clear that many of us feel called to help Africans.

Certainly, the help offered by American celebrities is a relatively recent phenomenon. Modern celebrity help for Africa began in earnest when Bob Geldof and other star musicians organized Band Aid (1984) and then Live Aid (1985) to raise funds for famine relief in Ethiopia. Since then, additional concerts and a steady stream of celebrity visitors (among them Bono, George Clooney, Mia Farrow, Angelina Jolie, Brad Pitt, Madonna, Guy Ritchie, Jessica Lange, Oprah Winfrey, and Simon Cowell) have helped call attention to many African issues. Whether or not these celebrities are sincere or merely seeking publicity at Africa's expense, it is clear that they succeed by tapping into the American desire to help Africa.

Yet is the Real Africa so helpless? Nigerian novelist Uzodinma Iweala says that while Africans appreciate help, we have mistaken the Real Africa.

> My mood is dampened every time I attend a benefit whose host runs through a litany of African disasters before presenting a (usually) wealthy, white person, who often proceeds to list the things he or she has done for the poor, starving Africans. Every time a well-meaning college student speaks of villagers dancing because they were so grateful for her help, I cringe. Every time a Hollywood director shoots a film about Africa that features a Western protagonist, I shake my head—because Africans, real people though we may be, are used as props in the West's fantasy of itself. And not only do such depictions tend to ignore the West's prominent role in creating many of the unfortunate situations on the continent, they also ignore the incredible work Africans have done and continue to do to fix those problems.[2]

Africans are not children and their problems are not natural to Africa. The problems have been created in a past that we Americans participated in, they are sustained by a present that we are involved in, and they will be solved only within a global context, by cooperation between ourselves and Africans (see Chapter 6).

Michael Holman, former editor of the *Financial Times*, a British newspaper, says that "celebrity aid" reinforces stereotypes by promoting gift giving rather than deep analysis of African problems. If we continue to see African problems as susceptible to redress only through aid, we will continue to see Africans as helpless and inferior. What message, for example, is sent when celebrities make high-profile adoptions from Africa? That Africa has no future? Holman suggests that celebrities could do the most good for Africa if they would abandon stereotypical help-for-poor-Africans strategies and focus on starting debates about questions that matter. Things might really be different, says Holman, if Madonna, who adopted a child from Malawi, would say,

> We should respond to the fact that the diaspora of Africa's educated is swollen by 60,000 a year. This has led to the bizarre, outrageous situation that more doctors who were trained in Malawi are practicing in

England's second city of Birmingham than in Malawi itself. If one of Malawi's main exports is health professionals, that is not in itself a bad thing—what is unacceptable is that there is no organised replenishment.[3]

Holman doubts that the celebrities' "armies of advisers and publicists and sponsors" would permit such statements. What do you think? I believe that intelligent entertainment celebrities (that's not necessarily an oxymoron) could help spark much-needed debates and still remain celebrities. George Clooney's work in Sudan seems to represent the best efforts, although he does not generally question the West's and others' roles in creating and sustaining Sudan's woes. Otherwise, for now, celebrities tend to reinforce Dark Continent stereotypes and thus keep us from addressing real issues concerning how the world is structured.

## Unchanging Africa

It's amusing to see a description of so-called traditional Africa that includes a statement such as "these age-old customs" or "as their ancestors have done for hundreds of years." If we find a Christian cross in an excavation of a tenth-century European church and find a similar cross in a twenty-first-century European church, would we conclude that today's Europeans are living as their tenth-century ancestors lived or even that they believe the same things about Christianity? Hardly. History works for Africans as it works for us. There is *both* continuity and change.

I like to ask Africans what they think Americans think about Africa. Here, for example, are excerpts from an interview with a Nigerian economics professor who teaches in the United States (and happens to like Americans):

*Q: How do you think that Americans perceive Africa?*
A: The Dark Continent.
*Q: Do people really say that?*
A: Oh yes. They ask me if I live in trees.
*Q: Do they really say things like that, or do they mean it as a joke?*
A: No, they really ask. They don't know. They ask, "Do you live with animals?" "Do you eat snakes?" Things like that. I've had colleagues

say to me, "Oh, you must not be typical." One person asked, "Is one of your parents white? The stuff you're telling me is not my idea of Africans."

Q: *Did you grow up with white kids at all?*

A: No. Once in a while we'd see an expatriate, a British or American person, coming to our little town. We would go out of our way to welcome them. But we would just say Hi to them and then leave.[4]

African students frequently report interesting questions they are asked by professors and other students. A professor asked a student from Ghana who had lived all of his life in an African city whether he was used to sleeping in a bed. A student from Cameroon was asked by fellow students whether there are houses in Africa: "They ask if we live in houses! And if there are cars in Africa, and it's really . . . [laughter]. I don't know if there is any country in the world now that doesn't have houses or cars."[5]

The way we treat African art tends to reinforce our views of Africans as unchanging. For example, visual arts specialist Carol Magee recently studied Disney's African Safari Lodge in Orlando, Florida. She found that "traditional" African art objects were carefully displayed and described throughout the lodge, while a few examples of modern African art were merely used as decoration in a restaurant.[6] The message is that the objects, often those associated with rituals, represent our fantasy of today's Real Africa, and, says Magee, this is really a re-creation of colonial Africa.

In the same manner, we are much more likely to see so-called traditional African art in museums, private art collections, and galleries than we are to see the work of modern African artists. Curators, collectors, and dealers highly prize the supposedly primitive qualities of traditional African art and want art that is old, in decent condition, and, most importantly, used by Africans, preferably in an important ritual. In other words, the best African art for a collector tends to feed on and reinforce stereotypes about Africa.

The system is self-perpetuating. If you are an African artist, your market is largely in copies of so-called traditional objects so there isn't incentive to be innovative. American galleries and museums are beginning to show us alternatives, but there is still a ways to go. Art collectors and dealers still scour the continent looking for the most desirable traditional pieces. Many African countries have laws that prohibit or restrict the export of such national treasures, but certain types of art have acquired so much value in the United States (and in Europe, Japan, and elsewhere) that sellers and customs officials in Africa can rarely resist the money they are offered. Thieves, smugglers, and forgers also find the high prices an encouragement to enter the market.[7]

## Exotic Africa

One definition of exotic is "strikingly unusual," which implies that something is either truly rare or merely unfamiliar. Cannibalism, if it existed (see Chapter 7), was truly rare while belief in nature spirits is common, though largely unfamiliar to us. Because we are unfamiliar with Africa, there will be much that is exotic to us. We can treat the exotic in one of two ways. We can focus on it and thus heighten its difference, or we can try to look at it in context and attempt to see it as familiar, human, and understandable (even if we don't approve). Very often, Americans choose the former. The student described at the beginning of this chapter found the Real Africa in an exotic past, ignoring the context of the African village and how the funeral ceremony fit into a changing Africa.

One place the exotic is emphasized is tourist Africa. Tourist Africa isn't the real Africa, just like tourist America isn't the real America. It is carefully managed, commercialized, and exoticized. The dancing and drumming of cultural performances are pitched to tourists' illusions of what they would like Africa to be, with seams covered up and a bit of quaint wildness added. Here's the 2008 rhetoric advertising one of the more interesting tours of West Africa:

*Its not the real Africa!*

> You'll feel you've stepped into the pages of *National Geographic* on this total immersion into the dazzling tribal world of Ghana, Togo, and Benin. This is a greatly under-visited destination, the richest of tribal Africa, and our itinerary is one of a kind.
>
> Watch voodoo priestesses whirl in trances at fetish altars, hike up a ridge to commune with a famous oracle, peer into the dungeons of a 15th-century slave castle, attend a flamboyant Ashanti funeral. . . .[8]

This tour might well be worth the effort and expense, but it is clear that the tour company will be seeking and emphasizing the exotic and that the tour won't be representative of most of today's African life.

Here's part of a similar blurb from a 2012 advertisement for a different tour:

> ElderTreks: Small group exotic adventures for travelers 50 plus.
>
> Travel to another place and time. ElderTreks 4-country journey to Niger, Benin, Togo and Ghana is simply fascinating, for those with a real spirit of adventure.
>
> This region of West Africa is the birthplace of Voodoo. Learn about the mysterious beliefs from encounters with Voodoo followers and priests. Explore fetish markets and visit temples and shrines to witness a Voodoo ceremony including the practices of chanting, drumming and the resulting trance.
>
> In Niger, visit the capital, Niamey and the bizarre market of Ayorou, with it's [sic] fascinating tribal offerings. Journey in search of the last wild herd of giraffes in West Africa. In Benin, encounter a rich tribal and cultural diversity. In Togo, visit Somba and Koutammakou, a World Heritage Site. Drive through the lush, beautiful mountains of central Togo, stopping to visit one of the famous Kabye blacksmiths.[9]

It sounds interesting, but the ad and trip clearly exoticize Africa and Africans.

## Sexualized Africa

Another way to construct Real Africa as close to nature is to portray Africans as hypersexual. This is certainly a legacy of a more racist era when black Africans were considered more animalistic and sensual, more natural and less intelligent than white Europeans. Indeed, it was common to believe that others in all different parts of the world were different sexually because of their biology. Now we aren't likely to express this sentiment, but others' sexuality is nonetheless a way we imagine difference.

For example, Dr. Ray Sahelian advertises yohimbe, an aphrodisiacal herb, on his website, saying, "Experience the orgiastic mating rituals of the

African Bantu."[10] In a book, Sahelian writes, "According to early histori-cal records, Bantu tribes ingested inner bark shavings of the yohimbe tree to sustain them during extended orgiastic mating rituals that would last up to two weeks."[11] What Sahelian doesn't say is that the "historical records" are late-nineteenth-century German reports and that the Germans were highly racist and evolutionist at that time and therefore untrustworthy ob-servers. Thus there's no accurate context for the sources *or* the culture. All this is exotic rubbish.

[*Sports Illustrated* has found a sexualized Africa to be useful for its swim-suit editions. It set at least two major swimsuit stories—1994 and 1998—in Africa] The 1998 article on the Maasai of Kenya shows swimsuit-clad white American women in semi-erotic poses with blanket-clad Maasai herders. The photographer prefaces his photographs with a paragraph that explains: "The idea was to capture the raw, unspoiled beauty of this place and this people." He wants an imagined Real Africa. Who is he kidding? His white guide arranged with the Maasai "chief" to pay $1,000 for a day of photography: "We won't bother anyone, and besides, it'll be fun! [The Maasai headman] had obviously had plenty of experience with what West-erners consider 'fun.'" So much for unspoiled Africa. Kenyan middle-class society is in fact very modest about sexuality, and the country has strict laws against pornography.[12]

Carol Magee, mentioned above, analyzes the 1994 swimsuit edition in detail in her 2012 book. In fact, she actually went to the South African lo-cation of the photoshoot. There she found that the photos were taken in an outdoor museum and that the actual South Africa, even in rural areas, simply doesn't look like the images in the magazine. Moreover, Magee comments on the fact that the darker-skinned Jamaican American model is more sexualized in the photos than the white American model.[13]

In 2013, *Sports Illustrated* photographed models on all seven continents for its swimsuit edition. On its website, it also posted additional photos, including photos of models with hunter-gatherers in Namibia. This time there was more controversy. A critical comment in a web blog was picked up by *ABC News* and turned into an evening news story. The blog by Dodai Stewart opined that "Using people of color as background or ex-tras is a popular fashion trope . . . but although it's prevalent, it's very dis-tasteful. . . . People are not props."[14] Professor Marc Lamont Hill of

Columbia University told *ABC News* that, "For me, the African picture was probably the most offensive because it played on some of the most old and stereotypical images, it showed the African as primitive as almost un-civilized."[15] *ABC News* was equivocal, noting that some people enjoy see-ing other people and places in the swimsuit edition. Nonetheless, *Sports Illustrated* felt it necessary to issue an apology, albeit a weak one.[16]

Sports Illustrated might argue that its goal is to capture "unspoiled beauty" (read *natural beauty*) of Africa and Africans, but such beauty is ar-tificially constructed to conform to our stereotypes. The same is clearly true for what the magazine does to construct mythical women, both white and black. Both African and Western women are turned into objects and naturalized. Yet the fact that both *ABC News* and *Sports Illustrated* re-cently took note of objections to such stereotyping shows that our atti-tudes are changing.

## Wise Africa

Westerners have constructed positive images of Africans and other non-Westerners for a very long time. As far back as classical Greece and Rome, Western authors idealized various peoples on the fringes of the known world. And from the era of European expansion onward, Amerindians, Polynesians, and other non-Westerners sometimes ap-peared in Western literature in the form of wise characters who critiqued Western civilization. The idea of the noble savage, which developed in the late seventeenth century, maintained that so-called primitives lived in a "state of nature"—healthy, happy, good, and free—as God intended all humans to live.

After about 1800, the widely held evolutionist myths made it difficult to sustain positive images of non-Europeans. Increasingly, Africans were seen as savages who needed to be controlled and, if possible, trained to do profitable work. Yet both colonial missionaries and secularists preferred to deal with Africans who were "uncorrupted" by the West. Government of-ficials frequently found that Western-educated "trousered blacks" and "mission blacks" caused problems because they could challenge the West on its own terms. And missionaries preferred Africans who were "inno-cent," meaning those who would accept Christianity in a biblically appro-priate "childlike manner."[17] Indeed, when Africans read the Christian scriptures, they sometimes concluded that it was the missionaries them-selves who were not following the Bible. Thus, for many colonists, the Real Africa was an illusionary place where Africans were good children—less evolved and more natural.

More recently, Westerners have attributed more dimensions to Africans, so that we now view Africans as more complex and more like us than ever before. Nonetheless, even our positive stereotypes still evoke dif-ference. For example, Malidoma Somé has become something of a celebrity in several American subcultures including the men's movement. Somé, a Burkinabe (a person from Burkina Faso) with doctorates in both political science and literature, became involved in the American men's movement. In his book *Of Water and the Spirit*, he describes how he was taken from his home as a very young child and raised by dictatorial French Jesuit mis-sionaries. Fleeing back home at age twenty, Somé could no longer under-stand his Dagara traditions or even his language. The elders struggled to reunite him with his people and culture through a dangerous initiation rit-ual. Eventually, Somé became a Dagara shaman and he now teaches Da-gara wisdom to Western audiences. One of his messages is that all males can learn from African initiation ceremonies how to mark the passage from boyhood to manhood, overcoming the crises of adolescence and becom-ing comfortable with adulthood.[18]

I find Somé an exceptionally interesting writer. Yet the book and his lectures are still problematic as a window on Africa, because they respond specifically to American longing for a place where life is wise, prime, basic, and good. Noble Africa stereotypes are still stereotypes. Here is a com-ment from Somé's website:

> The spark of this ancestral flame, which I have brought to the land of the stranger, is now burning brightly. Increasingly, I have been and will be encouraging westerners to embody these traditions as a testimony to the indigenous capacity to assert itself with dignity in the face of modernity. In this way the ancestors will know that this medicine has found a true home—that it is more than an honored guest.[19]

Somé's version of Africa might be an antidote for overdoses of some Dark Continent myths and of Western civilization, but it also falsifies and ob-scures contemporary Africa.

## Superior Africa

During the Dark Continent era, most African Americans more or less accepted the dominant European American belief in African backwardness.[20] The reasons are multiple. Because the general cultural climate in America promoted evolutionism, it would have been exceedingly difficult to see Africa in any other terms. Most African Americans were Christians and believed that most Africans, as non-Christians, needed salvation. Moreover, because whites gathered and interpreted nearly all the information about Africa, African Americans had little opportunity to imagine or discover a nonprimitive Africa.[21]

Even an unknown Africa, however, could symbolize "home" for African Americans. From the beginning, Africa represented freedom and played an important role in black American discourse about slavery, racism, and oppression in white America.[22] A prominent example of Africa's place in African American consciousness occurred in the 1920s when black Americans demonstrated widespread enthusiasm for the Back-to-Africa movement led by Marcus Garvey. Although Garvey's movement never sent emigrants to Africa, during its brief period of success it enrolled hundreds of thousands (some say millions) of African Americans in the cause of liberating Africa for the black race. Historian John Hope Franklin calls this "the first mass movement" among black Americans and notes that it indicated their doubts about ever achieving equality in America.[23]

Ethiopia also played an important positive role in African American consciousness. In the eighteenth and nineteenth centuries, both whites and blacks frequently employed the word *Ethiopia* as a synonym for Africa, following the biblical and classical traditions. In the early twentieth century, the country of Ethiopia (or Abyssinia) was the only part of Africa that remained independent of Western colonialism, a result of the crushing African defeat of an Italian army in 1896. Moreover, Ethiopians were mostly Coptic Christians, not the so-called pagans the Christians hoped to convert. Thus, the country could symbolize African American aspirations for their own, as well as African, freedom.[24] Historian William Scott notes that although black Americans knew little about Ethiopia itself, Ethiopianism was a "gospel of worldwide African redemption" that had been preached in black communities throughout eighteenth- and nineteenth-century America.[25] In the 1920s, Marcus

Garvey's Back-to-Africa movement tapped into widespread Ethiopianism, and when fascist Italy invaded Ethiopia in 1935, black Americans strongly protested.[26]

In the anti-Italian campaign, African Americans projected themselves for the first time into global politics. They campaigned for American support for Ethiopia and offered material aid and soldiers for the Ethiopian army. Yet this interest in the actual Ethiopia—rather than an idealized Ethiopia—caused many problems related to race. For example, Ethiopians, whose skin is relatively light-colored, did not consider themselves to be black, and they often treated black Americans as racial inferiors. Moreover, some black Americans opposed aid to Ethiopia because Ethiopians were not black enough. Many white Americans also had difficulties with the situation because they disliked fascist Italy but didn't want black Americans helping Ethiopians. They also used the Ethiopian claim of whiteness against African Americans.[27]

Until the mid-twentieth century, the few American voices that proclaimed the value of African achievements were usually African American. Even before the American Revolution, various black intellectuals described precolonial African history in positive terms. In the nineteenth century, such well-known figures as William Wells Brown, Frederick Douglass, and Martin Delany spoke of a civilized Africa. In the first half of the twentieth century, Carter G. Woodson and W. E. B. Du Bois became the preeminent American spokespersons for African accomplishments. Woodson founded the Association for the Study of Negro Life in 1915 and the *Journal of Negro History* in 1916, and his 1922 college text, *The Negro in Our History*, included a chapter on African history.[28] Du Bois championed African American consciousness of African greatness, and he promoted Pan-Africanism, a movement that linked black leaders in North America, the Caribbean, Europe, and Africa. At the same time, he opposed Garvey's Back-to-Africa movement because he felt that the African American "home" was America, not Africa. A focus on Africa, he said, would divert blacks from the struggle for equality in America.[29]

As Africans and African Americans gained power in the second half of the twentieth century, an increasing number of Americans, both white and black, came to understand that Africa has always contributed to global history. African American scholars played important roles in making accurate information available. In 1947, for example, John Hope Franklin published a widely read history of African Americans that opened with a solid discussion of African civilizations. African independence and the civil rights era of the 1960s helped reduce Dark Continent myths among black Americans. We can't say, however, that such myths are entirely gone. An African American teacher in the Washington, DC, public schools recently told me that his black students make fun of Africans because the students feel they are savages. This excellent teacher takes the time to show his students images of urban Africa as well as teach the students about African history.

Because American society is still race-conscious and evolutionist, the understandable temptation for some African Americans is to create countervailing myths about Africa.[30] In the extreme, some African Americans believe in an idealized superior Real Africa whose only problems are contamination, degradation, and exploitation by the West. In this superior Africa, Africans alone were responsible for the beginnings of world civilization, science, math, technology, law, government, ethical behavior, and so forth. Thus, the myth of superior Africa is constructed to compete with the equally mythical superior West, which defines progress primarily in terms of itself: its own great states, great cities, great wealth, great discoveries and inventions, complex technologies, universal religions, and so forth.

As with Ethiopia in the 1930s, however, the actual Africa poses problems for this version of a superior Real Africa. For example, several years ago I attended a workshop on Africa in which Afrocentrist graduate students verbally attacked the Africans who were presenters. The crux of the assault was that because the Africans had Western educations; because they were Christians, Muslims, or secularists; and because they were modern, they were not really Africans. The American Afrocentrists, who had not been to Africa, claimed to be the real Africans.[31]

## Where Is the Real Africa?

The Real Africa of our imaginations never existed. Nineteenth- and early-twentieth-century evolutionism created Africa as different—natural and primitive—and that idea hasn't died . . . yet. Such an imaginary Africa is kept alive by ignorance and by the benefits we get from myths about African difference. Yet the point here is not that today's Africa has no problems or that it has no difference. Indeed, Africa has more *visible* problems than any other region of the world, and Africa is the most rural of the continents except for Antarctica.

But Africa's problems and differences need context. First, Africa's problems are not inherent to Africa. That is, they are not natural. They were created in a history that included Western civilization as well as the civilizations of Africa. The West has been deeply involved in Africa for more than 500 years and has rarely taken Africa's real interests into consideration, despite a professed desire to help. This historical past, for better and worse, is very much a part of every corner of today's Real Africa.

Moreover, Africa is much more similar to us than our myths about difference allow. Africans in the past and present made and make decisions that are as rational (and irrational) as ours. And not only is today's Africa 40 percent urban, cities are growing faster in Africa than anywhere else. These cities imply roads, cars, bus lines, airports, water supplies, electricity, jobs, bars, nightclubs, movies, restaurants, popular music, factories, churches and mosques, hospitals, computers, cellphones, stock exchanges, and much more. Does everyone have reliable water, a job, a car, a computer, or a cellphone? Obviously not. But, to take an example, cellphone use is growing fastest in sub-Saharan Africa, where an average of 57 percent of adults have cellphones. According to a 2011 Gallup poll, usage is heaviest among urban males aged 18 to 45 years, but in some countries rural use is about the same as urban (for example, Ghana: urban 58%/rural 60%; Nigeria: urban 77%/rural 66%; South Africa: urban 82%/rural 86%).[32]

To take other examples, IBM is opening a research lab in Kenya where up to fifty scientists will study problems related to Kenyan traffic (vehicle congestion is a major issue), clean water supplies, and population density.[33] Nigeria, Kenya, and South Africa are exploring space programs so they can, among other goals, provide better information to farmers. The World Bank, while cautious, says "GDP growth in sub-Saharan Africa is back on track." The global prices of its exports are rising, there is strong local demand, new products are being developed (including many oil and gas discoveries), and governments are gaining experience in encouraging growth.[34]

Rural Africa, where 60 percent of Africans live, is rarely as isolated from modern Africa as we imagine. There are, perhaps, a few Africans who have stayed away from modern life either by choice, remoteness, or lack of opportunity. They too are part of the Real Africa, but they are more exceptions than representatives. For most rural Africans, there is frequent and increasing interaction with towns and cities. Most rural Africans are producing crops for urban areas or for the world market. Most rural children are going to school. And the vast majority of Africans practice either Islam or Christianity.

Is the Real Africa different from the Real America? Yes and no. Is a rural Midwest town different from New York City? Yes and no. It depends on what you focus on and how you tell the story. If you want to, you can turn the Midwest town into much the same mythical place as Africa . . . or New York City into a modern monster. Indeed, where is the Real America? From one perspective, we might even say that New Yorkers have more in common with the citizens of Cape Town, Nairobi, or Abidjan than with the people of the American Midwest. There are many Real Americas and many Real Africas.

Real Africa myths are understandable because they are "useful to think with." They can help us reflect on what our civilization does to us. They can make us feel better by telling us we are more evolved, more peaceful, more wealthy, or more (or less) something else. They can entertain us with the exotic. But although such myths are understandable in the American context, they are problematic for Africa.

# 6

# WE SHOULD HELP THEM[1]

I have sometimes shown my classes a short video about a village named Wassetake, located in northern Senegal.[2] The purpose of the video is to demonstrate how life in much of rural Africa is orderly and dignified. Viewers follow village families as they go about a typical day and year—keeping house, tending fields, going to Koran and French-language schools, entertaining guests, and making decisions that affect the village. The village is poor, but it is attempting to improve itself. For example, the elders discuss the construction of a larger school building and decide to request money for cement from some of the young people who have left the village to look for work in Dakar, the capital city.

Once, after I first began showing this video, a student came up after class and remarked, "We should help them!" Soon I discovered that quite a few students felt a desire to help this and similar villages. I was surprised because the video was not meant to elicit sympathy but to demonstrate that most Africans live satisfying lives and are working to solve their own problems. Many students saw poor people who needed help; I saw strong people coping with their lives. This interesting contrast in points of view is worth exploring. Does Wassetake village really need our help? What is wrong with life as they live it? What kind of help would be truly useful to them?

For the last 150 years many Americans and Europeans have gone to Africa to help. Our impulse to help is sometimes called our "civilizing mission." During the colonial era, Westerners assumed that helping

Africans become civilized could be only partially successful because of Africans' inferior race.[3] As the colonial era ended and racism declined, however, we came to believe that so-called civilization can be quickly diffused to Africans in a process called "development" or "modernization." Today, we continue to help Africa through efforts to make African societies look more like our own.

What we need to ask, however, is whether many of Africa's contemporary problems might be a *result* of our efforts to help. Perhaps our assumptions about becoming modern are faulty and our approaches actually *contribute* to Africa's problems. Perhaps becoming more like us is not really the goal Africa ought to be striving for. The point is not that our modern civilization has nothing to offer Africa. Rather, by assuming that we know what Africans need and by trying to help Africans from the outside in, from the top down, we may in fact distort the process of change so badly that the result is an African *inability* to develop.

To explore these ideas, we look at five different models of assistance to Africa: authoritarianism, the market economy, gift giving, conversion, and participation. In addition, we briefly discuss military help. The purpose here is not to be comprehensive but to point out that helping Africa is not as easy as we might at first assume.

## Authoritarian Help

All sorts of Africans participated in the independence struggle against Europe, but those who gained control of the newly independent states in the 1960s and after tended to be "modern men." These new elites had Western educations and professed a modern vision for their countries. At last, they proclaimed, Africa would "catch up" with the West. What they envisioned, for the most part, was economic development defined as industrialization. But since the majority of Africans were uneducated traditionalist farmers, most new leaders assumed that the only hope for rapid industrialization lay with the state. The model of apparent success at state-sponsored development in the Soviet Union was readily available. Moreover, leading theorists in the new Western discipline of development studies focused on capital accumulation as the engine of economic growth. The key idea for Africa was that governments should raise capital through taxes, borrowing, and foreign aid and then invest it in education, health care, roads, state-run factories, and other development projects.]

This top-down plan turned out to be a recipe for disaster because it funneled development resources through the hands of small groups of African leaders who were neither disciplined nor skilled at implementing such policies. The plan allowed the leaders to divert funds to other purposes, such as increasing their own wealth and power, often exacerbating the many social divisions in their countries. In a short time, bureaucracies, police forces, and military forces grew dramatically; independent voices were squelched; and leaders used divide-and-conquer tactics among their own peoples by appealing to ethnic, religious, regional, and class loyalties. Moreover, the top-down method of industrialization reduced profit incentives and efficiency and concentrated resources in urban areas so that poor rural people streamed into already overcrowded cities. The West complained but nonetheless cooperated because it needed the support of African leaders in the Cold War, because raw materials and profits still flowed toward the West, and because Westerners assumed that Africans were backward and thus unable to manage any better.

By the 1970s, the continent as a whole was slipping badly. Adding to the internal mismanagement by African governments were sharp rises in the price of oil imports, sharp drops in the prices of exports, and global inflation. Underpaid, underserved, and overtaxed farmers decided to grow fewer crops, resulting in even less income for governments. Cash-starved governments borrowed money, hoping that a turnaround in world prices would allow them to repay their loans. This didn't happen. There simply wasn't enough money in Africa to repay the debts, maintain national economies, and support the by-now-institutionalized corruption. As a result, communications, water, power, and transportation systems deteriorated and collapsed. Spare parts, fuel, pesticides, and fertilizer grew scarce. Food had to be imported to feed the urban populations. A few elites lived like royalty while most citizens barely survived.

[ Most important for our discussion is that the failed authoritarian model of development in Africa was deeply conditioned by the West's evolutionist ideas of development and by the West's efforts to help. Colonial systems were schools for demonstrating government centralization of politics and economics.] And after independence (we promoted industrialization as the road to development, supported dictators (or anticommunist rebels) in the Cold War struggle, and endorsed the assumption of the new African elites that ordinary Africans were too backward to know how to develop on their own. New studies in the 1960s and after, however, revealed to economists that African farmers make rational market decisions. Thus, it now appears that African governments, not farmers, lacked the skills and attitudes to promote economic growth. Authoritarian development failed because those who were supposed to make it work made evolutionist assumptions, because they could not be held accountable to the ordinary citizens they claimed to serve, and because they depended on global political and economic systems that did not support development.

## Market Help

The West could not afford to allow Africa to descend into chaos in the 1980s. Our own self-interest and humanitarianism required some kind of new help for African problems. Therefore, Western political and financial leaders decided on a new plan, one that would get the inefficient African governments out of the way. Deeply in debt and unable to repay, Africans were told that if they wanted Western help, they would have to abandon the goal of quick industrialization and return to an emphasis on the production of raw materials. For the most part, African leaders complied because without Western help they could not remain in power.

The new plan was largely implemented through two giant international agencies run by wealthy Western countries, the International Monetary Fund (IMF) and the World Bank. Country after country had to adopt a "structural adjustment plan" (SAP) that would reduce the government's role and shift economic growth to private hands. This entailed drastic changes that included lowering taxes and tariffs, cutting education and health care budgets, selling government-owned businesses, devaluing currencies, and ending urban food subsidies. Farmers were allowed to charge higher prices in an effort to stimulate food and cash-crop production.

The outcomes of structural adjustment in Africa have been uneven and controversial. By some measures, SAPs produced economic growth and more income equity. Shrunken governments, for example, had less ability to fleece the African people, and programs saved money by shutting down schools and health clinics. Higher prices for raw materials encouraged the production of crops and supply of minerals that could be sold to Westerners. The lifting of government restrictions made space for new, small-scale African businesses. The sale of unproductive government-owned businesses allowed economic rejuvenation by efficient new private owners. Some African countries began to slowly pay back some of the billions of dollars of debt they owed the West.

On the other hand, Africa's modest recovery was extremely fragile and vulnerable to external factors such as weather and global economic conditions. Moreover, SAPs produced enormous economic and social disruption. They required radical surgery, more extreme than belt-tightening or even shock therapy. In the many countries in which they were applied, SAPs suddenly took away the safety nets of millions of people. Many lost jobs. Steep inflation destroyed the value of local currencies. Educational, health care, and social welfare systems were gutted. One Nigerian observer, Claude Ake, protested, "These grim notions of policy reform can be inflicted only by people who do not belong to the adjusting society or by those who are immune to the impact of the reform."[4] Indeed, many Africans who condemn the rapacious behavior of African governments also ask whether the goal of structural adjustment was to help Africans or to help the West. The West reaped the rewards of African raw materials, investments, and interest on bad loans, while Africans struggled to survive. Many Africans argue that the West used the economic crisis to once again impose foreign ideologies and force Africans to produce raw materials for Western powers, as in the colonial period.

As parts of Africa became even poorer, the International Monetary Fund, the World Bank, and other international financial and development institutions realized that structural adjustment had gone too far.[5] The debt incurred in the 1970s and 1980s was simply too large for many African countries to repay no matter what reforms they undertook. Moreover, without health care, education, and basic infrastructure, Africa was indeed doomed. The "debt crisis" had to be addressed, and the only way to do so was through debt cancellation for the many "heavily indebted poor countries" (HIPCs) in Africa. But the lending countries found it difficult to cancel the debt of the HIPCs. Lending countries had long realized they would never get their money back, but by canceling debt, they would lose leverage over African countries. Since about 2000, a few of the HIPCs have received cancellation in return for economic reforms, and more are under consideration. SAPs still exist, but in a more moderate form, and are now called Poverty Reduction Strategy Papers.

In trying to implement a market economy in Africa from the top down, the West has run into all sorts of difficulties. Educated, urban, and well-connected Africans, as well as foreign corporations, have benefited most from the forced transition to market economies. They understand what is happening and can, for example, move quickly to buy up bankrupt government factories or claim as their own the collective land of family lineages. They are most able to manipulate the government bureaucracy to promote their schemes. A top-down market agenda, even when inspired by well-meaning experts, can crush people who are less advantaged and who lack the cultural knowledge that would allow them to either protect themselves or succeed in the imposed market economy.

We should also note that the rich countries have subsidized their own agriculture, often making African agricultural products too expensive to export or even to sell on local markets. Journalist Regina Jere-Malanda calls it an "obscenity" that "every European cow receives $2 per day from governments while 1.2 billion people live on less than $1 per day." She adds, "It is indeed bizarre that it is cheaper for a Ghanaian to buy an imported European-raised chicken than a locally raised one." Under pressure, the Ghanaian government passed a law in 2005 that curtailed poultry imports, but the IMF forced cancellation of the law.[6] Thus between 2002 and 2011 poultry imports quadrupled and the Ghanaian domestic poultry industry declined dramatically.[7]

Although the new market orientation was supposed to help ordinary people, it has in many cases done enormous violence to them. Under such circumstances, it is easy to see how Africans might doubt that so-called market solutions are the answer to their economic problems.

## Conversion Help

Does the conversion model of assistance produce better results? It is certainly less violent, based as it is on persuasion rather than state-imposed capital formation or a foreign-imposed market. On the other hand, the conversion model still constructs an evolutionist world in which African cultures are inferior and their goal should therefore be to become more like the West.

The prototypical conversion experience is, of course, religious, and it continues throughout sub-Saharan Africa to this day. There are, however, more secular forms of conversion, such as education and commercial advertising that attempt to convince Africans to adopt new ways. Africa is bombarded with messages that suggest lifestyle alternatives. Schools teach Western history, philosophy, and economics. Development workers promote scientific methods of nutrition and hygiene. Billboards advertise Mercedes, Coca-Cola, and Marlboro. Television in some countries broadcasts American shows such as *CSI*, *Extreme Makeover*, *Desperate Housewives*, *Baywatch*, and CNN news, while radios play the music of Western stars. The Voice of America and the British Broadcasting Corporation, run by the United States and the United Kingdom, respectively, proudly teach English and spread Western points of view.

Under the best of circumstances, those who are converted gain skills and ideas that can enable them to cope better with the world. Africa could not defend itself in a global arena without its many Western-educated professionals who speak the same intellectual language as the West. Likewise, one would hope to spread knowledge about safe sexual practices in the face of AIDS and other sexually transmitted diseases. But not all conversion is beneficial. In one infamous example, in the 1970s the Swiss-based Nestlé Corporation advertised that bottle-fed babies were healthier than breast-fed babies, targeting mothers throughout the developing world. As a result, thousands of infants died each year from malnutrition (because families could not afford sufficient formula) and from gastrointestinal disease (because families used unsafe water to dilute the formula). An international boycott of Nestlé products produced an agreement in 1984 in which the company agreed to abide by a World Health Organization (WHO) code. However, the company continues to market its products in Africa and elsewhere by trying to convince mothers that bottle feeding is good for babies. Nestlé is still a target for a boycott led by Baby Milk Action, a British-based group supported by a number of churches and child-focused nonprofit organizations.[8]

In any culture, it is painful to see people converted to self-destructive tastes and habits. This is particularly so in Africa because of the limited resources available. To see people drink Coca-Cola or smoke Marlboros when their children have inadequate nutrition is troubling. And while American tobacco companies are increasingly restricted in the United States, they are expanding their advertising campaigns elsewhere.

Conversion poses another danger. Frequently, those who gain specialized modern skills dissociate themselves from their villages and countries. The brain drain of African professionals who have emigrated to Europe and America is legendary. Tens of thousands of educated Africans leave Africa each year. Even more damaging are those who become Westernized and then use their knowledge to exploit ordinary Africans. For example, churches in Africa often sponsor young people in achieving Western educations, so they can later return and serve the church. But once they are trained, the youths often either abuse church positions of trust or leave the church entirely and use their educations to become privately wealthy. This is not surprising, given human nature and the individualist values implicit in Western education, but it is a major pitfall for those who want to help by converting Africans to Western ways. In my own teaching experience in Congo (Kinshasa), I probably trained as many functionaries for the oppressive central government as I did citizens who aspired to promote development in their communities.

With all of the strong conversionist messages bombarding Africa, one wonders on what cultural foundation Africa could best build its future. Scholar Ali Mazrui has considered the confusion that arises in the clash between African, Western, and Islamic cultures and concludes that "Africa has lost its way."[9] The modern assault that individualism, consumerism, and alternative lifestyles pose is even more problematic for Africans than it is for ourselves. Presumably, Africans will find creative solutions in the midst of the confusion, but cultural harmony has not been a hallmark of this era.

## Gift-Giving Help

A popular misconception holds that American foreign aid is a huge government expenditure. Actually, in 2011 US government foreign aid amounted to 1 percent of the US government budget. All US foreign aid to all developing countries amounted to only 0.20 percent of our gross national income, fifth from the bottom of the twenty-three industrialized countries that are members of the Organisation for Economic Cooperation and Development (OECD). The average contribution was .46 percent,[10] while the United Nations goal for industrialized countries is .7 percent. Only because we have such a large economy do our small percentages still represent more in absolute terms than what others give. And only because private American citizens are generous do our overall contributions remain substantial.

The question of whether to give aid is one of the most debated topics in our relations with Africa, and critics point to numerous reasons why aid is too much, too little, misdirected, useless, or harmful.[11] Most of the issues with giving aid fall outside the scope of this book, so here only a few of the issues can be mentioned. We should note, for example, that most aid packages have an evolutionist basis in that they assume the transfer of resources should be "downward" to help Africans "catch up." Moreover, except for disaster and debt relief, aid is rarely a true gift. Most frequently, aid is connected to donors' ideas about what is good for Africa and either explicitly or implicitly requires Africans to change their societies so they can make use of what is given. Ideally, Africans are supposed to receive exactly what they need for development. More frequently, gifts are mixed blessings.

Examples of failed aid projects number in the many hundreds. In the 1970s, for example, development workers began to realize that most aid for relief and development was reaching African men but not women because of Western assumptions that men were the breadwinners and would share with women. In much of Africa, however, men and women keep separate accounts, and property and roles are sharply divided along gender lines. Women do most of the work of growing, storing, and preparing food. This means that aid going only to men contributed to a long-term decline in the status of women and the condition of children.[12] In a similar manner, a 2006 fact-finding trip to Kenya by two British members of the European Parliament revealed that aid tends to flow toward commercial agriculture and disaster relief while leaving out poor farmers and herders.[13]

In a further example, a large American religious organization decided to build classrooms in Congo (Kinshasa). American builders arrived, and schools quickly rose in four or five villages. The villages used the classrooms but did not take care of them because they had not built them. When the buildings fell into disrepair, there was no motivation or organization to fix them. A request to the United States for more money and another builder went unanswered; the American organization had moved on to other projects.

Clearly, gift giving can promote ideas and tastes that are not good for Africa, foster dependence, weaken local initiative, and empower people who are not legitimate leaders. It can promote superior-inferior relationships between the West and Africa. And it requires an "aid industry" of foreigners interested not only in helping Africans but also in maintaining their own influence and employment. In fact, aid failures are so numerous and successes so few that some observers have asked whether *all* of our aid efforts have been misguided and ought to be halted. Most, however, would argue that aid has a potentially important role to play in helping Africa. What we need is a better sense of what kind of aid is really helpful.

We should take note of the efforts that have worked well. Four examples related to AIDS must suffice here. (1) Two retired doctors, Bill and Peg Hoffman, who volunteered at a clinic in Tanzania introduced the use of drugs that prevent the transmission of AIDS to unborn children. Their work became a model for the country and has saved countless children.[14] (2) The Global Fund to Fight AIDS, Tuberculosis and Malaria has funded effective campaigns mounted by a number of government health ministries in Africa against these diseases.[15] (3) The Clinton Foundation's CHAI (Clinton HIV/AIDS Initiative) and UNITAID (a UN-funded European agency) helped Africans pool their purchasing power to achieve a 2007 agreement with two pharmaceutical manufacturers to provide antiretroviral medications (ARVs) at low cost to millions of people in Africa and elsewhere.[16] (4) The President's Emergency Plan for AIDS Relief (PEPFAR), a US government program, has sponsored a campaign in Rwanda whereby patients receive ARVs, and the use of cellphones assures that each patient receives a daily dose. It had been assumed that ordinary Africans would not adhere to a daily dosage schedule, but in Rwanda adherence is better than in many countries with better education systems.[17] Whether through personal, nonprofit, commercial, or government assistance, aid *can* help Africa.

One recent shift on the part of government donors has been from "project aid" toward "program aid." Program aid is given to African governments or economic sectors that maintain programs to support development, such as the recruitment of teachers or higher pay for nurses. Such programs require fewer skilled managers and have much lower start-up and maintenance costs than projects, and therefore use resources more efficiently. They also provide much-needed support over time rather than the once-and-done support of projects. Program aid is also increasingly tied to performance targets rather than policies, thus providing measures of a country's success in using its aid. However, program aid is generally given on a year-by-year basis and thus relies on the vagaries of yearly appropriations battles in donor countries. By contrast, because aid for individual projects is appropriated all at one time, it is more secure.[18]

# Participatory Help

In recent years, one of the buzzwords of development aid to Africans has been *participation*.[19] Participation implies that development must be a bottom-up rather than a top-down process and that it cannot be done *to* or *for* someone. Those who are developing must therefore take part in deciding what they need, what they are willing to build, and what they can maintain. Most definitions of participatory development also include the idea that successful development is "self-reliant," meaning that it receives only small amounts of outside help. Here is one such definition:

> Self-reliant participatory development is an educational and empowering process in which people, in partnership with each other and with those able to assist them, identify problems and needs, mobilize resources, and assume responsibility themselves to plan, manage, control and assess the individual and collective actions that they themselves decide upon.[20]

Participatory development assumes that local people have knowledge and resources and that their greatest needs are self-reflection, self-confidence, organization, and self-discipline, rather than gifts or conversions. If outside funds, equipment, or knowledge are provided, they should come only in small, "appropriate" forms and amounts, and they should go only to local groups that have already had small successes on their own.

To some extent, participation is now recognized as an important component of every development project in Africa. At the local level, however, real participation is difficult to achieve. The everyday work of development is most often done by development agencies, mostly nonprofits, commonly known as nongovernmental organizations (NGOs). Many have familiar names—World Vision International, Save the Children, Care, Bread for the World, Food First—but there are hundreds more, both African and foreign, both nonprofit and for-profit. It is now common for the agents of foreign NGOs to ask for grassroots participation, frequently in the form of surveys or focus groups. But most NGOs have their own agendas (such as mosquito nets, vaccines, clean water, or nutrition) and need fast, concrete, and impressive results that appeal to contributors. Thus, agents often construct a facade of participation that hides what is essentially top-down development. They ask questions and make suggestions based on the NGO's preconceived ideas about what the target villages need. Or participation is elicited, but those who participate are the "important people" in a village, who may have their own agendas. Some development researchers mockingly turn *participate* into a passive verb, saying that Africans "are participated" in such top-down projects.

It is difficult to find NGOs and individual agents willing and able to facilitate true bottom-up participation for ordinary village people and the urban poor. Effective work usually requires actually living in villages and learning African languages. Progress is often slow because true participation requires that villagers develop themselves with only minimal input from agents. It is a complex and even dangerous process, since every community has its own hierarchies of power that will be upset when real development occurs. When one group (such as women, poor farmers, or wage laborers) gains wealth and power, others (such as men, richer farmers, employers, or government agents) may feel deeply threatened.

In spite of these difficulties, most development experts now call for more attempts to facilitate real participation. NGOs are working on ways to increase Africans' participation levels and educate their Western contributors about the benefits of participation and patience. Many NGOs are adopting the slow-but-effective participatory policies that have long been used by such low-profile agencies as Heifer International and the Mennonite Central Committee.[21] Even Western governments are channeling more of their development dollars through NGOs rather than through African governments, the US Agency for International Development, or Western corporations. Slowly, African development is coming to be viewed as a bottom-up enterprise.

One kind of bottom-up development effort is found in the relatively new social entrepreneurship movement.[22] Social entrepreneurs use entrepreneurial principles, but they count their profits in social value more than in money. Perhaps the best known of the social entrepreneurial projects is community banking. Inspired by Muhammad Yunus, winner of the 2006

Nobel Peace Prize, community banks now make small loans—microloans—to poor people in Africa and elsewhere. With a small loan, often only $100 or less, a person can start a small business such as raising goats, sewing clothes, or milling grain. Poor people, who were once considered untrustworthy and without collateral, now repay their loans more faithfully than borrowers in Europe and the United States. Their collateral is social pressure, because those who do not repay make it impossible for others in a borrowing group to get credit. In small-scale communities, social pressure is very strong.

There are many other social entrepreneurship projects in Africa. For example, in 2012 the Schwab Foundation for Social Entrepreneurship awarded five prizes for African projects: (1) an Ethiopian who trained hundreds of people to make stylish footware, for sale in international markets, from recycled tires; (2) a Rwandan who organized villagers to sell pedal-rechargeable LED lights; (3) a South African who set up a chain of roadside health clinics for long-distance truck drivers in ten countries; (4) a South African who trained young people in environmental management and set up an environmental sustainability certification program in several African countries; (5) a Burkinabe (a person from Burkina Faso) and a Frenchman who taught villagers how to make houses entirely out of bricks, thus providing many jobs and saving the trees that were formerly used for roofs.[23]

Each of these examples and many others demonstrate that ordinary Africans can change their own lives if given the opportunity. Most social entrepreneurs are ordinary people who see a problem and on their own decide to address it from the bottom up. It is possible, however, for American students to study social entrepreneurship. For example, the online journal *Poets and Quants* describes and ranks eleven top graduate programs in nonprofit management that teach social entrepreneurship.[24]

## Military Help

The military help we offer Africans is not directly related to the kind of development discussed above, but it nonetheless represents how Americans think about Africa. During the Cold War we gave military advice and aid to cooperative African governments, most of which were oppressive. The

Soviet Union did the same for its African clients, increasing domestic oppression and fostering proxy wars between our friends and theirs. One could argue that weak African governments needed support and that stability was better than chaos. One might also argue that support for anti-Soviet "liberation" groups helped end the Cold War. Until the end of that war, however, our military help generally promoted oppression rather than democracy.

The US military currently operates in dozens of African countries. In 2007 the United States announced plans to establish a separate Africa command structure for its military operations—AFRICOM—with headquarters based permanently somewhere in Africa. The reason given was the promotion of African security, government stability, and development, but the US government doesn't give such "help" without having its own interests in mind. In this case, China, terrorism, and resources are in play.

The Chinese have rapidly moved into Africa in search of markets and raw materials. Across the continent, Chinese traders sell cheap goods desired by Africans. The Chinese, not Americans, produce the cheap bicycles, motorcycles, foot-powered sewing machines, everyday cooking equipment, and other tools that Africans need. Thus Chinese traders undersell African and Western traders. Furthermore, the Chinese government is providing large amounts of aid to Africa in an effort to win friends. More troubling, however, is the Chinese practice of buying rights to African resources, generally considered the property of African states, with little regard for whether the governments that profit are oppressive.

The United States is increasingly concerned about Chinese influence in Africa. Of course, the irony is that the Chinese are doing essentially what the West has done in Africa for centuries. But given our interests, the United States must respond, and one response is to increase military presence in the region. AFRICOM may help increase security and stability for some, but AFRICOM's primary goal is revealed by the fact that it originally intended to establish its headquarters somewhere near the Gulf of Guinea, the location of oil fields rivaling the huge fields of Saudi Arabia. Many Americans are concerned that increased US military presence in Africa will further militarize Africa and send the wrong message about peaceful African development. African countries, with only two exceptions (Liberia and Ethiopia), do not want the AFRICOM headquarters on their territory.

Of course another goal of the US military is to deal with terrorism and political instability across the continent. We are rapidly building our capacity to wage special operations warfare in what is sometimes termed our "secret war" in Islamic areas.[25] As a result, we seem to be entering an era in which we once again support oppressive governments and cause increasing numbers of Africans to resent us, because we do not address underlying issues of poverty and oppression. It is clear that our primary goals in Africa are not to stop genocide in Sudan, end the brutal conflict in eastern Congo (Kinshasa), or capture the ruthless bandit Joseph Kony. One might ask, in that regard, why it is necessary to allow exceptions to the 2008 Child Soldiers Prevention Act for Chad, Congo (Kinshasa), (South) Sudan, and Yemen. We look the other way when children fight for our causes. And how do you suppose most Africans feel about the title of a 2009 American military university report: "Irregular Warfare on the Dark Continent"? Such an insult and the shallow and inaccurate analysis contained in the report show how far we still have to go.[26]

## The Failure of Help

In the 1970s a friend of mine was staying at a mission guesthouse in Dar es Salaam, Tanzania, where he made the acquaintance of another guest, an elderly white man who was visiting the country to see old friends. Remarkably, before Tanzanian independence in the early 1960s, this man had been the missionary who ran the guesthouse. Rather than experiencing a joyful return, however, the old man was distraught because the guesthouse, now run by Africans, provided dreadful service and was falling apart. All his years of caring for the place had only resulted in this. "I tried," he said, almost crying.

We might sympathize with this man. After more than a century of the West offering help to Africa, many of the stereotypes we have about today's Africa—war, disease, famine, corruption—have some basis in fact. In the midst of our concern for Africa, however, we must be careful not to fall back on our old assumptions about helping Africans. Our cultural myths would have us blame Africans for their failure to become more like us. This is another version of evolutionism. But the problem is less about Africans than about the project we undertook and the methods we used. Like the missionary, we focused on the guesthouse while we should have been focusing on something else. Or, to paraphrase Mark Twain, if your only tool is a hammer, all your problems appear to be nails.

The elderly missionary defined development as a well-run and well-maintained guesthouse, and he had tried to teach Africans how to accomplish this. But these were the missionary's goals and methods, imposed on people who had their own cultures and their own ideas about what development meant. The point is not that modernity, technology, and assistance are useless. Nor is it that Africans should be left alone to live however they choose. Abandoning Africa would be cynical (and impossible) after the centuries of mutual involvement that have shaped today's Africa and world. Rather, we need to throw down our hammer and find different tools, different concepts, and different methods of development. The model of development defined as "catching up" has not worked well.

Such thinking is also problematic in that it replicates the nineteenth-century error of measuring Africans by what they lack, while measuring ourselves by what we appear to do well. As a result, we focus our gaze away from our own problems. For example, if we portray all of our actions in Africa as "helping Africa develop," it becomes difficult even to imagine that we might be exploiting Africa. Thus, we have in good conscience supported dictators who fought our Cold War, configured African economies so that raw materials exports continue to flow, sold Africans products suited to our culture but not theirs, and employed thousands of experts who provide top-down advice. Instead, we need to remind ourselves that our modern way of life produces problems that we ourselves have not been able to solve or curb, such as economic inequality, violence, and overconsumption of resources. Our planet simply cannot sustain a world full of people living as we do.

Overall, our five decades of post-independence assistance have produced poor results. Africa has improved its literacy rates, primary school enrollment, and child survival rates, but not as quickly as other developing areas have. Foreign investment in Africa is still low, while the level of development assistance needed, as well as Africa's debt, is extremely high. We do not yet know what really helps in the African context, and an astonishing number of voices—both African and Western—have suggested often-conflicting versions of how to achieve development.

# Rethinking Development

There are numerous ways to help Africa—including the methods described above—but many current practices need to be rethought and reconfigured. One way to approach the problem is to explore alternatives to our assumptions about development. We could, for example, begin to reconsider the *metaphors of relationship* implied by development. Our helping interventions in Africa have mostly relied on hierarchical, unilineal evolutionist metaphors such as parent-child and patron-client, distinguishing between the "developed" and the "underdeveloped." New metaphors of relationship might imply respect for difference and equality of purpose. I have, for example, heard "teacher-student" used to describe our role in Africa. The point in this case was that the failures of Africa's SAPs were due to our failure, as teachers, to understand the culture of Africans, our students. Perhaps this is an improvement over the parent-child metaphor of colonial days, but it is still paternalistic and hierarchical. And it won't work, because it implies that we are taking responsibility for what Africans must figure out and eventually do for themselves.

Health researchers Andrea Cornwall and Rachel Jewkes recommend that we relate to Africa in a "collegial" manner, "in a process of mutual learning where local people have control over the process."[27] Likewise, the image of "partnership" is appealing because it suggests that people are working toward a common goal and that each partner has something to contribute. "Friendship" might work: it is a "no strings attached" model in which our friend's well-being is the only stated goal. Perhaps "neighbors" might apply as well. Or it may be that there are African models of cooperation that we are not yet acquainted with. There are, of course, those who abuse collegiality, partnership, friendship, and neighborliness. We must not do so ourselves, and we must choose our partners carefully. And somehow we must also watch out for our own interests.

In rethinking development, we might also explore new names for our goal. The current term, *development,* is too closely associated with Western concepts of economic wealth. To broaden the term's meaning, it might be useful to pair it with a modifier, such as in "human development," "alternative development," "sustainable development," "just development," "ecological development," or "participatory development."[28] A number of development specialists talk of abandoning the word altogether, but as yet no substitute word or phrase has been found that carries the full meaning we need to express. Belgian scholar Thierry Verhelst has suggested that what we should be striving for is "a good life," not development, but this term has not caught on.[29]

It is more probable that we will have to retain the old word and give it new life. We cannot know exactly what meaning might emerge, but we can explore new definitions. In fact, many development theorists and practitioners have begun this work. One such effort is a textbook published by the World Bank, an institution frequently criticized for being a tool of industrialized countries. Titled *Beyond Economic Growth*, the book is designed to help readers understand indicators of development, such as birth and death rates, education levels, income equality, and sustainability, that are not strictly related to economic growth.[30]

This new thinking may also be seen in the Millennium Development Goals for 2015, adopted in 2000 by 192 member states of the United Nations. These goals aim to (1) eradicate extreme poverty and hunger; (2) achieve universal primary education; (3) promote gender equality and empower women; (4) reduce child mortality; (5) improve maternal health; (6) combat HIV/AIDS, malaria, and other diseases; (7) ensure environmental sustainability; and (8) develop a global partnership for development.[31] These goals show that we have learned lessons from the failed efforts described earlier in this chapter. Even if only partially achieved, they will mean significant positive changes for Africans and others.

Nonetheless, I believe that we still have a ways to go in actually *defining* development. Following is my own short, incomplete list intended to suggest possibilities for a new meaning for development:

1. All individuals and cultures, including our own, need development. The criteria for development should include broad goals that *all* cultures can aspire to rather than only the so-called underdeveloped cultures of today.
2. Development includes material comfort, but economic growth, efficiency, and wealth should not be its primary goals. Adequate definitions of development must also include *human values* such as those associated with learning, self-confidence, health, aesthetics,

spirituality, and community. Development will mean different things for different people.

3. Development empowers communities and ordinary people. This implies that responsibility for the development process lies with participants, not with outsiders or the powerful. Development can include roles for outsiders who provide resources, but these should be minimal so as not to interfere with the process. The development agenda, the primary energy, and most resources must come from those who are developing.

4. Development is equitable. Developed systems benefit a broad base of people rather than just those who are clever, efficient, or powerful enough to respond to opportunities. In a world in which survival depends on peaceful coexistence, individuals, groups, or societies who exploit others cannot claim to be developed no matter how developed they feel or appear to be. The development of one must sustain the development of others.

5. Development improves the environment. Our physical world is so fragile that we need to go beyond the current term *sustainable development* to ensure that we are well within the margins of environmental sustainability.

## Helping Out

This is a good place to return to the questions posed at the beginning of this chapter: Does Wassetake village in Senegal really need our help? What is wrong with life as they live it? What kind of help would be truly useful? Although I was surprised at first by my students' comments, I actually came to agree that "we should help them." But the way we should help is not what one might at first think.

Surprisingly, we might be of most help to Wassetake if we act here in the United States to ensure that the policies of our government, our corporations, and our NGOs are not exploitative. This would first require study. How, for example, do US subsidies for American peanut farmers affect the prices Wassetake farmers receive for their cash crops? In what ways might we be supporting a Senegalese government bureaucracy that is insensitive to villagers? How might the opportunities of the market be unavailable to Wassetake? Which foreign corporations operate in Senegal and what methods do they use? How do the international organizations that we control affect people in Senegal and Wassetake? How can we define development in ways that are more constructive to both Africans and ourselves?

In 1989, Pierre Pradervand offered a preliminary list of partnership issues for industrialized countries that is still relevant:

> Real partnership would include a general agreement on a series of key issues, which until now have been negotiated in a haphazard manner, if at all. Key issues include the cancellation of debts or their rescheduling, the pricing of raw materials, technology transfer, the "brain-drain," capital flight, access for African products to markets in the [industrialized countries], immigration policies, food aid, human and political rights, and many others.[32]

Other suggestions for helping Africa and other developing regions include regulating international corporations; creating an international information system that gives inexpensive Internet access to Africans and assures news from Africa is accurate and balanced; establishing a system within which NGOs and Africans compete for aid dollars based on success in delivering on aid promises; and reforming international economic organizations—including the IMF, World Bank, and World Trade Organization—to include more representation by poorer countries.

If we want to help Wassetake village more directly, we should begin, once again, with study. Ideally, we might learn their language and quietly live in the village. Over time, we would certainly discover that Wassetakeans have their own valid ideas about what "the good life" means. We would also discover that they are intelligent and creative actors, not just backward victims. We might learn how to help without getting in the way.

Few of us, of course, will choose to go to Wassetake or even to Africa. Instead, we can help by working through one of the many NGOs already in Africa and already sensitive to the issues of development. This brings up the question of which NGOs to support. Disaster and crisis relief is of first priority, but beyond emergency help we can seek out those NGOs that have a philosophy of participatory development and that actually practice it. Again, this requires study on our part. We must get to know the agencies we support. What are their philosophies of development? Do they actually do what they say they do? How much of their budget actually goes toward work in Africa as opposed to paying for fund-raising and administration here in America?[33]

Helping Africa requires more than gifts of money. It requires knowledge of oneself, of others, and of the environments in which others operate. It also requires will, effort, organization, knowledge, participation, and community. We might even say that helping others develop requires the same skills as development itself. Learning to help Africans is an opportunity for developing ourselves.

## PART THREE

# FURTHER MISPERCEPTIONS

# 7

# CANNIBALISM

## *No Accounting for Taste*

Many Americans believe that cannibalism existed in Africa in the not-too-distant past, and some believe it exists today. Sixty percent of preservice social studies teachers who were surveyed about their knowledge of Africa associated the word *cannibalism* with that continent.[1] In spite of general belief, however, we do not know whether Africans ever practiced cannibalism, because we have no reliable evidence. Nineteenth-century explorers, especially those in Central Africa, were certain that cannibalism existed, and many reported having witnessed it. But, as this chapter shows, modern scholars are not sure such reports can be trusted.

Most references to African cannibalism in our own time occur in humor. The Internet, for example, contains many cannibal joke sites. Most cannibal jokes fall into the same category as Polish jokes and other forms of ethnic humor; although we may laugh at such jokes, few of us really believe that Poles are stupid or that today's Africans are cannibals. In fact, it seems that most (but certainly not all) of today's cannibal jokes have been stripped of any specific identification with Africa, or with any other part of the world for that matter. Our cannibal "tastes" have changed from the 1950s, when cannibals and Africans (and missionaries) appeared regularly in the same jokes. A cannibal joke now is more likely to be obscene than to be about Africa.

Here are four examples that are not specifically African, not copyrighted, often repeated, and—in the interest of decency—not obscene:

> Cannibal: "Shall I boil the new missionary?" Chief: "No, he's a friar."
> When do cannibals leave the table? When everyone's eaten.
> Did you hear about the cannibal who loved children? He just adored the platter of little feet.
> Why did the cannibal refuse to eat the accountant? There is no taste for accounting.

Computer programmers and mathematicians also seem to find cannibal situations amusing. For example: "Three missionaries and three cannibals are on one side of a river. Their boat can take one or two people at a time. If the number of cannibals on either side ever outnumbers the missionaries, the cannibals will eat the missionaries. Get all of the missionaries and cannibals across the river without any snacks in the process." A puzzle involving cannibals is admittedly more interesting than, say, one with foxes and rabbits.

A number of modern studies assert that cannibalism was prevalent in pre-colonial Africa, especially Central Africa. In his book about the Congo River, for example, journalist Peter Forbath said that Africans commonly submerged their victims chin-deep in streams before cooking them, "since suffering was believed to tenderize the meat for the cooking."[2] And David Levering Lewis, in his history of the European conquest of Central Africa, explains that "cannibalism had always been a predilection among some of these [Congo River Basin] peoples: enemies captured in war were often eaten, and the flesh of slaves was sometimes consumed to give strength to ailing persons. But until the Swahili infestation, it had been held in check by traditions of warfare and ritual."[3] With the chaos of Swahili slave and ivory raiding in the 1880s, Lewis argues, a "wave of flesh-eating" occurred "that spread from inveterate cannibals like Bakusa to Batetela, the Mangbetu, and much of Zande."[4]

These recent descriptions of historical African cannibalism rely not on careful fieldwork in Africa but on nineteenth-century European accounts that were deeply prejudiced by Dark Continent myths. They are unreliable. One anthropologist who has taken an interest in this subject, William Arens, claims that despite frequent reports from explorers, missionaries, and travelers, there has never been a substantiated case anywhere in the world of cannibalism as a regular cultural practice. Except in extreme and isolated cases such as the Donner Pass incident,[5] Arens concludes, cannibalism never existed.[6] Arens is supported by Philip Boucher, who asserts in *Cannibal Encounters: Europeans and Island Caribs, 1492–1763* that although Columbus's description of Caribbean island peoples as cannibals has seemed plausible to Europeans from 1492 to the present day, it has no basis in fact. Columbus's cannibals influenced the work of Shakespeare, Hobbes, Locke, and Rousseau, but they were mythical cannibals.[7]

Some scholars support the idea of cannibalism as an established human practice. For example, anthropologist Marvin Harris believes that cannibalism did exist in our ancient past, either as a source of protein or as a threat to neighbors. He writes that for a small-scale society concerned about self-defense, the warning "We will eat you!" is a powerful deterrent to enemies. But, he says, when societies become larger and more powerful, they seek to incorporate their enemies, not frighten them, and so they adopt a more welcoming message: "Join us and you will benefit!"[8] Personally, I believe that human culture is flexible enough that under the right circumstances whole societies might condone and engage in cannibalism. In the extreme conditions of warfare, we should not be surprised to find cannibalism anywhere on Earth.

Like Arens, however, I am skeptical about whether cannibalism ever existed in Africa as a *regular* practice. I have spent most of my time in Africa with the Mangbetu, a people living in Central Africa and identified by historian David Lewis as "inveterate cannibals." Georg Schweinfurth, a German who in 1870 became the first Westerner to visit the Mangbetu, reported:

> The cannibalism of the Monbuttoo is the most pronounced of all the known nations of Africa.... The carcasses of all who fall in battle are distributed upon the battle-field, and are prepared by drying for transport to the homes of the conquerors. They drive their prisoners before them without remorse, as butchers would drive sheep to the shambles, and these are only reserved to fall victims on a later day to their horrible and sickening greediness. During our residence at the court of Mbunza the general rumour was quite current that nearly every day some little child was sacrificed to supply his meal.[9]

Schweinfurth visited the Mangbetu for only a few days and could not speak their language. Yet his information was accepted as truth by subsequent visitors to the Mangbetu and by many others, so that the Mangbetu soon became the most infamous of African cannibals.[10]

I am convinced that Schweinfurth and other Westerners never saw a cannibal feast nor likely even a roasted human leg or hand. One would expect such persistent and widespread events to show up in African oral histories, yet they do not. *If* cannibalism existed in the nineteenth century among the Mangbetu or any other Africans, I suspect it was limited to ritual cannibalism intended to frighten enemies, honor the dead, or assist in acquiring attributes of the dead. For Europeans, however, the idea of African cannibalism alone seemed to justify the conquest of Central Africa. They believed that they had come upon a truly depraved practice that demanded their intervention. Reports of African cannibalism increased in the 1870s and 1880s, when Europeans were on the verge of conquest, and declined precipitously in the late 1890s, after conquest had ended. By 1900, Europeans were claiming that there was much less cannibalism in Africa because they had stamped it out. In fact, whatever cannibalism had existed was largely in the conquerors' own minds. Once they felt in control, they no longer needed to imagine Africans as cannibals.

It is entirely possible that in the late nineteenth century, Westerners in Central Africa actually thought they had seen cannibal meals because they were predisposed to believe that such events occurred and might have mistaken another kind of meat for human meat. But even if late-nineteenth-century Westerners in Africa did not witness cannibal feasts, they nonetheless would have had good reasons to say they had. People back home were convinced that cannibalism pervaded the Dark Continent, and an explorer, soldier, or missionary who had no experience with it would have been suspect. Without descriptions, discussions, and condemnations of cannibalism, their books would not have been as interesting or have sold as well.

Africans themselves often added to Western suspicions by using metaphors of cannibalism. In Cameroon, for example, some people I spoke with believe that sorcerers dig up the dead and eat them. It is also common in many places to say that someone "ate" something, meaning that a person stole or used it up carelessly—as in "He ate the money." But even though people may have taken such metaphors literally, cannibalism didn't necessarily exist.

The conviction that others are cannibals has not been a one-way street. Indeed, many Africans came to see Europeans as cannibals. The idea that slaves were taken from Africa for use as European food was apparently common for centuries. Schweinfurth himself mentioned that the Mangbetu were suspicious of him when he wanted to buy skulls for scientific experiments.[11] In the 1980s, elderly Mangbetu men told me that in the past they thought the pictures of people on containers of baby food, corned beef, and oatmeal sold by whites might indicate the contents. An informant among the neighboring Budu said that during the colonial period the Belgians caught African children on the roads and put them in their cellars in town to fatten and eat. As with most tales, he said he hadn't seen it himself, but he knew someone who had.

Here, I think we come to the crux of the issue. Cannibalism is one of the strangest practices *anyone* can think of, and therefore it is potentially one of the most powerful of symbols. Adding the practice of cannibalism to a ritual makes that ritual seem sacred in a way that nothing else can. If a new king eats human flesh as part of his inaugural ceremony, he becomes godlike, different from his ordinary human subjects. Indeed, the Christian act of communion is so powerful because it is metaphorical cannibalism: "This is Christ's body, broken for you." Here, cannibalism is a symbol of incorporation. In baser circumstances, cannibalism can come to symbolize the barbarism of others, or our fear of others. The more different others are, the more likely they are to be accused of cannibalism.

Because of the mutual accusations by both Westerners and Africans and the lack of evidence on either side, whether cannibalism ever existed in Africa is more or less irrelevant. What is important is that *accusations* of cannibalism existed. Thus cannibalism, as an extreme metaphor for otherness, became an idea that was used by both Westerners and Africans to think about the other.

Africans, too, make jokes about cannibalism. In fact, Mangbetu elders today are quite aware of their notorious reputation, and rather than fight it—deserved or not—they often derive enjoyment from it. A researcher friend told me he was present when a group of Swedes traveling across Africa camped overnight at a Mangbetu chief's compound. Around an evening fire, the tourists asked about local customs including cannibalism, and the elders present began to mock the tourists' misperceptions. They had fun with standard Mangbetu gags such as how monkey meat tastes "almost as good as human," and the tourists ate it up (oops!) in all seriousness.

I've heard a number of such humorous stories in conversations with Mangbetu elders. Once, I was asking some Meje men (the Meje are Mangbetu neighbors and speak the same language) about the first white man to visit them, an American soldier named Thornton who worked for the Belgians during the conquest period of the early 1890s. I had read official colonial documents from the era reporting that Thornton had been killed and eaten, and I was curious about the incident. Here I was, interviewing the sons of the supposed cannibals, now old men. So I asked whether the reports were true. After a small private conference, a spokesman said that they had killed Thornton because they feared the Belgian invasion. They were going to eat him and first boiled his boots, thinking them to be a part of his body. But the boots turned out to be so tough that they didn't bother with the rest of him!

This great joke deflects the question and shows that the Meje recognize the powerful emotions connected with cannibalism. It also reflects parallels with our own cannibal jokes. Yet it is also a sad comment, because it represents an inequality between African and American myths about cannibalism. This African humor is largely defensive, intended to defuse accusations that are probably false to begin with. Western humor tends to be offensive in two senses of the word: not only does it distort reality, but it does so in order to justify exploitation.

American cannibal humor has changed as we have become increasingly aware of its negative ramifications. In the late 1970s, two *Frank and Ernest* cartoons showed the pair cooking in African cannibal pots. In one cartoon, Frank says to Ernest, "One way to look at it—it's a *very* fitting end for a consumer advocate."[12] In the other, a father with a young child says to Frank, "Don't be such a grouch—say 'Snap, Crackle, Pop' for the kid."[13] In the late 1980s, however, the *Far Side* cartoons that featured generic "natives" included no cannibals and invariably made fun of us, not of others. Today's cannibal jokes contain fewer specific references to Africa and more self-critical references.

As with other accusations of savagery directed toward Africa in the past, accusations of cannibalism have diminished in recent years because of increasing awareness and protest. But the use of cannibalism as a veiled symbol for African otherness still appears in our culture. It will likely remain so, if we continue to mistake Africa for something it is not.

# 8

# AFRICANS LIVE IN TRIBES, DON'T THEY?

When African students arrive at the college where I teach, one of the first questions they are asked is, "What tribe do you belong to?" The African students usually respond happily until they discover that the American idea of *tribe* is much different from theirs. Then they become amused or angry at American ignorance and stereotyping. For us, to be part of a tribe sounds exotic and somewhat primitive. The label *tribal* can imply an unthinking, primal attachment to kin. As this chapter reveals, however, Africans understand *tribe* in a different way. Modern Africans have attachments to their kin, but they also have professional, religious, regional, national, and other loyalties. Moreover, contemporary African tribes are just that, contemporary. They bear only superficial resemblance to the organizations that existed fifty years ago or to those that Europeans found more than a century ago when they conquered the continent.

Most scholars of Africa have, in fact, abandoned the term *tribe* as too confusing and inaccurate. They fear that if they were to use the word in the African sense, they would be understood in the American sense. Indeed, many scholars see the almost knee-jerk American association of Africa with *tribe* as our most salient stereotype about Africa. The myth of Africa as tribal confuses us because it relies on outmoded concepts formed during a more racist and imperialist era. If Americans are to understand Africa today, we need to abandon our old ideas about tribes.

For this reason, it would be helpful to investigate what *tribe* means and why it came to be associated in the American mind with Africa. We can also examine the alternative words that scholars now prefer.[1]

## A Textbook Definition

The word *tribe* is used today by some anthropologists, so first, we ought to be clear about what it refers to in a technical sense. One anthropology textbook designed for college students has defined *tribe* as one of five major types of political organization: band, tribe, chiefdom, confederacy, and state. A tribe, says the author, is "a political group that comprises several bands or lineage groups, each with similar language and lifestyle and each occupying a distinct territory. . . . Tribal groupings contain from 100 to several thousand people."[2] Tribes consist of one or more subgroups that have integrating factors but are not centralized upon a single individual, as they are in a chiefdom. Frequently, such groups organize themselves through kinship (vertical unity) and associations and age grades (horizontal unity). Some tribes are integrated by a "Big Man" who holds the group together loosely by the force of his personality and whose position is constantly contested and not hereditary.

According to this somewhat technical definition, Africa is not full of tribes; about half of African societies would be excluded because, historically, they were organized in bands, chiefdoms, confederacies, and states. And many of the remaining societies do not fit the definition of *tribe* for other reasons. For example, the Amba of Uganda and the Dorobo of Kenya are sometimes called tribes, but the Amba have two languages, while the Dorobo live among the Nandi and Maasai and do not have their own territory. Moreover, strictly speaking, tribes cannot exist at all in modern Africa because all African peoples live in modern states, which hold ultimate sovereignty over their populations.

Classifying types of societies is an extraordinarily difficult task that requires scholars to understand how each society operates and then to select a few characteristics that are equally representative of several societies so as to make up a category. But reality is vastly more complex than classification schemes, so *any* scheme will be partly inaccurate. In a sense, we *impose* our classifications on reality, and some categories fit better than others. In Africa today, *tribe* barely fits at all.

## A Word with a History

The word *tribe* has a very long history. It comes from a Latin root, *tribus* (plural, *tribi*), used to describe a unit of the Roman state. Originally, Roman tribes were based on territory—at first there were four urban and sixteen rural tribes—and each territory-tribe was considered to have its own culture. The tribes performed administrative functions such as tax collection, conscription, and census taking. By 24 BCE there were thirty-five rural tribes, and more were added as the Romans conquered new territories. Later, people could also formally *enroll* in a tribe, indicating the loss of tribes' primarily territorial and cultural bases. Increasingly, different tribes lived among each other. The lower classes and freed slaves tended to join urban tribes.

The Latin derivative *tribe* entered the English language through Old French in the thirteenth and fourteenth centuries. It was often used to translate Hebrew and Greek words that signified the organizational units of ancient Israel and Greece, as in "the tribes of Israel." It appeared in translations of the Bible and occasionally in Shakespeare. *Tribe* was a useful word: it could summarize the very different political organizations of Israel, Greece, Rome, and other ancient societies.[3] Similar developments occurred in other European languages.

The word was also useful for describing many of the peoples whom the British encountered as they began to establish their global empire after 1600. Thus, distinct groups of Native Americans, Africans, South Asians, and others were referred to as tribes. At this time, however, the word still had a neutral meaning and was interchangeable with the words *nation* and *people*. The terms all meant a generalized group of people who shared a culture, and they were applied to Europeans as well as non-Europeans.

These words began to diverge in meaning in the late eighteenth century. Europeans, who increasingly thought of themselves as more advanced than other peoples, needed words to distinguish themselves from others. The word *people* retained its general usage, but *nations* came to be thought of as larger groupings with more complex social structures and technologies. The word *tribe* was reserved for groups that were smaller and, supposedly, simpler and less evolved. Our modern ideas about primitives and the Dark Continent emerged in the same era. By the mid-nineteenth century, the word *tribe* had assumed a negative meaning that implied political organizations that were primordial, backward, irrational, and static. A person didn't join a tribe, but was born into it. People in civilized societies could actively select from among different, creative courses of action, but tribal people followed tribal customs without thinking. It was indeed fortunate for tribes that they had such customs to guide their actions, because members were so limited intellectually. Of course, "tribalism" was expected of such people. In other words, to be tribal was to be genetically incapable of more advanced thought or political organization.

In the twentieth century, the meaning of the word *tribe* as applied to Africa developed in two directions. The first, favored by white politicians and colonial administrators, was a variation of the nineteenth-century definition of tribes as having closed boundaries and unchanging customs. Administratively, this viewpoint allowed colonialists to make sense of and create order out of the bewildering variety of African political organizations. Administrators, seeking easier ways to control Africa than by using force, opted to reorganize African reality to fit the tribal model.

Writing of colonial rule in British Tanganyika (today's Tanzania), historian John Iliffe notes that in the 1920s, administrators believed that all African social organization was ordered by the kinship principle. To them, "Africa's history was a vast family tree of tribes. Small tribes were offshoots of big ones and might therefore be reunited."[4] And all tribes needed to have chiefs, theoretically because chiefs were more advanced than village councils, and practically because white administrators could rule Africans more easily when they could work through a clear chain of command. When the British were done, Tanganyika had been fully tribalized. British administrators in the 1920s did not consider themselves to be doing violence to African political organizations. Rather, they intended to help Africa by putting it *back in order*.

Because the reordering was based on history that didn't exist, however, history had to be extensively reinvented to fit it. For this task, the British had the cooperation of many Africans. Indeed, Africans—like all peoples—had long been adept at reinventing their histories to suit current political needs.

Since the major integrating principle was kinship, groups that were combined or split manipulated their genealogies creatively to make sense of the new arrangements. In the same manner, Africans who sought power as chiefs could be quite sure of finding historical "proof" for their claims. Likewise, because colonial rule disrupted African cultures, many Africans were looking for new identities for themselves and found them in invented historical roots.[5] We now speak of the invention of tribes in Africa. Many studies in the past several decades have described how tribal self-consciousness developed during the nineteenth century and the first half of the twentieth century.

As an administrative tool, the ideology of tribe caused a great deal of difficulty for both Europeans and Africans. The emphasis on tribal consciousness had two contradictory purposes—to change and to remain the same. Wanting docile Africans who would produce cash crops, administrators sought to transform Africans into orderly "tribesmen." But *tribe* implied a childlike people, something Africans were not. Whenever Africans resisted, the British could apply the ideology of African childishness to justify the use of force: those who didn't cooperate needed firm parental discipline. Yet the need to use force revealed the fundamental contradictions in the idea of colonialism as a progressive institution.[6]

The second direction in the development of the word *tribe* was favored by anthropologists. In the 1920s, some anthropologists began to live with Africans and to take their day-to-day lives more seriously. Their experiences revealed the nineteenth-century definition of tribe to be deeply flawed. They found that tribal peoples were neither unthinking nor less evolved than Westerners, and they learned that tribes were constantly changing and adapting, just as their own societies were. Anthropologists have sometimes been called servants of colonialism, because they provided the information and categories necessary to organize African peoples. Although this negative label has some validity, it is also true that anthropologists were among the first to recognize that African complexity was creative and purposeful rather than irrational and chaotic.

## The End of the Tribe

Studies of African tribes in the 1960s took on a new urgency as most African countries became independent and colonial definitions became clearly irrelevant.[7] Anthropologists focused on the flexibility of various

African tribal organizations, which linked or separated small groups as needed. The evidence—already gathered in administrative reports and ethnographic studies—needed only reinterpretation to support the new model. Colonial administrators had used African flexibility in this area to form and re-form administrative units. And the field anthropologists of the colonial era had recognized that Africans frequently used invented traditions to reconstitute their political organizations.

Morton Fried argued in the same decade that tribes did not evolve by themselves out of simpler forms, as had been thought. Most tribes, he said, form in reaction to *external* pressures, not internal ones. Tribes become as cohesive as those described by our traditional definition only when groups of people are forced to unite for self-defense. And, Fried asserted, when major external pressures are applied by larger political units. He concluded that colonialism *caused* many tribes to form.[8]

Also beginning in the 1960s, some scholars argued for the abandonment of the word *tribe* in reference to *urban* Africa, where Africans live more modern lives. The major contender to replace *tribe* was *ethnic group*. Surprisingly, the terms *ethnicity* and *ethnic group* are not very old, having been initiated by North American sociologists after World War II. The terms were invented to describe the kind of cultural consciousness that a group might develop in a modern city. Urban ethnicity was seen as more fluid and diffuse than the group consciousness of people in rural areas. The word *tribe* was, then, reserved mainly for rural peoples.[9] By 1970 *ethnic group* had the solid acceptance of many Africanists. In that year, two Northwestern University professors published an extensive proposed syllabus for university-level African studies courses that made the distinction between *ethnic group* for towns and *tribe* for rural areas.[10]

This distinction did not last. *Tribe* was so widely recognized as imprecise and tainted with primitivism that it largely ceased to be employed by Africanists. By the late 1970s, anthropologists, sociologists, historians, art historians, ethnomusicologists, political scientists, and other scholars had switched to the term *ethnic group*.

This new usage also won the support of many African intellectuals. Usually educated in Europe or America, these Africans knew of the popular Western association of *tribe* with savage, and they also knew about the complexity of the situation in Africa. Moreover, they wanted to help defeat so-called tribalism in Africa. For such Africans, the concept of the clearly definable tribe—developed as a tool of colonial domination—was a primary obstacle in postcolonial domestic and international politics. What Africa needed was to break down the rigid "tribes" that were not, in fact, African. A new image of Africa in Europe and America that downplayed tribes would help, because foreigners would see Africa more accurately and because they could not continue to dominate Africa by playing one so-called tribe against another.[11]

## Contemporary African Uses of *Tribe*

For Americans, one of the confusing aspects of modern Africa is that ordinary Africans continue to use the word *tribe*. This would seem to suggest that Africans themselves recognize that they live in tribes. To some extent they do: contemporary political and social systems are derivatives of earlier systems. We should be careful, however, not to assume that Africa's idea of tribe is the same as ours. Most Africans do not generally equate tribes with the savage or the primitive. Their use of the word seems more like that of our phrase *ethnic group*. Moreover, Africans are aware that they have *various* identities and loyalties including kinship, language, region, religion, country, town, continent, school, profession, and class. *Tribe* takes its place among these other factors to form complex and changing patterns.

As pointed out at the beginning of this chapter, one of the first things an American often asks an African is what tribe he or she is from. We assume that one of the most important subjects to Africans is their tribe and that this topic will help us connect. However, the question can reveal our ignorance and can be insulting. Most Africans in fact do not think of themselves as part of a tribe so much as part of a lineage. The tribe is large and diffuse, whereas the lineage is small, cohesive, and immediate. In addition, because most Africans have layers of identity, asking about their tribe may be puzzling to them. Why would you want to know immediately about tribe and not, say, about family, region, religion, or profession?

The question can be insulting because many Western-educated Africans know that the word *tribe* is frequently American code for primitive. Moreover, in the African political context, the bold question "What is your tribe?" can create tension. It would be like asking a new acquaintance in the United States, "What is your socioeconomic class?" instead of "What do you do for a living?" Likewise, if we saw someone whose race was not clearly evident, we would not immediately ask, "What is your race?" At least for public purposes, we strive to act out our belief that "all persons are created equal," because we know it is essential for public order.

Of course, some Africans, like some Americans, broadcast their ethnic identity. It is still possible to find Africans who are *creating* tribes for many of the same reasons they were created during the colonial period. This brings up a thorny problem. To see Africans demand to be identified first by their tribe tends to confirm the American cultural suspicion that in Africa, we are facing a primal force that is uncivilized, undemocratic, and unmodern. We react similarly to anyone who demands to be identified first by her or his race, sex, or class. But, once again, there is more to consider.

Mainstream Western white culture has long used the concept of the primitive, in reference to tribe, race, sex, disability, abnormality, and so forth, as a way to maintain power over others. Those who strike back by wearing their difference as a weapon seem threatening. On college and university campuses in the United States, for example, white students sometimes complain about African Americans or Hispanics who have their own organizations or who sit together at lunch. Yet if whites have similar, whites-only organizations, they are labeled racist. It may be regrettable that we live in a society that fosters such self-segregation, but the fact is that this behavior is thoroughly modern and not a throwback to so-called tribal times. In the United States, being self-consciously ethnic has provided many minorities with psychic and even physical protection against the frequently hostile larger society.

Some modern Africans have also felt it useful to be self-consciously ethnic. The writer Ken Saro-Wiwa, for instance, long identified himself as a Nigerian and participated in the wider Nigerian culture. But in the 1990s, he felt it necessary to publicly declare himself Ogoni in order to defend Ogoni people against exploitation by the Nigerian government and Shell Oil. He protested the loss without compensation of Ogoni oil and the pollution of Ogoni land. The government responded that it was acting on behalf of all Nigerians, who should share the oil. It branded Saro-Wiwa a tribalist, traitor, and instigator of violence, and, to the world's horror, he was executed in 1995. It is clear now that the oppressive military government framed Saro-Wiwa so it could be rid of him.

A question we might ask in the context of Saro-Wiwa's execution is what resemblance, if any, his version of tribalism bears to what Americans currently conceive of as African tribalism. The answer is, very little. The Western definitions of tribe recall precolonial African political structures, and do that badly. But our inaccuracies in describing the past are mild compared to our inability to describe the present. Today's worst "tribal" conflicts have taken radically new, modern forms. Saro-Wiwa acted in a modern arena defined by cities; by state bureaucracies and armies; by newspapers, books, radio, and television; by automobiles, airplanes, telephones, video cameras, fax machines, and computers; by foreign corporations and foreign governments; and by Western-educated Nigerians. He acted and was executed for quite modern reasons.

Africa's contemporary tribes and tribal conflicts are simply not captured by the American understanding of these words.

## Other Tribes

You may note that we continue to use the word *tribe* for Native Americans and that there is little protest. There is a difference, however, because our concept of a Native American tribe is not the same as our concept of an African tribe. In the nineteenth century, Native Americans were considered just as primitive as Africans, and they were herded onto reservations or killed. But in modern times, Native Americans have become more mainstream in American culture, or they have become almost sacred to many Americans as shamans, ecologists, artisans, and artists.

Interestingly, under different circumstances most Native Americans would probably not use the word *tribe*. United States history has made the term politically useful, however, so Native Americans have embraced it publicly. A 1946 decision of the US Supreme Court obligates the federal government to compensate those Native Americans who can claim exclusive occupation and use of their land since time immemorial. Such compensation is legally due to only bureaucratically defined tribes. "Under these circumstances," says Morton Fried, Native Americans "have vested interests in the concept of tribe and are obliged to provide the deepest history for it."[12] Providing such deep history is easier if people consider themselves tribal today. Thus, the terms *tribe*, *tribal council*, and *tribal elder* are common in public discourse, even though other terms might be more accurate or preferable.[13]

*Tribe* is also used to designate minority groups in Latin America and across Asia. In some cases it is applied technically, as a description of social organization, and is not meant to connote primitiveness. This is how anthropologists might apply it. But more frequently, *tribe* is employed by a majority to imply that a minority is primitive. In the latter case, the term seems similar to our application of it in Africa.

The continued use of the word *tribe* around the world, varied as its meanings are, may help us understand why we find the word acceptable for Africa. Because most so-called tribes do not complain, why should we change? We have to remember, however, that the peoples labeled as tribes usually cannot complain, because they lack the tools and opportunities to make their voices heard.

## African Tribes in America

In the 1970s, American use of the word *tribe* in reference to Africa dropped dramatically. Apparently, the media were listening to Africanist scholars and Africans themselves. Yet the word *tribe* and tribal analysis still appear here and there, even in such prestigious publications as the *Washington Post* and the *New York Times*.[14] Likewise, when television news comments on events such as those in Sudan, Rwanda, or South Africa, the word is sometimes considered an appropriate tool of both description and analysis. It also tends to appear in other places where the intended audience is the general public and the author is not a scholar of Africa, such as museum exhibit labels, documentaries, movies, and music recordings. Judging from first-year college students, I would guess that it is in frequent use in high school social studies classes.

The persistence of the word *tribe* has at least two roots. One is our lack of awareness that the word does not fit African reality. Many Americans are well-meaning but ignorant. Even if not always well-meaning, Americans have shown themselves willing to drop derogatory terms for the sake of political correctness. We no longer find it acceptable to use certain racial, ethnic, or gender labels in public, even though prejudice is still very much a part of our society. If we knew that so-called tribal peoples around the world objected to being referred to as such, many of us would change our words in order to avoid being publicly offensive.

But there is a second, deeper reason for our failure to change: Americans still equate *tribe* with *savage* and believe that modern African problems can be explained by African primitiveness. In this sense, the word we use is irrelevant. If we substitute *ethnic group* for *tribe* but continue to apply it in the same way, there is no gain. In fact, some reporters who have abandoned the word *tribe* out of political correctness continue to analyze African situations from a nineteenth-century point of view.

For example, early press reports on the 1994–1995 civil war in Rwanda frequently called it a tribal war or, if the journalist was more aware, an ethnic conflict. Much was made of the fact that Tutsi and Hutu slaughtered each other in brutal ways that were incomprehensible to civilized Westerners. The conflict was portrayed as having origins in ancient tribal animosities. In reality, the war was vastly more complex. This is not the place to fully analyze the situation in Rwanda, but such "tribal analysis" grossly distorts Rwandan facts. Reporters should have situated the war within the contexts of European colonialism, the Cold War, neoimperialism, class structure, personal and clan power struggles, global markets for raw materials, arms merchants, and a number of other factors. The most important factors include the following: (1) Belgian colonialism created Rwandan "tribal" problems and dependence on foreigners; (2) the manner of the Belgian exit provoked a 1960s civil war and massacre; (3) Cold War support for military dictators deepened these problems; (4) dependence on the global coffee market impoverished local farmers, pushing them to the economic edge; (5) competition between the United States and France led France to secretly arm and encourage Hutu extremists in the 1990s; and (6) international pressure to hold multiparty elections terrified urban Hutu politicians, who feared losing their grip on the privileges of power.

Ethnic consciousness played a large role, but not "age-old" ethnicity. This ethnicity was created and maintained in modern times. And it was not the kind of ethnicity that Americans think of when they use the terms *tribal war* or *ethnic war*. Not only do Hutus and Tutsis share the same language and culture, but their relationships are mediated by modern institutions such as states with armies, identity cards, state-run newspapers and radio, cash-crop markets, and, for the Hutus, a secret hate-radio station. Moreover, there has been considerable regional and urban-rural tension *among* the Hutus.

To mistake the Rwandan civil war for a stereotypical "tribal" war reflects a dangerous misperception of what really happened. The United Nations, along with the United States and other governments, now admits that no one acted quickly or decisively enough to stop the slide toward genocide. Last-minute efforts were too little and too late. But considering that Western governments did not really understand the problems in Rwanda to begin with, this is not surprising.

Perhaps a major reason that tribalism colors our first analysis of an African political problem is that we do not adequately prepare our news reporters. Reporters who do not know much about Africa, let alone individual countries such as Rwanda, are likely to fall back on stereotypes and other simple ways to convey complex events. Surely they are not unsympathetic to Rwandans as people. They are just unprepared and in a hurry, and so is their audience. In Rwanda, it was as though the news teams had just arrived on the scene of an accident and were trying to figure out quickly what had happened.

In a deeper sense, however, we quickly resorted to portraying the Rwandan conflict as primordial, because such a response reinforces our American view of the world. Specifically, by portraying African conflicts as age-old, we Westerners do not have to take responsibility for our share of the *causes* of modern African history. Moreover, if the causes of a conflict are so basic as to be tribal—meaning primitive—then we can imagine that *solutions* will be almost impossible to find. Thus we can congratulate ourselves for relief efforts for victims, but not feel responsible for addressing even the African causes, let alone the Western ones. Some problems are just too deep to resolve, we can rationalize. Tribal analysis walls off African crises from modern history, making it appear as if Africans do not participate in the same world in which all the rest of us participate.

During the Rwandan crisis a congressman asked me to brief him on what was going on. I prepared a ten-minute presentation on background causes and alternative analyses of current events. My presentation was basic because he knew little about the situation in Rwanda. When I arrived, I found that he did not really *want* to know what was going on. His only concern was whether the brewing "tribal" trouble between the Hutus and Tutsis in neighboring Burundi might in some way spill over into his world and necessitate involving US troops.

I can sympathize with Anthony Appiah, a Ghanaian scholar living in the United States, who suggests that the way we use the word *tribe* facilitates exploitation of Africans. He writes that "race in Europe and tribe in Africa are central to the way in which the objective interests of the worst-off are distorted."[15] What he means is that we have an interest in actually promoting tribalism and the myths of the tribe in Africa. This effort may be conscious or unconscious, but by keeping ourselves thinking that tribe matters, Africans will be easier to ignore or exploit.

Wole Soyinka, a Nigerian and winner of the Nobel Prize for literature, has applied the same logic to Western considerations of African governments. He criticizes scholars who say that Africa's ethnic divisions *require* dictators in order to keep the peace. The supposed African tribal mind becomes an excuse for the West not to hold African leaders to international standards.

## Alternatives to *Tribe*

Soyinka recognizes that our word *tribe* is a problem for Africa, but rather than criticize us, he throws the word back at us. He has started calling white and black Americans the white tribe and the black tribe. Soyinka knows that we will immediately recognize that identifying Americans as living in tribes, at least the kind we think of, is threatening to our social order. It oversimplifies, promotes division, and hinders our ability to solve our *many* kinds of problems. Africans respond in the same way to our use of the term for them.

Soyinka's counterattack will not make the word disappear, however. It is too ingrained in our consciousness and too widely used around the world. What we can hope for is that Americans become aware of the word's *various* meanings. Yet we should not use the word in reference to Africa, because African reality, both past and present, is not accurately described by *any* of the word's meanings. *Tribe* distorts African reality and therefore makes it impossible to understand the continent.

As mentioned above, the principal contender to replace *tribe* is *ethnic group.* But if we elect to substitute *ethnic group*, will this new term serve us well? Its primary advantages are its lesser negativity compared to *tribe*, its applicability to groups all over the world (making Africans seem more like people elsewhere), and the purpose for which it was invented, to describe people's group consciousness in modern societies.

The main drawback to *ethnic group* is that the term is just as ambiguous as *tribe*. How can a single phrase apply both to a European American's mild sense of attachment to the "Old Country" and to the intense feelings of hatred that have arisen between warring factions in the former Yugoslavia? The only real connection among the many different uses of *ethnicity* is that the term describes a feeling of closeness to one's own group that arises in the face of contacts with other groups. It does not, however, describe the intensity of the feeling or even its precise nature. And it does not adequately describe the nature of the group itself. Moreover, if we use *ethnic group* in Africa in the same ways we have used *tribe*, we accomplish little. *Ethnic group* may just hide the fact that we still think that African groups, whatever our name for them, are composed of primitives.

Are there other options? A genuinely useful word would help us distinguish different kinds of situations and different kinds of groups. It would help us understand the negotiations and conflicts between groups and also the negotiations and conflicts between individuals and their groups. Regrettably, no such word has appeared yet. It is for this reason that we must be especially careful. To pick one word and let it stand for many different situations is to mistake Africa.

A variety of words are now used by those aware of the problems with *tribe*. *Ethnic group* is just one. Other possibilities include *people* (as in, the Zulu are an African *people* who live in southern Africa); *group* (the Ogoni are a *group* in Nigeria); or simply the name of the group (the *Tiv* of Nigeria live near the confluence of the Niger and Benue Rivers).

With any of these alternatives, you still must be careful. *People* and *group* are emotionally neutral words with sufficiently vague definitions that they can serve in most contexts, but they are not precise enough for careful analysis. If you identify a person by the name of a specific group, that person might be offended that you picked out this characteristic as important rather than some other. A Tiv might prefer to be called a Nigerian first, or an author, or a mother, or by a clan name. Moreover, by using *Tiv* you might be implying that the Tiv are all uniform, with one set of customs, one attitude, and so forth. The Tiv, like other African peoples, are quite diverse.

Sometimes you might not want as inclusive a word as you at first think. For example, consider using some of these words and phrases, which have more specific meanings: *community, society, village, farmer, herdsman, rural people, rural dweller, urbanite, citizen, local people, kin group, clan, lineage, family.* And when discussing precolonial Africa, words such as *band, chiefdom, kingdom, empire, state, ministate,* and *city-state* might convey a more exact meaning.

You might be tempted to use the word *nation*, because in the United States and Canada, *First Nations* is sometimes employed to dignify Native American groups. In the modern African context this would not be a good idea, however. Throughout the world, most people think that nations ought to have their own sovereign countries and that countries ought to be composed of only one nation. By this logic, if you identified the Tiv as a nation, you would imply that the Tiv should form their own country with their own state government. If you were Tiv and held such beliefs, you would be considered treasonous by the Nigerian government, which is trying to foster a feeling of Nigerian nationality.

The basic problem is that we need labels but almost all labels are inaccurate and easily contested. There really is no satisfactory way to solve the labeling problem. We can, however, make a reasonable attempt to be fair to Africa if we remind ourselves of two principles. First, beware of analyses that emphasize only one or two factors. Tribalism is much too general a category with which to explain modern Africa. As we learn more about specific situations in Africa, we see that many factors are likely to be relevant. Second, strive for precision. Learn the meanings of words and try to use them appropriately. Many terms are more accurate than *tribe*, even if they are not themselves entirely satisfactory.

One final note: you may be curious about how Africans you meet orient themselves in the world they live in. Do they consider themselves part of a tribe? Should you ever ask? That would depend on the context. You probably should not go directly to the T-word. You can ask about country, region of the country, and hometown first. Since most Africans you meet in America will be city or town dwellers, you might ask what part of their country their family comes from originally. This is a relatively neutral question, and they can answer by revealing as much as they want about themselves. Such answers can help you discover a great deal about ways that people conceive of themselves. If you feel you must ask about tribe, you might get a small lecture on why ethnicity should not be important, why *some* people think it is important but *they* do not, or why Americans ought to stop thinking of Africans as primitives. On the other hand, most Africans will take your question kindly. For them, ethnic diversity is a fact of life, and *tribe* does not have the same adverse connotation as it does for us. Many people will be thankful that you have simply taken the time to show interest.

# 9

# SAFARI

## *Beyond Our Wildest Dreams*

One of the major ways we connect with Africa is through its wild animals. Most Americans easily associate Africa with images of lions and elephants and with words such as *safari* and *simba*. In fact, brief reflection reveals a surprisingly large number of ways Americans "interact" with African animals. We are sometimes hunters and photo-tourists in Africa, of course, but here at home we are also visitors to zoos and animal parks; viewers of nature programs on television; purchasers of products that use elephants, lions, and other African animals as "salesbeasts"; and patrons of movies like *The Lion King* and *Madagascar*. Even *Sesame Street*, a television show comparable to mother's milk for American children, has had a segment featuring an outline map of Africa that morphs into a lion, a hippo, and an ostrich while a voice repeats, "Africa, Africa, Africa."[1] Images and experiences of African animals deeply shape our understanding of the continent and support our evolutionist myth of Africans as close to nature and somehow less advanced than Americans.

My purpose in this chapter is to investigate the ways we interact with African animals. I am particularly interested in exploring whether our interactions have common meanings or whether each kind of experience— safari, zoo, movies, or the like—stands on its own. This problem was first posed by a student who told me he was a hunter and was interested in going to southern Africa to kill big game. In hunter culture, southern Africa is one of the most attractive destinations because of the availability of large animals such as lions, elephants, and Cape buffalo. This student— I'll call him Richard—had dreams of hunting Cape buffalo somewhere in South Africa, Zimbabwe, Botswana, or Namibia.

I was interested in knowing how Richard would describe what hunting in Africa meant to him. His major point was that facing down a Cape buffalo would be the most "real" experience he could ever have. This animal, particularly known for its vengeful ferocity, will literally stomp you to a pulp if you don't succeed in killing it. Richard shared the thoughts of hunter guru Jeff Cooper, who argues that for humans, "danger—not variety—is the spice of life. Only when one has glimpsed the imminence of death can one fully appreciate the joy of living."[2] Richard also directed me to *Meditations on Hunting* by Spanish philosopher José Ortega y Gasset, which, in brief, asserts that hunting is the only real way by which humans can become their "natural selves." Modern humans are condemned to live in society, says Ortega y Gasset, but by hunting, they become animals again and thus momentarily rejoin nature.[3]

Richard added that hunting has nothing whatever to do with the more popular photographic safaris or, for that matter, with American zoos, nature TV, or *The Lion King*. Hunters criticize those who view nature in cages or through a camera's eye as mere observers rather than actual participants in nature. From Richard's perspective, hunting is a unique experience that focuses on only the hunter's union with nature.

## Where the Wild Things Aren't

Our quick association of Africa with wild animals is not an invention; Africa does indeed harbor the greatest number and variety of large, wild mammals on Earth. Vast savannas teem with elephants, zebras, wildebeests, rhinoceroses, antelope, lions, cheetahs, and a variety of other animals. Likewise, rivers and lakes harbor crocodiles and hippos, and in rain forests, leopards stalk. By contrast, the Americas and Australia are poor in large mammal species because of large-scale extinction during the late Pleistocene era (about 11,000 years ago). Perhaps 80 percent of the big animal species in the Americas died out, for reasons that are unclear but that are probably related to human activity. In the past 5,000 years, populations of megafauna in Europe and Asia have mostly disappeared as a result of human agency.

We should, however, dispose of the stereotype that animals are plentiful all over Africa. The animals of Africa live either at the margins of human habitation or where they have been protected from humans by modern wildlife management techniques. This means that most African animals are found in Central Africa or in the north-south corridor along the east coast from Kenya south and across to Namibia. Even in these regions the natural habitat is shrinking rapidly. Especially fragile environments, such as those of the mountain gorilla or those adjacent to dense human populations, are under extreme threat. Most Africans see far fewer animals than we could view in any moderate-sized American zoo.

## The Good Old Days

As mentioned above, the African hunting safari is a thoroughly Western experience. A good example of this comes from the life of Theodore Roosevelt, our twenty-sixth president. Roosevelt was both hunter and conservationist—avocations not as antithetical to each other as they might at first seem. Roosevelt's intense interest in nature showed itself early. As a boy he created his own natural history museum, which eventually included over 2,000 specimens. The adult Roosevelt undertook trips to the American West, where he killed large mammals such as bison; there he came to understand the importance of preserving our lands for future generations. Roosevelt became our first conservation president, adding five national parks, sixteen national monuments, and fifty-one wildlife refuges to federal management.

As mentioned in previous chapters, when he left the presidency at the age of fifty, Roosevelt turned first to Africa. He decided to organize and lead an enormous hunting safari to East Africa so he could visit "these greatest of the world's great hunting-grounds."[4] He also wanted to introduce African wildlife to the American people through the preservation of specimens for the Smithsonian Institution. Thus, for a full year, from 1909 to 1910, he shot and collected wild animals in newly colonized East Africa.

Up to this point in the description, Roosevelt's safari seems almost heroic: the exploit of an ex-president who could do anything he wanted, but who nonetheless desired to do good for humanity and so provisioned a national museum with scientific data. There are, however, deep contradictions in Roosevelt's story. His colorful dispatches from Africa, sent regularly to American newspapers to help pay for the expedition, give the impression that the safari was about more than a love of nature and hunting. Roosevelt was certainly interested in science and conservation, but he was also interested in exploitation and conquest.

Roosevelt's account of his African safari begins with a commentary based on nineteenth-century Dark Continent myths. Like his early-twentieth-century contemporaries, he views Africa as an unevolved world where one may experience a pristine environment and where the backward inhabitants benefit from colonization by superior whites. He then describes his safari, one of the largest ever undertaken. The safari required hundreds of Africans—numbering two thousand over the course of the year—who served as trackers, gun bearers, guides, porters, tent boys, horse boys, cooks, skinners, and soldiers. Roosevelt lauded the "strong, patient childlike savages" who as porters transported tons of salt for curing hides, hundreds of traps, ammunition, food, tents, beds, books, animal specimens, and a bathtub. Roosevelt insisted that each day "a hot bath, never a cold bath, is almost a tropic necessity."[5] It was not unusual in safaris at that time for each white person to require as many as thirty porters, each of whom carried about sixty pounds of supplies.[6] The safari thus could not move more than about ten miles a day. At every campsite, the African workers set up a small tent village.

Roosevelt was a sensation in East African colonial circles. An American president, even an ex-president in the days before the United States became a world power, was a major celebrity. Both Roosevelt's rugged individualist personality and his legendary conversational ability fit well in white Kenyan frontier society. But even in a colony renowned for the excesses of its whites, there was something in the president's behavior that disturbed many. For example, Roosevelt frequently took wild shots from his horse at great distances, without stalking, and he used ammunition too liberally. He also killed many more animals than was necessary for a good-sized collection. In southern Sudan his party shot nine white rhinoceroses, animals Roosevelt knew to be in danger of extinction.[7] Elsewhere, Roosevelt noted that the British East Africa colonial government was trying to protect elephants and that "it would be a veritable and most tragic calamity if the lordly elephant . . . should be permitted to vanish from the face of the earth."[8] Yet his party killed more elephants than he needed for the collections he was establishing.

Many white East Africans attributed Roosevelt's demeanor to his Americanness. Americans had long had the reputation for general excessiveness and for being more interested in good results than good technique. The British settlers emphasized the sport rather than the kill. Animals needed a "fair chase," which implied that the hunter had to discipline himself to keep on relatively the same level as the animals. This attitude was made law when, after the motorcar was first used for hunting in the 1920s, the colonial government ruled that hunters had to be at least two hundred yards from the vehicle before they could shoot. By the 1960s, the rule had been expanded to require the vehicle to be at least five hundred yards away from the animal. Contrast this approach with a hunt in the 1920s in which two infamous Americans killed 323 lions between them and caused the Tanganyika government to limit hunters to five lions apiece.[9]

Yet there was really not much difference between the Americans and the British. Big-game hunting in Africa quickly became a sport in which white men directed Africans in the mechanized and commercialized conquest of African nature, while hoping that not too many other white men would want to do the same thing. Whether conducted with British sportsmanship or American brute efficiency, the safari was more about colonialism and the subjugation of nature than about conserving or understanding nature.

For Americans, Roosevelt's famous safari occurred in the context of similar stories of African adventure. The missionary David Livingstone had a well-publicized hand-to-claw encounter with a lion in the mid-nineteenth century. The explorer Henry Morton Stanley shot game almost daily as he searched for Livingstone ("Dr. Livingstone, I presume"), traversed the continent, and opened the Congo River to European commerce and conquest. The British author H. Rider Haggard penned widely read African adventure stories such as *King Solomon's Mines* and *Mogambo*, in which the heroes were white big-game hunters.

After Roosevelt, more stories and more famous Americans followed who linked Africa with hunting in the American mind. Dozens of Edgar Rice Burroughs's Tarzan stories inspired young men from the 1920s onward to yearn for African jungle adventures.[10] And beginning in the 1920s, the safari appeared in hit films such as *King Solomon's Mines* and the extensive Tarzan series. In the 1930s Ernest Hemingway described his version of the safari in *Green Hills of Africa* (1935) and in two short stories, "The Snows of Kilimanjaro" and "The Short Happy Life of Francis Macomber" (1936). The early 1950s were banner years for safari films, with the appearance of a Hollywood remake of *King Solomon's Mines* (1950) and *Mogambo* (1953). The MGM on-location filming of *King Solomon's Mines* in East Africa entailed the largest safari since Roosevelt's, but it was soon outdone by the expedition for *Mogambo*. All in all, the stars (including Gregory Peck, Joan Bennett, Susan Hayward, Ava Gardner, Grace Kelly, and Clark Gable), the big movie releases, and the stories kept the safari and its glamour in the public eye.[11]

The white hunter in Africa became a minor American genre in the same way the cowboy in the American West became a major one. Indeed, one could argue that about the time the American West had been conquered, Africa under colonial rule was opened up to white hunters. The African safari became analogous to the conquest of the American West, in the sense that both demonstrated the Western urge to dominate man and nature. The similarity is only partial, however, because the celebrated hunters of the American West were solitary, were not wealthy, and did not need a caravan of assistants.

## The Decline of the
## Great White Hunting Safari

In the American popular mind, the big-game safari was associated almost entirely with the British settler colony of Kenya, even though it was possible to hunt big game in many other places. As white power in Kenya receded after World War II, the glamour of the hunting safari declined. Bartle Bull's sympathetic history of the Kenya safari identifies the conditions for the successful safari: dissatisfaction with the intensity of modern life, yearning for adventure and freedom from domestic life, confidence in the future, wild nature in abundance, and the subservience of other men. As white colonialism faded and modern life crept in, the illusion could not be maintained. Kenya's anticolonial struggle in the 1950s and its independence in 1963 physically disrupted the land and drastically reduced the influence of whites. More important, Kenyan independence, together with the eventual independence of all tropical African countries, took a psychological toll on whites and made the safari more like "just hunting" and less like the ultimate experience of dominance over man and nature.

Since the 1970s, other factors have modified the safari experience. Continued modernization and rapid population growth in Africa have severely threatened many habitats and forced Africans to manage wildlife ever more carefully. The Kenyan government decided in 1977 to ban hunting entirely in order to preserve what wildlife remained. Such bans have become a contentious issue, however. Hunters and many conservationists argue that when hunting is allowed, the profits from licenses can help finance conservation and development projects, which, among other results, help convince ordinary Africans that animals are their cohabitants and benefactors rather than their competitors.

It is still possible to go on a hunting safari in Africa. The client will probably still have a white guide—now called a "professional hunter" instead of a "white hunter." But otherwise, the surface experience is considerably different from the classic white man's safari of past decades. Hunting parties no longer go out with huge retinues, and Land Rovers substitute for porters. Camps tend to be permanent and may consist of modern lodges rather than tents. The license fees for killing are extraordinarily high. Most such hunting is now done in southern Africa, where safaris are closely regulated by governments and frequently undertaken on private property. The clientele is also different. Bartle Bull writes that "for most, [today's] safari is a holiday in which stress and hardship may not be desirable. Often it is easier for a professional hunter to set standards of moderately luxurious camping and undemanding hunting, which can then be adjusted either for the really spoiled or for the serious hunter."[12] There are a few places outside southern Africa and Tanzania where hunting is possible. In Sudan, Congo (Kinshasa), and the Central African Republic, for example, hunters may sometimes make arrangements to fly into camps that we would consider extremely remote. Bull writes about a hunter who pursued game in southern Sudan under conditions he considered exceptional: the human population had fled the area in a civil war in the 1960s and 1970s, and forest regrowth had allowed game to repopulate.[13] Such "luck" in finding abundant hunting grounds outside game preserves is increasingly rare.

# The Tourist Safari: Animals in Pictures

Photography has been a part of the hunting safari since at least the 1890s. Hunters love to capture themselves on film with their trophies, but the camera also produced a whole new kind of safari experience. Eventually, the nature film and the camera safari became American staples. Few are the days now when no African nature film is being shown on cable television, and most upper-middle- and upper-class Americans know at least one person who has been on a photo safari in Africa. At a time of growing environmental consciousness, we might conclude that the photo safari and the nature film are positive developments for Africa. In a sense they are. Africa's rich wildlife heritage is a global treasure that not only deserves preservation for the sake of maintaining the planet but also gives Africa the positive attention it otherwise rarely receives in the West.

A look at advertisements for television programs and tourist safaris, however, reveals that their main attraction is not an understanding of nature but a sense of adventure and exoticism. Tourist safaris tend to focus on picture-perfect nature, interesting experiences, mild adventure, and comfort. Tourists are frequently promised that they will experience "native" or "tribal" customs. Nature programs on television tend to focus on the wildness of nature and the adventure of being near it or studying it. Certain animals get photographed again and again, particularly lions and elephants. Viewers are frequently assured that the film was made in the *best* place to see a particular animal and that what they are viewing is extraordinary.

Hunters often criticize photo-tourists and nature photographers. Bartle Bull summarizes the hunter's point of view as he contrasts photographers with hunters:

> The photographer is concerned with light direction, a clear view of the animal and, above all, a retainable object for the future. The hunter or stalker must be concerned with wind direction and a protected approach. He is committed to the present. You can have a brilliant day's hunting with no trophy, and even no shooting, but the photographer must have a picture. The photographer benefits from a tamed, accessible animal that will appear wild, but the hunter wants truly wild, elusive game. Much of even the best game photography is done from vehicles, itself an abandonment of the intimacy of the chase.[14]

The point here is that photography tends to turn African game preserves into giant zoos where game is managed but where *real* wildness no longer exists. A public television program on South Africa illustrates this point. In this TV tour, an American couple is shown on safari in Londlozi, perhaps the most expensive and exclusive of Africa's game parks. At $500 a day, visitors feel they have the right to experience something extraordinary. They are not disappointed. Night photos reveal leopards and lions so used to being in a Land Rover's spotlight that they disregard humans. It is even possible to sit in an open vehicle right next to the animals, providing a sense of being out in "real" African nature. The white guide notes that this represents "many, many years of work and a lot of respect on our part."[15] This kind of intimacy is shaped deeply by human management of nature. We may indeed ask whether this *is* natural.

## The Safari from a Distance

On the ground, the hunting and tourist safaris may seem attractive and rewarding. But from a distance, we can see the same patterns of Western experience in Africa discussed in earlier chapters. In both types of safari, the experience of Africa and nature is mediated by Western technology, commerce, and management techniques. Visitors arrive by air, approach by four-wheel-drive vehicles, shoot with modern guns and ammunition, view with binoculars and high-tech cameras, and retreat to hot-water showers, food cooked on gas-fed stoves, beds covered with mosquito netting, and telephones. They are cared for by African employees who drive, cook, track, and clean. If they become ill, they are evacuated to modern hospitals in Africa or beyond.

The game is wild, but managed. Hunters are part of the management plan and must follow management rules. There is danger—hunters and tourists sometimes die from animal attacks—but it is managed danger, not the same danger faced by the African farmer or herder who is more vulnerable to nature's raw edges and is less equipped.

The hunter and the tourist go to Africa for similar reasons even though they scoff at each other's motives. The hunter claims that photographers cannot perceive what nature is really like because they are observers and not participants. The photographer replies that hunters are predators who upset nature's reality. Yet both imagine that they can glimpse life as it was before humans became too numerous. Both kinds of visitors intend to stay in Africa for only a few days or weeks, and in this short time they attempt to experience life in fuller measure than they can back home. Both return with bragging rights, each bringing back material tokens of their conquest: the hunter, a trophy, and the photographer, a picture.

And what about the zoo, the animal amusement park (such as Disney's Animal Kingdom), the natural history museum, and animated films (such as *The Lion King*)? What is their relationship to the safari? On the ground, of course, there is little comparison. These experiences are much further removed from nature than the safari. The animals in the museum are dead, the zoo and amusement park are caricatures of Africa, and *The Lion King* is mythical. Yet from a distance—again, where the details are less likely to clutter our overall view—the patterns of Western behavior are similar. African animals in these other places are also mediated by Western technology, commerce, and management techniques. Each experience is heavily technologized, requiring special equipment for presentation and access. Each requires large sums of money for maintenance, and most allow access only upon payment.

The zoo and the amusement park safari are extreme cases of management, with human care substituted almost entirely for nature. The natural history museum, an artifact of Roosevelt's day, is supremely Western in its attempt to understand through science the workings of nature. We might even say that *The Lion King* gives children an introduction to management of African wildlife, since the movie is not about nature as it really is.

And each of these genres is heavily mixed with entertainment. There is something for everyone. The more intellectual patrons might like the museum; the more active, the zoo or amusement park; the children, *The Lion King*. Advertisements for all but the movie stress both education as well as entertainment, but entertainment is in the forefront even in the museum. Like the African safari, each focuses on personal pleasure to the extent that it mistakes African nature.

A safari rarely lasts more than a few days or weeks, and it would be hard to argue that in such a short time a tourist could learn much that is intimate about nature. If we want to learn about how nature operates, we would probably do better to spend more quality time with nature in our own backyards. It is quite likely, therefore, that the tourist to Africa, and even the hunter, interprets African nature based on preconceived notions.

We may feel we are seeing the world as it was at the end of the Pleistocene era. We may feel we are witnessing the balance of nature. We may have the illusion that we have momentarily become a part of nature. We may view the big predators as proof that nature operates in a survival-of-the-fittest mode (a lion as a capitalist entrepreneur). We may see the lion as a manager, as in *The Lion King*, and we may see our commanding position in the food chain as proof that nature is arranged hierarchically rather than in a web. We may even believe that we are seeing the last remnants of true nature, a leftover from the time before human colonization of the entire planet.[16]

The whole safari experience seems much more about us than about an attempt to learn about nature. If we take account of the larger structure of the experience—who can afford to go, how they get there, what they do, what they focus on, and what they think—we can see it as part of the whole Western pattern of experiencing the world. As such, it reconfirms what we already believe about Africa, as do zoos, natural history museums, animal amusement parks, nature television, and even *The Lion King*.

## Hunting Africa

My first reaction to my hunter student Richard was that in his pursuit of a highly personal and Western goal, he was going to participate in the Western domination of Africa. Even if killing a charging Cape buffalo is the ultimate experience of being alive, which I doubt, we should not necessarily do it at Africa's or nature's expense. Moreover, the African hunting safari is clearly a Western experience, not a universal one, and in its contemporary form it still frequently mimics the efforts of Roosevelt's safari to gain dominion over Africans and animals.

In further investigating this question, however, I have come to a deeper appreciation of Richard's position as a hunter. Hunters get one thing right that many tourists seem to miss. They know it is dangerous to read our view of the structure of reality into nature. The Cape buffalo will kill the hunter who misreads nature and whose technology fails. We need to become part of nature in order to survive. A short hunting safari in Africa cannot suffice to learn about African nature, but the impulse to be *in and of* nature seems correct. At the heart of the matter is the necessity not to be a spectator and not to turn nature into an object.

These ideas can be extended to the way safaris treat Africans. Whether for hunting, photography, or just sightseeing, the modern safari tends to consider Africans as objects rather than as people. Although individual Africans may profit from the jobs and fees that result from safaris, Africans as people are only ancillary to the enterprise. Tourists and hunters arrive in Nairobi, Harare, Gaborone, or Johannesburg and leave town to get to the game parks as quickly as possible. They interact with Africans primarily as employees: drivers, trackers, cooks, waiters, maids, and gift-shop salespersons. What contact there is with African culture occurs mostly through idealized re-creations of the African past in the form of dances, art, food, and "ritual."

And so there are parallels between the ways we tend to see African animals and how we view African people. Real African animals and real African people are not allowed to interfere with the tourist illusion of how nature and society ought to be. They do not hit us full in the face, causing us to question our relationships with African animals or people. In "safari Africa" we do not get involved with either animals or people in ways that challenge us to become partners on a shared planet.

# 10

# AFRICA IN IMAGES

This chapter presents a few examples of the way Africa is portrayed in images. Over the course of three decades, several generations of students and friends helped collect these and other images.[1] We generally found such images with little trouble on the Internet, in magazines and newspapers, and in books from the period we were studying.

In the two previous editions of this book, this chapter provided images from current sources, mostly advertisements. These images illustrated that Dark Continent ideas are still available in what we read every day or on the products that we buy. I've included some of those images in this edition, but my intent here has changed a bit. This time I present a more historical approach. Beginning with images from the nineteenth century and continuing to recent times, you will see that our popular views of Africa have become less racist and evolutionist. In fact, it is increasingly rare to see advertisements evoke African primitiveness and/or wild animals other than in travel and photography ads. This is progress. Nonetheless, you will also see that Dark Continent myths persist.

Before you read the chapter you might look at the images and try to analyze them for their Dark Continent messages. How do these messages illustrate the ways we "use Africa to think with"? How have ideas changed? What is being said about Africa? Is it stereotypical? Does it promote a better understanding of Africa?

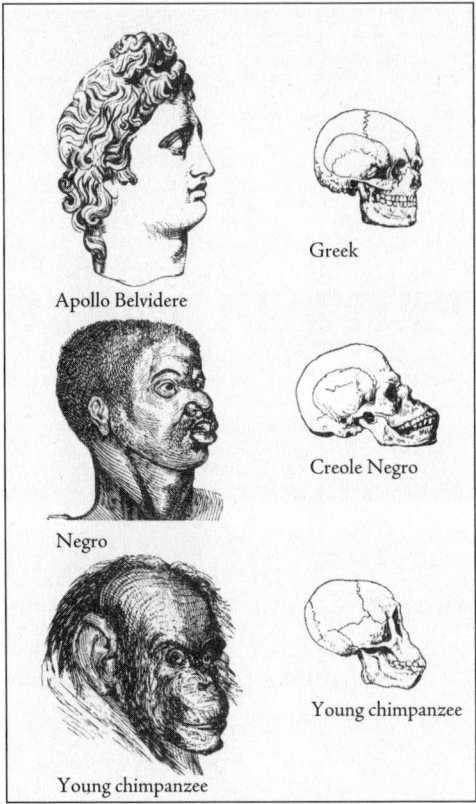

PHOTO 1

## Photo 1:
# Indigenous Races of the Earth[2]

This image, published in Philadelphia in 1868, represents the state of American evolutionary "science" at that time. In fact, until the mid-twentieth century it was common for white Americans and Europeans to think of Africans (and African Americans) as biologically inferior. About this image specifically, biologist Stephen Jay Gould says that "the chimpanzee skull is falsely inflated, and the Negro jaw extended, to give the impression that blacks might even rank lower than the apes."[3] In his well-known book *The Mismeasure of Man*, Gould demonstrates again and again that scientists of the nineteenth and early twentieth centuries falsified data to "prove" that Africans and others were biologically inferior.

PHOTO 2

## PHOTO 2:
## "Affectionate Curiosity of the Rosako Women"[4]

Here is a scene imagined in 1889 by Illinois author James W. Buel, an "armchair explorer" who retold and illustrated the exploits of Henry Morton Stanley, the best-known African explorer of the era. Buel created over five hundred drawings to accompany his work, *Heroes of the Dark Continent*, which was published by at least four different American publishers in 1889 and 1890.

This image seems designed to titillate, but it doesn't represent what happened to Stanley. Traveling into the interior of East Africa in 1871, Stanley wrote that he had heard that sometimes Africans would be very forward in touching explorers' possessions and asking what they were used for. Once in a while he reported that people were indeed curious about him and all the many things he brought along. But he doesn't say that the Rosako men or women were especially curious or that the women tried to touch him or fondle his beard.[5] In Buel's image, ordinary curiosity turns into something more primitive and sexual, thus entertaining the American reader and reinforcing stereotypes of Africa.

Other images from this era frequently depict Africans as violent, irrational, disorganized, fearful, venal, dirty, sensual, childlike, and so forth. Of course, Westerners are shown as the opposite. Moreover, images often celebrate the advance of Western "civilization" in the face of African primitives.

## PHOTO 3:
## *Tintin in the Congo*[6]

Given the recent appearance of the movie *Tintin*, it is interesting to reflect on Tintin's trip to Africa. Hergé (Georges Remi) published the comic *Tintin va au Congo* in 1930 in "Le Petit Vingtième," a weekly youth supplement to a conservative, Catholic, procolonial, anticommunist Belgian newspaper. *Tintin in the Congo* has subsequently appeared in numerous translations into many languages worldwide, often well after 1960, the end of the colonial era in Congo. The most recent English edition was published in 2010.

The cartoon is charming and fun, but also full of colonial stereotypes of Africans. The plot is that Tintin goes to Africa as a reporter for "Le Petit Vingtième" and in a series of adventures captures a group of bad white men. The many Africans in the story are depicted variously as helpless, stupid, irrational, lazy, silly, childish, happy, hospitable, power hungry, and evil. A modern biographer of Hergé defends him as paternalist rather than racist, but that is hard to accept given the era and the racist climate in Europe and America.[7]

PHOTO 3

Most of the *Tintin in the Congo* story is set in villages or jungles. In the images shown here, however, some Africans are in a rickety train and the engineer is not paying attention. Tintin's car has stalled on the tracks. When the train hits the car, it's so decrepit that it falls off the tracks without harming the car. Tintin apologizes while the Africans, who are wearing Western clothing in weird ways, complain in broken English (French) about the "wicked white man." Tintin suggests that together they fix the train, but the Africans are lazy and don't want to get dirty. Tintin organizes the Africans to put the train back on the tracks and tows it to a village.

The messages are fairly clear: Africans can't be trusted with modern technology. Africans adopt Western ways but don't really know how to be Western. Africans are lazy and make excuses. Africans call white colonialism bad, but need whites to organize them to get work done.

As in the exploration and conquest eras, the colonial era produced images in which Africans were primitives and Westerners were helping to bring "civilization." Typical scenes involved new roads and bridges, Western justice, mission stations and churches, children in schools, and destroyed "fetishes." There were also many images calculated to show why Africans needed Western help.

## Photo 4:
## Map of Central Africa[8]

As African colonies became independent countries in the 1950s and 1960s, images began to be more favorable. The change was much slower than we might expect, however. Here is a map of Central Africa published in a 1964 geography textbook for American middle-school children. After more than seventy-five years of Belgian colonial rule, the map's only icons are "natives," wild animals, and mineral resources. And yet, at the time of independence in 1960, Congo had large towns and cities; extensive road, rail, and river transportation systems; schools and newspapers; a university; and so forth. The text mentions some of these, but focuses on Western help for primitive Africans.

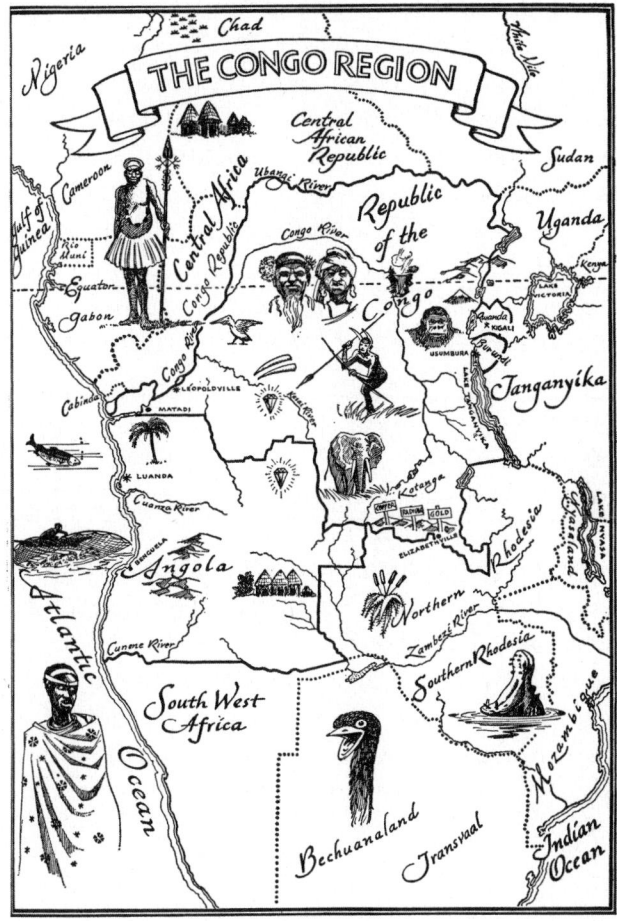

PHOTO 4

And for African history, the accompanying text is equally primitivizing. For example, the ancient kingdom of Kongo, first contacted by the Portuguese in 1482, had a complex history that included a large capital city, a bureaucracy, conversion of many Kongolese to Catholicism, and collapse under pressure from the slave trade. But the text highlights "Bantu natives" and "pagan beliefs" and badly mangles the facts. Here's an excerpt:

A half-century [after the Portuguese arrive and convert the king] passed peacefully. Then the Ba-Ngala came. They were a fierce cannibal tribe from the north. They ate all of the Portuguese missionaries and many of the native Christians. The others quickly became pagans again. Only their Catholic crucifixes were treasured, for they were considered some form of white men's magic that would keep away evil spirits.

That was long, long ago. Today there are many missionaries and Portuguese settlers in Angola. Some of the native Angolese have become Christians and learned European customs. Many more continue to believe they must offer sacrifices to dead ancestors, whose spirits come back to haunt the living.[9]

I find humor in the reference to cannibalism, because it is so blatantly stereotypical. But it isn't really funny because the whole passage is deeply inaccurate, stereotypical, and primitivizing. Moreover, the text totally omits the negative impact of the slave trade and oppressive Portuguese and Belgian colonialism. When I realize that I'm old enough that the first edition of this textbook (1952) could have been used when I was in middle school, I have two reactions: First, many of our current leaders and citizens were brought up on this fare, which explains a great deal about why stereotypes persist. Second, we have come quite a way despite the lingering effects of such mistaking of Africa.

### Photo 5: "Tarzan: Moon Beast"[10]

In the original 1912 story, Tarzan's parents died and he was raised by "apes." Thus the meaning of the tale is that Tarzan's white noble blood (his race) triumphed over the culture taught him by less evolved apes and Africans. Thus he became the superior white male, the "king of the jungle." In many later stories, Tarzan saves good-but-helpless Africans (and white women), usually from wild animals or bad whites who collaborate with bad Africans. Tarzan is like Tintin in that he still promotes myths about Africa. Today both Tarzan and Tintin have active fan clubs. But Tarzan

PHOTO 5

is even more influential in America, because he is always associated with Africa, because he appears more frequently (in books, films, cartoons, comics, and oral culture), and because he has an American creator, Edgar Rice Burroughs.

In the 1973 DC Comics "Moon Beast," shown here, Tarzan is framed by a powerful medicine man of the "B'Tunga tribe" and has to save himself. Naturally, the evil Africans and animals are very evil and the good ones need Tarzan to either direct or save them. All are primitive. The cover, shown here, illustrates the stereotypes openly promoted only forty years ago. Today there are fewer primitive Africans in Tarzan creations, but the strong association of Africa with nature persists.

## Photo 6:
## "Africa. A Political Jungle"[11]

By the late 1970s when this image appeared, all of Africa was independent except for three white settler colonies in Southern Africa (South Africa, Namibia, and Zimbabwe/Rhodesia). Scholars had debunked most of America's common myths about Africa, but the popular media was slow to follow. In this 1978 *Time* magazine cover we can clearly see remnants of Dark Continent stereotypes. Carter is a missionary, Castro a guerilla, Brezhnev an explorer, and Giscard d'Estaing a legionnaire. There are lion and jungle references to evoke African wildness and survival-of-the-fittest stereotypes.

This cover was probably meant to be amusing when it appeared. But how did it become so? In 1978 the amusement was in the hilarious caricatures of world leaders as stereotypical colonists and the clever equation of African politics and the African jungle. At that time, we were consumed with the Cold War and Africa appeared to Americans as too uncivilized and close to nature to resist communism by itself. But note the similarity of this "news" magazine cover to the Tarzan comic cover above. Africa's primitiveness was still assumed, as was the need for Western intervention against bad Africans (and bad whites: Cubans and Soviets). Do you suppose that a cover like this could appear today?

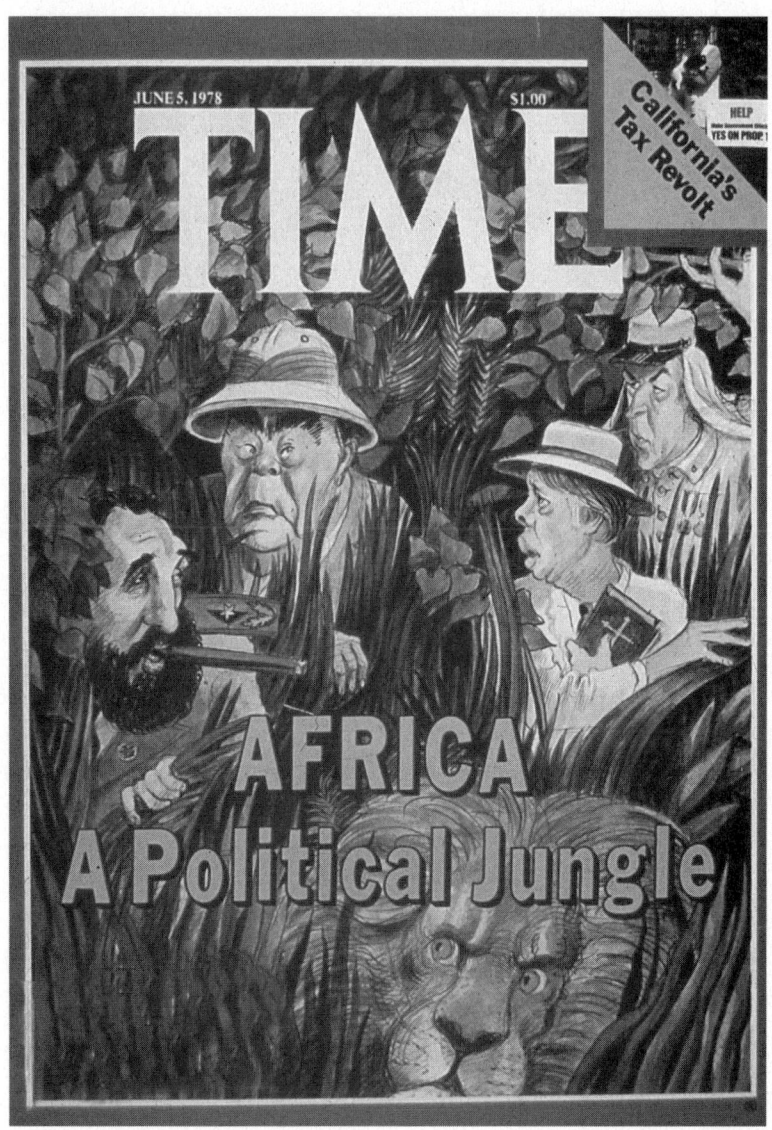

PHOTO 6

PHOTO 7

## Photo 7:
## "Lose Citicorp Travelers Checks in Maputo . . . "[12]

In the case of advertisements, Africa is, of course, only one of the subjects that ad agencies treat in stereotypical ways. Indeed, advertising in general thrives on its ability to represent our culture's fantasies and myths about the world. Advertising is a dreamland where our hopes, fears, and illusions about reality and unreality appear. Thus it is also a place where we can look into the corners of the American mind.

Ad agencies presume we do not read every ad and might only glimpse their ads in passing. Therefore, the ad must grab us, if only for a fraction of a second. The designer of this 1980 Citicorp ad did a good job in that regard, but what does it say about Africa? In 1980 Mozambique had been independent for four years. Maputo, the capital city, had skyscrapers, paved roads, traffic lights, banks, and other modern features. Moreover, Mozambicans had recently fought a war of liberation against the Portuguese using modern weapons, not spears and shields. The ad is funny even today (why? because we still associate Africa with "natives" and jungles?), but it is quite unfair to Africans. Moreover, it promotes stereotypes that made (and make) it difficult for Americans to understand today's Africa. Search the Internet for images of Maputo today, and you'll see a much different Africa.

PHOTO 8

# Photo 8:
# "Ankle-biting Pygmies"[13]

It was a cute idea, but this 1997 ad primitivized and naturalized Africa. "Ankle-biting Pygmies"? Please. Pygmies couldn't talk back so it was safe to mock them. Moreover, the Pygmy metaphor is used even today by self-important Americans who dismiss and diminish those who criticize them. And what about the jungle, the disease, the ants, and the spiders? Packard Bell unashamedly re-created the Dark Continent. But this Dark Continent is not in the past. It's still out there to frighten us, said Packard Bell.

"Wouldn't *you* rather be at *home?*" Was Packard Bell telling us that we could experience nothing and still know everything? Or perhaps the message was that we should only go places where we feel comfortable. With this attitude toward the world, could we expect American interest in and knowledge of global affairs to be adequate? Most of Africa is actually very safe and well worth the effort of leaving home.

PHOTO 9:
## "If Carlos Knows He's Half Irish, . . . "[14]

At first glance, this IBM ad makes no sense. Upon more careful inspection, it still makes no sense. The only way in 2007 to discern the meaning of the statement that Carlos, likely an American of mixed European ancestry, is

PHOTO 9

also Tanzanian was to go to the referenced website. There we were told that IBM and *National Geographic* teamed up for a five-year research project that intended to trace how we are all biologically related and how our common human ancestors dispersed from Africa. The Genographic Project researchers planned to collect DNA samples from randomly selected people around the world and identify their similarities and differences.[15]

IBM continues to be involved in the Genographic Project, and the work is important. But the sentiment expressed in the ad's caption seems wrongheaded. Neither Carlos nor the majority of participants in the project are citizens of Tanzania. Moreover, our distant ancestors were not Tanzanians any more than they were citizens or residents of any other modern country in Africa or the world. They didn't even look like modern Tanzanians. But it's worse than that. While we do share a common biological kinship with all others through our African roots, equating modern Tanzanians with our African ancestors fosters the myth of an *unchanging* Africa, close to nature, where we may still find our ancestors living.

IBM certainly didn't mean to send this message, and the subtlety of this ad can give us hope that Dark Continent myths are dying. But we are also reminded that Dark Continent myths often persist even when we intend to do better.

# Photo 10:
# "I Am African"[16]

Gwyneth Paltrow is surely among the least African of American celebrities. This ad would not be quite so surprising if it featured Akon or Don Cheadle. It's the celebrity's blonde highlights and freckles that capture the viewer's attention: how can she claim to be African? Oddly, reading the text of the ad doesn't answer this question.

Like IBM, the Keep a Child Alive organization has good intentions. It raises money for antiretroviral drugs that can help Africans fight HIV/AIDS. The "I am African" campaign features celebrities (Alan Cumming, Liv Tyler, Tyson Beckford, Lenny Kravitz, and others) photographed with face paint intended to make them look like Africans. But in trying to get its point across, the campaign mistakes Africa. You must go to the organization's website to find the full meaning of "I am African":

PHOTO 10

"Each and every one of us contains DNA that can be traced back to our African ancestors. These amazing people traveled far and wide. Now they need our help."

As in the IBM ad, the "I am African" campaign is sorely wrong. Those who live in Africa today are not the "these amazing people" referred to in the ad, nor are they our ancestors. To say they are is an evolutionist perspective (described in Chapter 3). Moreover, to be African does not imply that one is suffering and dying. Furthermore, how does wearing face paint make one African? The number of today's Africans who use face paint is miniscule, unless you count the millions who, like us, use modern cosmetics. The "I am African" campaign may attract our attention to Africa and may even contribute to supporting the lives of the needy, but it fails to educate us about African diversity, African culture, or our true relationships to Africa.

## PHOTO 11: "Experience Africa"[17]

Detect lions, conquer a mountain, visit villages. The ad offers ten-day safaris starting at a moderate price, and describes the "experience" of Africa in terms not exactly objective. Rural Africa may indeed be a fascinating place for the open-minded traveler, and GAP Adventures should be congratulated for helping tourists connect with more than wild animals. But this is not the real Africa any more or less than the skyscrapers of Nairobi are. And such heavily charged words as *remote* and *tribal* derail the attempt at objectivity. This ad urges the traveler to look at rural Africans in a stereotypical way, as curiosities to gawk at or as remnants of an ancient world to be studied for meaning in contrast to contemporary life.

The imagery of this ad presents a cultural fragment, a group of rural Kenyans from "Samburu Village" engaged in a dance, and a young Western woman learning by imitation. The purpose is clearly to show that the GAP tourist can actively participate in the culture of the Africans pictured. But the village is not pictured, and learning a dance in a tourist-oriented village is not learning to live in a different culture. Moreover,

PHOTO 11

Samburu women don't dance by jumping, so what is a Western woman conveying when she imitates the men?

Traveler Marie Javins tells of a conversation she had with a tour operator who once took tourists to a village near the Samburu. The operator said, "The tourists were always disappointed by the T-shirts and jeans the locals wore, so the nomads had taken to changing into traditional clothing exclusively for the tourists. It got to the point where I was calling them on their mobiles to say, 'Take off your shorts and T-shirts because I'm bringing tourists by.'"[18]

Why is it that travel ads such as these focus on only the remote and the unmodern in Africa? And why do they presume that nothing in urban Africa will draw our interest? One can hardly blame GAP Adventures and other tour companies for advertising what we want to buy. Yet advertisements such as these flatten an entire continent of diverse lifestyles and environments into mere dusty savannas full of wild animals and villages of dancing families. This is harmful both to Africans and to those American travelers who genuinely want to learn about Africa from experience.

## PHOTO 12:
# "We Face Challenges All over the World"[19]

ExxonMobil has indeed contributed to health initiatives in Africa, including efforts to mitigate the effects of malaria. Yet to put the corporation's 2007 ad in perspective, 18 percent of ExxonMobil's oil and gas production came from Africa, and its profits were the largest of any company in the world, ever: $25.3 billion in 2004, $36.1 billion in 2005, $39.5 billion in 2006, and $40.5 billion in 2007.[20] While down a bit in 2009, profits were back to $41 billion by 2011.[21] Considering the company is capitalized at over $400 billion, the profits may not be excessive. However, given the amount and the source of the profit, $40 million over seven years to help Africa is a paltry sum: an average of .014 percent of profits per year.[22]

ExxonMobil has also been associated with a good deal of exploitation and corruption on the continent. Payments for extraction of oil in Equatorial Guinea go into dictator Teodoro Obiang's personal bank account, from which he spends lavishly on himself and his family while his citizens remain desperately poor.[23] One of the most corrupt countries in the world, Equatorial Guinea is considered our ally.

A 2012 book by Pulitzer Prize–winning author Steve Coll describes ExxonMobil's poor record in Equatorial Guinea, Nigeria, Chad, and other countries around the world. He says that considering its enormous power in poor countries (exceeding the US government, he argues), ExxonMobil needs to act more responsibly. For example, they should insist that local governments make public their records about profits from oil and about where the money goes.[24] ExxonMobil, a company itself shrouded in secrecy, replied that they are only about energy development and won't tell local governments what to do.[25] This sounds like the 1980s justifications for US companies doing business in racist South Africa: "We follow all local laws. We don't get involved in politics."

ExxonMobil is not the only bad corporate citizen advertising its good works in Africa. For example, you might have seen Chevron television ads showing smiling Angolans who explain how the company helps them and their country get ahead. But what does Chevron really do in Angola, or in Nigeria and many other countries in the world? Each year, a large group of human rights and environmental organizations publishes "The True

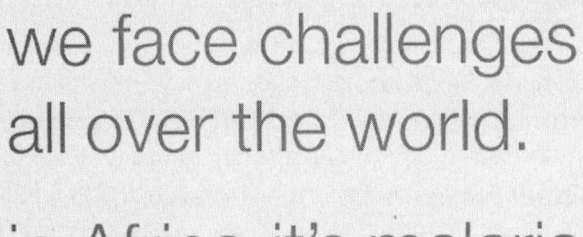

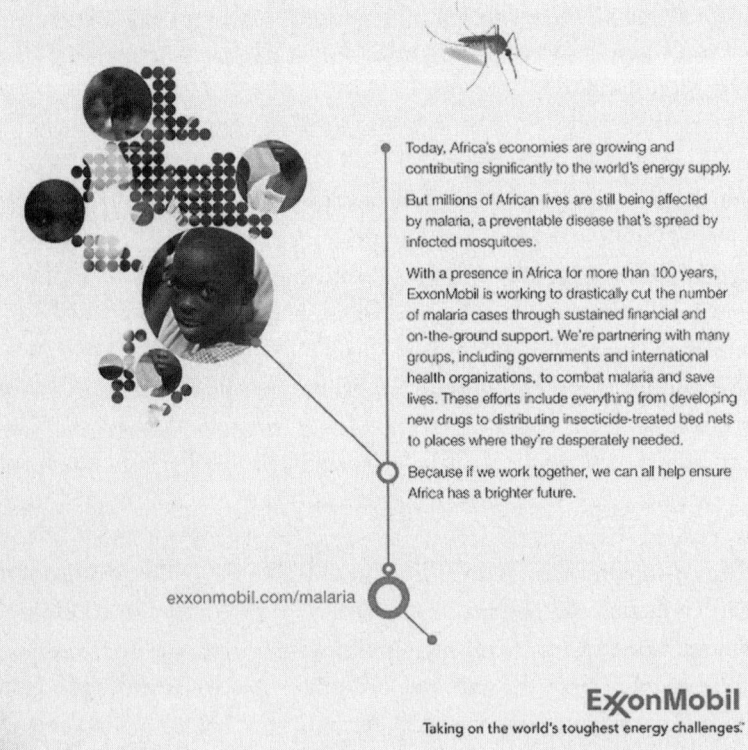

Cost of Chevron: An Alternative Annual Report" to counter the image Chevron likes to project. This report portrays a much different story, one that is truly damaging to Africans and their environments.[26] Considering the controversy over the activities of ExxonMobil and Chevron, can we call their tiny efforts to help Africa humanitarian gestures, or are they marketing strategies that draw attention away from the crises they are fueling on the continent? Moreover, is it possible for us to criticize China for its African deals that ignore human rights, if this is how we act?

PHOTO 13

## Photo 13: "Jewelry With a Global Flair"[27]

This ad appeared in 2012 in several fashion magazines and is available on the web. On the surface it seems harmless enough and is effective because of the contrast between the elaborate, colorful bracelet (emeralds, diamonds, and platinum) and the simple, monocolor African background (mostly light browns).

But what does the ad tell us about Africa? That Africa is nature and natives? The African here is an icon rather than a person, and she lives peacefully with lions. And why this instead of an urban African scene? Could it be that the emeralds, diamonds, and platinum were mined by this African? Hardly. Or are we supposed to be reminded that these materials could well have come from Africa? And is the ad's title supposed to be ironic? "Adler, Jewelry With a Global Flair." Do we suppose that the African here could afford or would normally wear the bracelet or that we objectify this African while wearing the bracelet?

## Photo 14: "Elegant"[28]

Not all images mistake Africa, of course. This excellent ad by the Village Banking Campaign of FINCA International helps to correct some of our stereotypes. It shows Africans connected to us through their clothing style and through the goods they are selling in their shop. We also see urban Africans who live in Kampala, the capital of Uganda. In addition, the Africans in the ad are improving their own lives with just a bit of outside help. Here is an opportunity to help Africans that promotes African dreams, rather than our own, and allows Africans to take responsibility for their own development. FINCA International is rapidly expanding its village banks in Africa and elsewhere.[29] For a discussion of micro lending and community banking, see Chapter 6.

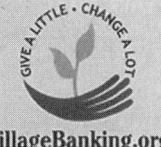

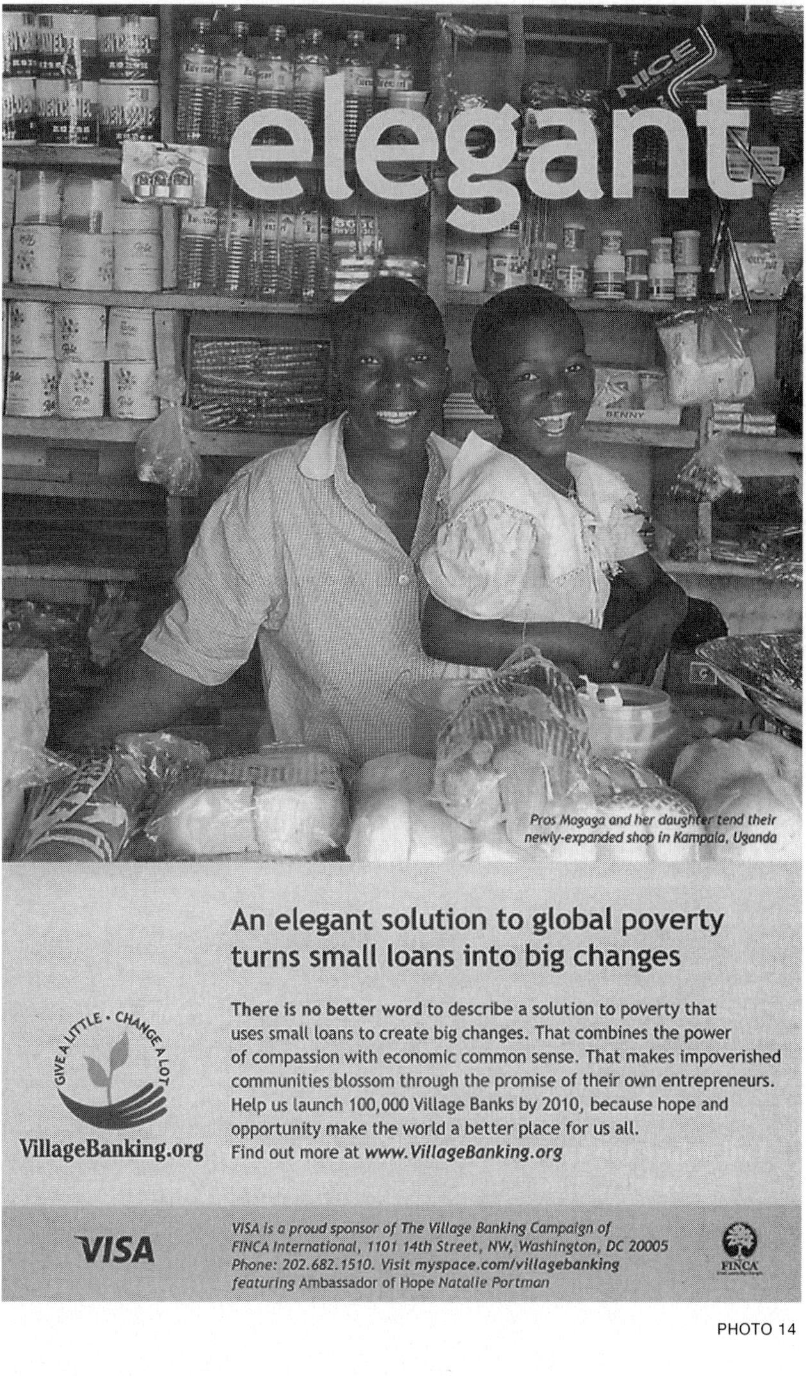
elegant
Pros Magaga and her daughter tend their newly-expanded shop in Kampala, Uganda
An elegant solution to global poverty turns small loans into big changes
There is no better word to describe a solution to poverty that uses small loans to create big changes. That combines the power of compassion with economic common sense. That makes impoverished communities blossom through the promise of their own entrepreneurs. Help us launch 100,000 Village Banks by 2010, because hope and opportunity make the world a better place for us all.
Find out more at www.VillageBanking.org
GIVE A LITTLE • CHANGE A LOT
VillageBanking.org
VISA
VISA is a proud sponsor of The Village Banking Campaign of FINCA International, 1101 14th Street, NW, Washington, DC 20005 Phone: 202.682.1510. Visit myspace.com/villagebanking featuring Ambassador of Hope Natalie Portman
FINCA

PHOTO 14

## PART FOUR

# NEW DIRECTIONS

# 11

# RACE AND CULTURE

## *The Same and the Other*

Until only a few decades ago, the idea prevailed in Europe and North America that some humans were more biologically evolved than others. The resulting racism, Dark Continent stereotypes, and evolutionism are major themes of this book. Today, most Americans believe or want to believe that others are biologically the same as we are, yet few can explain the origins or significance of obvious differences among people and cultures. How is it that people can be so different and still be the same? We frequently see others doing such strange things that it is difficult for us to imagine that we all have the same basic biology.

Since this book deals with American attitudes toward a continent about which questions of race and culture have been prominent, it is important to consider the underlying nature of our differences. What follows is not a detailed study but a discussion of ideas we can pursue.

## Race

When it comes to facts about the nature of race, much remains unclear. Scientists don't know for sure when or how races developed, and they are not entirely sure why. Nor can they prove that the biological differences between population groups play no significant role in who we are. But science is like that. Whereas racism begins with belief, science begins with questions and doubt.

Strong evidence suggests that *Homo sapiens* emerged first in Africa about 200,000 years ago and that modern *Homo sapiens* began to spread across the world as recently as 50,000 years ago, eventually differentiating into what are perceived to be today's races.[1] But what is clear and important for our discussion here is that our original African ancestors were not the "black people" we associate with sub-Saharan Africa today. Today's blacks, like today's whites and others, are offshoots of our early common ancestors.

Why did we eventually differentiate into so-called races? Evolutionary theory proposes that differentiation occurs for adaptive reasons, but it also notes that many genetic traits are adaptive-neutral, meaning that they are neither particularly adaptive nor maladaptive. Whether adaptive-neutral traits persist or change is not important for the survival of a species, at least in the short run. For some traits, such as skin color, it is difficult to know whether they are adaptive and, if so, what their functions are. Our best guess is that skin color is an adaptive trait, a result of biological reaction to the sun. Darker skin seems to protect against skin cancer and folic acid depletion at the sun-drenched equator. Thus our common ancestors, who lived near the equator, were likely dark skinned. Lighter skin allows humans closer to the sun-poor poles to synthesize sufficient vitamin D and thus avoid rickets, a potentially fatal bone disease. The fact that Eskimos, Inuits, and others living in the far north are darker than Scandinavians does not contradict this theory, because the former migrated from southern parts of Asia in relatively recent times and have presumably sustained themselves in the reduced sunlight by eating a fish diet rich in vitamin D.

In any case, skin color is not much of an indication of what we are. First of all, when we say that we see a particular skin color, we usually see not what is in nature but what our culture says is there. "Black" skin, for example, ranges from blue-black to all shades of brown to almost white, and so-called blacks display a wide variety of physical types. "White" skin ranges from white to pink, orange, and olive, and likewise, "whites" include a whole range of body types. Moreover, someone considered black in the United States might be considered white in another culture. In fact, our whole system of race classification—Caucasoid, Mongoloid, Negroid, Pygmoid, and so forth—is a cultural artifact of the era in which Western

Europeans attempted to substantiate their own racial superiority.[2] Our limited categories virtually blind us to the infinite differences within races and to the similarities across races.

If we locate different genetic factors geographically, the map rarely corresponds to the races as we know them. Instead, our genetic traits, most of which are invisible, cross racial lines and scatter among populations that appear homogeneous on the surface. In short, the map is quite jumbled.[3] Moreover, thanks to recent advances in molecular genetics, we have learned that the average genetic differences among individuals of different "races" are actually smaller than the average differences among individuals within the same race or even ethnic group. Here is one summary of our genetic similarities and differences:

> On average there's .2 percent difference in genetic material between any two randomly chosen people on Earth. Of that diversity, 85 percent will be found within any local group of people—say, between you and your neighbor. More than half (9 percent) of the remaining 15 percent will be represented by differences between ethnic and linguistic groups within a given race (for example, between Italians and French). Only 6 percent represents differences between races (for example, between Europeans and Asians). And remember—that's 6 percent of .2 percent. In other words, race accounts for only a minuscule .012 percent difference in our genetic material.[4]

To put it another way, the concept of race simply doesn't provide very much that is scientifically useful. Indeed, scientists have abandoned the term when discussing humans and instead talk about *regional* or *continental* characteristics. Divergent characteristics help *a little* in understanding why some individuals have certain physical features or are susceptible to certain diseases. But differences in most human traits can be more easily explained by one's family genetics and environment than by larger-scale characteristics. *Race* as we know it is mostly skin-deep.

Given our obsession with race, it is ironic that genes account more for our sameness than for our differences. And our sameness is vast. One person who has spent his life thinking about human sameness, human behaviorist Desmond Morris, asks what similar traits the human animal displays worldwide. In his now-classic book *The Naked Ape*, Morris includes discussions of sex, child rearing, fighting, feeding, exploration, and comfort that provide ample evidence of the many fundamental traits shared by all humans.[5] His television documentary series *The Human Animal* covers similar topics and is rerun frequently.[6] Morris's research demonstrates that our common human traits, including our attachment to groups (whether based on our race, clan, or friendship), must certainly be a result of common biology.

Those who have attempted to test whether different races have different mental abilities have always failed to obtain meaningful results. Proof of this hypothesis requires a test that reliably takes into account a person's physical and cultural environment, but such a test has yet to be devised. The problem is that humans not only are biological animals in the sense that Desmond Morris has described but are also individually affected by environment (for example, nutrition and disease); history (for example, wars, slavery, and colonialism); and culture (for example, child-rearing practices and preferred forms of logic). In addition, there are the idiosyncrasies of one's individual family and community to take into account. For these reasons, to devise a fair intelligence test would require an analysis that accounts for different environments, histories, cultures, and families. The task would be infinitely complex, and thus virtually impossible.

We have arrived at two modern assumptions about human reality. First, because we know there is more genetic difference among individuals of the same race than among individuals of different races, we assume that race is more a cultural than a biological construct. Second, because there is no reliable way to test for mental differences, we assume that all humans operate with the same basic capacities. As far as I know, today's science can provide no absolute proof that these two assumptions are correct. Remember, however, that scientific inquiry begins with doubt about its hypotheses. In the social sphere, reliance on the assumption of sameness seems safer than to sink into the dangerous contentiousness of imputed racial difference.

This is why those who study other cultures have generally concluded that there is no such thing as a primitive human being or even a primitive human culture. They assume that minds of similar capacity are working in all societies to solve the problems of life, and that the answers these minds arrive at will be similarly effective. On the other hand—and this is the hard part—we must avoid the trap of believing that once we all recognize our biological sameness, we will easily get along. It's a small world, but a world marked nonetheless by significant differences among cultures and peoples. We must take into account the influences of environment, history, and, most important, culture.

# Culture

Other animals operate on instincts more than we do; our capacity for thinking and learning—that is, our ability to supplement and overcome instinct through culture—is much greater than theirs. We rightly take pride in our ability to learn practically anything. Indeed, our cultural capacity is so great and so adaptive that—though outclassed in terms of speed, agility, and strength by many of our competitors—we have colonized the entire globe and are reaching for the universe.

Our great capacity for culture depends on a number of physical abilities including speech, bipedalism, and finely coordinated hands. Our cultural capacity is also shaped by our instincts, which encourage us, for example, to share with each other and live in groups. Some version of the Golden Rule is perhaps necessary in any human culture, but if we were not also programmed to cooperate, society as we know it would not be possible.

When it comes to culture, our crowning glory—literally—is our brains. Our capacity for culture is largely possible because of two mental traits: thought and memory. Thinking is usually regarded as the more important of the two, because it helps us determine what works in a specific situation and gives us our prized imagination and sense of freedom. Chris Stringer and Robin McKie write that the key to the evolution of modern humans was our development of new ways of thinking. They note that "to a Neanderthal, a cave bear was a cave bear. To a modern human, it was not only a threat, or possibly a source of food, it was a god, an ancestor, and who knows what else."[7] The modern humans who emerged about 50,000 years ago marked the beginning of a more "fluid and generalized" ability to think.[8] With our more developed brains, we could use ideas in one intellectual domain to think about ideas in another. We could eventually turn our hunting-and-gathering instincts toward job searching or grocery shopping. And we could turn our ability to keep track of what was going on among our neighbors toward storytelling, novel writing, and history writing. We could learn to use art, music, and religion to comment on who we are and how we want to live.

The other trait particularly significant to the development of human culture is memory, which deserves greater attention if we are to understand the problems of race and culture. Each of us has complained that he or she cannot remember well, but in fact our whole world is largely created by memory. Let me give two simple examples. In Kenya, light switches move up for off and down for on, which is the opposite of switches in the United States. When I go to turn on a light in Kenya, I must stop and think. And thinking seems inappropriate and unnatural when it comes to a task I do automatically all the time. I get momentarily confused and then annoyed. Another example is that cars in Kenya travel on the left. When I am a passenger in Kenya, I sit on the side of the car where I would be driving in the United States, but I have no steering wheel or brake pedal. Roads are narrow, cars pass frequently, and they come straight toward me. I am terrified. If I were to drive in Kenya, my body would take months to adjust to the point that I could trust my reflexes in the same way I do when driving in the United States.

These minor examples illustrate how dependent we are on memory. What would happen if we had no memory? What if we had to think about every small task we face such as how to brush our teeth, put on clothes, make breakfast, or cross a street? We would become exhausted from thinking, or more likely, we wouldn't even be able to think because we wouldn't remember what a toothbrush, shoe, or street was. And what would happen if those around us were similarly incapacitated and forgetfully drove on the wrong side of the road?

It is not just in our daily actions that memory constructs our world. Humans learn religion and develop ideas through memory. We couldn't deal with the natural world without memory. The societies we grow up in construct whole fields of memories that tell us what the world is and what it means. Although you might think a tree is a tree, the ways trees are used and what trees mean differ from one *memory system* to the next—that is, from one *culture* to the next. Our agriculture, industry, and science all rely on our cultural memory systems. Even such fundamentals as our logical and emotional behavior are deeply shaped by memory, so that different cultures prefer different behaviors. And when we encounter something new, we tend to reach into our memories to find an analogy or metaphor that allows us to categorize the new experience.

When it comes to action, the kind of memory we call *habit* is particularly important. Thankfully, most of our daily activities—turning on lights, crossing streets, brushing teeth—are governed by habit, so we can use our thinking ability to work on new ideas. And happily, people around us have similar habits, so we can predict ahead of time, more or less, what they are going to do. Habit is, in a sense, a cultural equivalent of instinct that allows humans to get along with each other, to build different worlds, and to adapt to many different kinds of environments. The capacity for habit helps us feel comfortable in our world. Indeed, we talk about our habits as "second nature," thoughts and actions we have learned so well that they feel instinctive.

But what happens when we meet a person or a whole society with different memories and habits? When faced with the need to deal with such difference, humans try to make sense of it on several levels. Our conscious minds may think, "These people are OK. They are different only because they have learned different ways to look at the world. They have a different culture." But on an unconscious level our minds notice that we are not comfortable, that our habits are unable to keep us safe, and that every signal given by others has to be consciously evaluated. We feel threatened because even our smallest acts don't have the same results as they do when we are with "our own kind."

This threat is not just a threat to our ideas, however. It is actually felt as a threat to our physical body because we have *become* our habits. In other words, our culture has come to feel *natural* even though it is learned. This is why living in or dealing with an unfamiliar culture commonly produces "culture shock," a physical sense of being unsettled and a desire to withdraw. This happens even to those who consciously desire to be in the new culture. Life seems *un*natural and demands more thinking than we can tolerate, leading some even to fall into depression.

At this point, we experience a critical moment. If we are not aware of what is actually happening, we might wrongly conclude, consciously or unconsciously, that the other culture or persons actually have a different nature from ours because they belong to a different race or because they are witches, or animals, or monsters, or aliens. Or we might conclude that others need us to show them how to act more naturally, more like we do. We may have similar responses even to people in our own culture if we perceive them to be much different or if we have to interact intensely with them. Numerous problems occur, for example, when two people get married and neither has had much experience with the other's gender, subculture, family, or personality type. After an initial euphoria, the differences begin to cause wear and tear on the relationship.

## On Being Human

We are not equipped with instincts to handle a great deal of difference even if we are naturally curious about how others live. Most of us do not mind being spectators of difference (via movies, novels, gossip columns, travel, and so on), but we do not wish to actually experience too much of it. Our instincts have evolved to help us live in small communities, and most of us subconsciously try to create for ourselves small circles of family and friends that make up a comfortable band or clan. One researcher estimates that the ideal biological size for human communities is about 150 people.[9] We tend "naturally" to be clannish (or tribal, race-oriented, parochial, partisan, nationalist, or whatever).

We must somehow learn to deal with difference if we are going to survive in the global society that is growing up around us. Fortunately, a significant feature of human beings is that our instincts are relatively weak, and through thinking and the influence of culture, they can be channeled in new directions and even be overcome. When survival demands it, our cultural ability allows us to develop a second nature to deal with new environments. My presumption is that we will be happier and safer if we do not just *think* about how to deal with difference but actually develop the habit, the *memory*, of successful negotiations of otherness.

Learning to deal with difference can begin at a distance through reading, watching television, eating at restaurants, attending classes, and engaging in other experiences that are relatively easy to accept. But the deepest explorations necessitate placing ourselves in situations in which we must physically experience the fact that others who also belong to the human race see the world in significantly different ways than we do. The first step is to teach our conscious minds what I discuss above—that for humans, culture becomes habit and habit feels natural even if it is not. The second step is to teach our unconscious minds, our memories, and our bodies to recognize the same thing. This second step is more difficult, and we may need to put ourselves in potentially painful situations to give our bodies the chance to adjust to difference.

Some people are born with little fear of cultural difference, and some families, communities, and societies are better than others at teaching members how to cope with and enjoy such difference. Most of us, however, have to learn about difference for ourselves. I was fortunate to learn at a young age that at least one kind of cultural difference was good. My mother's parents were recent immigrants and spoke American English with a thick Danish accent. I was also lucky in that my family was not openly racist, although I remember that they associated certain traits with certain races. It was not until I was in college, however, that I spoke in any seriousness with a person from another American subculture or from another world culture. Because I wanted to experience the world, I volunteered to room with a "foreign" student, as international students were called then. Life as a freshman with an older roommate from Kenya was rocky, to say the least. I recall my roommate's sighing assessment of my level of awareness: "You just don't know!" He was right; I didn't. By the time I graduated, I was better at negotiating difference, but I felt the shock of difference again when I lived in Africa after some graduate study. For weeks after my arrival in Congo, where everyone was black, I felt *very* white, like a thousand-watt lightbulb. Later, however, I remember being surprised when looking in a mirror and finding I was white, not black like those whom I associated with all day.

An often-quoted lyric from the Rodgers and Hammerstein musical *South Pacific* says, "You've got to be carefully taught to hate." The song implies that those who are not taught to hate will naturally like others. My own experience shows that this view is much too simplistic. We also need to be trained to deal with and appreciate difference. The training begins at day care centers with a child's feelings of separation and even panic, an early experience of culture shock. It continues as we go to school and eventually leave home—perhaps to attend college, to work at a job, or to be married. All of this separation, this experience with difference, may be interpreted as pleasurable and exciting, but it is usually painful, too. Fortunately, most of us succeed in becoming full members of our communities and, in doing so, also become more comfortable with living in the wider world and interacting with it.

Americans are being asked to go even further in accepting difference as we mix with each other in our neighborhoods, organizations, and jobs and as our society is increasingly entwined with the affairs of other societies. But evidence suggests that we don't go nearly as far as we could in exploring either the difficulties or the benefits of difference. We usually do what is appropriate when the boss says, "This is your new coworker," but we rarely choose to go much further than the situation requires. In fact, for most of us the painful transitions toward living with difference—from our experiences in day care to those in our jobs—take place out of necessity rather than choice. After each transition we settle into living in and enjoying our new situation. Moving onward, toward *more* difference, may still be painful and may remind us that our knowledge and skills are often shallow.

The rewards for putting ourselves in such potentially painful situations are great, however. They include not only the excitement of difference but also the satisfying newfound skills of negotiating difference. It is indeed a pleasurable experience to speak a new language, whether in the literal sense or in the sense of being able to cope comfortably in a different culture. But even more than this, learning to negotiate the difference of another culture allows us to reflect more deeply on our own culture and selves and on what it means to be human. Indeed, we can discover that difference at its deepest levels doesn't make as much difference as we once thought.

# 12

# FROM IMAGINATION
# TO DIALOGUE

I spent time in the 1970s researching the history of the Mangbetu people of northeastern Congo (Kinshasa). My best informant was a very old man named Iode Mbunza. Lame and frail, Iode was one of the brightest and gentlest men I have ever met. As a youth he had been interested in the history of his people, so he stayed home to listen to the elders when other young men went hunting. Iode knew stories. One evening, sitting around a fire, he told of a flying craft that had visited the Mangbetu in the 1930s, hovering briefly over the forest. People on the ground could see into the front window of the flying machine, where a white man stood reading a book. Astonished, I asked whether this had perhaps been a helicopter or dirigible, and he assured me that it had not.[1]

Such a machine carrying white men over Central Africa in the 1930s is outside my understanding, even if today someone might suggest it was a UFO. Iode himself was also unsure of the meaning of the event, but unlike myself, he had no problem imagining that what he remembered was true. He could easily conceive of the reality of such a craft because he knew only a little about white men, books, and machine technology. The strange white colonizers had brought the equally strange books and airplanes to Central Africa, so why not a white man reading a book in a hovering craft?

Contrast Iode's experience with that of Chief Batsakpide, a man I met in the same region in the late 1980s, after Iode and his generation had passed away. Chief Batsakpide, a young man of about thirty-five, had served in the Congolese air force and had studied aeronautical engineering in France. Well educated and with good employment prospects in urban Africa, he had nonetheless responded to the call of his people to be their leader. In a part of Africa remote from cities, he was helping a population of about 4,000 cope with the changing world around them. As I had done with Iode, I sat with Chief Batsakpide around an evening fire. But instead of stories of inexplicable aircraft, he taught me Western astronomy and pointed out the many man-made satellites that streaked across the clear African sky.[2] The difference between the two Africans was striking.

Iode easily imagined a white man reading a book in a flying machine. Writing and machines were at the heart of the white man's power in colonial Africa. Iode also imagined that white colonizers had been cannibals and that whites in general had magic that made them powerful. Understandably, Iode interpreted *our* civilization from the perspective of his own. In contrast, Batsakpide, the aeronautical engineer trained in the West, was familiar with our technical culture and would never have imagined that we possessed levitating craft in the 1930s, that we are cannibals, or that we have powerful magic.

Most Americans have been more like Iode when it comes to thoughts about Africa. We have imagined what Africa is like by using limited knowledge and limited categories of reality. There is one major difference, however. Iode visualized us from a position of powerlessness, whereas Westerners have visualized Africa from a position of power. Iode imagined that whites acquired control through magic. We have imagined that we acquired control because Africa was primitive.

## Evolutionism

The concept of primitive originated with the modern belief in evolutionism, which proposes that all things evolve along a single line and that some races and cultures are farther along that line than others. Evolutionism, a product of Western civilization, presumes that Westerners—especially white, male, upper-middle- and upper-class Westerners—are farthest along the line. This system uses the term *progress* to describe movement toward Western culture and Western ideals. Although Westerners themselves frequently disagree on the specific content of their ideals, an underlying Western belief persists that others *advance* as they become more Western. In other words, evolutionism assumes that the truth about reality is best embodied in Western culture.

Evolutionism emerged in the West in the late eighteenth and early nineteenth centuries, as we discovered that the natural world had evolved and as we struggled to understand what that meant for us. If we evolved, was it only by chance that we became human? Was there no purpose to evolution? For most, this idea was unthinkable. Rather, evolution needed to be fit into larger schemata of meaning. For many, evolution was seen to be God's plan for working out His purpose; for others, it was nature's plan for perfecting life. In either case, however, Westerners easily imagined that there was a plan and that they were at the forefront of its realization.

In the evolutionists' eyes, others—including Africans—were less evolved. To state it another way, blacks were essentially whites at a much earlier stage of development. Here we see the critical role of *time* as the link between races.[3] Africans were seen as living ancestors, present in this time yet representative of another time. Or they were seen as perpetual children, not yet adults and therefore only marginally significant in contemporary time. In the nineteenth century, the root cause of Africans' backwardness was considered to be their race. Most whites believed, for example, that Africans lacked philosophy because they lacked the biological capacity to produce it. Over *time*—a very long time—blacks would evolve the ability to philosophize like whites, to create real art, and to rule themselves, but until that moment, the best that could be done was for white men to accept the burden of control and care, as one might do for children. In practice, of course, the "white man's burden" of taking care of Africans turned most frequently into the "black man's burden" of suffering exploitation. Because Africans were presumed to represent a more primitive time, most Westerners, including most Americans, could easily accept African subjugation and overlook African contributions to history.

The idea of African racial inferiority dominated Western thinking until at least the 1960s and still has some currency in American and European society. As the twentieth century unfolded, however, the importance of race was challenged. Biologists emphasized that evolutionism is not the same as the scientific theory of *evolution*. Whereas evolutionism proposes that all forms of life lie along a single pathway, evolution proposes that life spreads out in a weblike fashion. And whereas evolutionism describes progress and assumes that all history is moving toward a single goal, evolution emphasizes *adaptation* and *interdependence*. The scientific theory of evolution does not assume that biological history has a goal or plan but instead assumes that the complete extinction of any and all species is a real possibility. In the twentieth century, biologists also explored genetics and concluded that all humans are indeed the same species.

Meanwhile, anthropologists who lived with and studied non-Western peoples found that nonracial factors such as history, environment, and culture could explain almost all the differences between Westerners, Africans, and others. And Western societies in general—having experienced two world wars, the loss of their colonies, civil and human rights movements, and the challenges of urban, industrial culture—became less certain that whiteness or Westernness alone conferred the capacity for solving human problems.

Increasingly, Americans have abandoned race as a primary explanation for why others are different. We have not, however, totally abandoned the idea of evolutionism. Race evolutionism has largely been replaced by cultural evolutionism. In its negative version, cultural evolutionism encourages us to imagine that African societies are less developed and need to catch up to ours. Moreover, the modern development model has largely assumed that ordinary Africans have little to offer to development theory or practice and that it is up to us to help Africa modernize from the top down. We still frequently assume, for example, that Africans are woefully mired in static and irrational tribalism when, instead, we should understand how their lives have been dynamically shaped by colonialism, urbanization, technology, international markets, contemporary politics, and many other factors.

Cultural evolutionism also encourages positive myths and stereotypes of Africa. It is easy to believe, for example, that before Africans were corrupted by Western civilization, they led lives that were whole and even magnificent when compared to our lives today. Rural Africans, whom we imagine to be insulated from the West, are used as positive examples by critics of Western cultural patterns—whether of our excessive materialism and individuality, our medical science, our religion, or our imperialism. In this model, we can aspire to recuperate our essential goodness by studying African history and culture or by visiting isolated villages where the true, "unspoiled" Africa remains.

# A Kind of Equality

Most Americans are still steeped in the kind of cultural evolutionism that overtly compares cultures to one another in terms of progress. That is, we openly presume that one society is ahead of or behind another. There is, however, still another way that some Americans mistake African culture. The events of the twentieth century have led an increasing number of us to believe that all cultures are equal. Many Americans now say that African cultures (and other cultures) are "not inferior, just different." My students frequently espouse this point of view. Perhaps this kind of perceived equality is helpful; it reflects an attempt to give others space to be themselves. It is not, however, the solution to evolutionism.

Sociologist Bernard McGrane has noted that the "not inferior, just different" model has a long history. It was, he says, first worked out in the eighteenth century as a way to maintain Western feelings of superiority in the face of increasing knowledge about other cultures. As exchanges with non-Europeans intensified, Westerners had to cope with the fact that others saw reality in significantly different ways. But rather than engage others' ideas, a move that would have challenged Western culture, Westerners developed the "just different" explanation of other cultures. That is, if others were *not inferior*, neither were they *superior*, just different. This reasoning allowed an intellectual distance that preserved Western cultural cohesiveness and feelings of superiority.[4]

Behind this "just different" explanation of other cultures was the hidden assumption that others actually were inferior. "For the sake of good-conscience," writes McGrane, eighteenth-century Westerners maintained the myth that all people, including those in other cultures, were equal.[5] At the same time, however, those who were ignorant of recently discovered Western notions about democracy, individualism, natural rights, private property, the free market, and the material nature of reality were considered inferior. Thus Westerners believed themselves to be the same as others, but with superior truths that allowed them to look down on others and justify their domination.

In the twentieth century, say McGrane and many other critics, the anthropologists who largely formed our modern notions of culture took a similar position. That is, although these anthropologists abandoned racism and argued that other cultures were equal, they *acted* as though Western culture was superior. Anthropologists learned *about* others but did not believe that others could make valid comments about the nature of reality or, especially, about us. "Equal, just different" was another way to avoid real discussions with others about the meaning of life. In McGrane's words, such a view of equality is "not a moral nor an intellectual victory but rather a great trivialization of the encounter with the Other."[6] This seems a bit harsh, considering the significant contributions some anthropologists made to destroying Dark Continent myths, but the point must be considered seriously.

We can use this perspective to examine how Americans think about Africa today. After learning to avoid Dark Continent and Wise Africa images of Africa, we still might imagine Africans to be "equal, just different." We might be "objective" and seriously study Africa to learn about its various environments, histories, customs, politics, and economics. In learning about Africa, we might even become sympathetic toward African problems and act to be helpful. But our viewing Africa objectively and helping Africans do not necessarily mean that we take Africa's differences seriously. If we treat Africa objectively—that is, as an object—that outlook continues to isolate us from Africa, because we still specify the categories of study, set the agendas for interaction and help, and define what constitutes progress.

Moreover, thinking in the "just different" mode allows us to say that Africans should live their way while we live ours. This sort of cultural individualism would seem to imply respect for African cultures, but ultimately it does not. We do not really mean that others can do whatever they want. As in the eighteenth century, contemporary Western culture insists that certain universal rules of reality can be deduced from nature. In a sense, our proposing that African cultures are "equal, just different" is analogous to South African whites proposing that Africans who had political and cultural autonomy in their "homelands" also had equality. In this extreme example, the realities of interaction and exploitation are easy to see. In the broader world context, the fiction of the "separate but equal" arguments may be less clear. Nevertheless, the reality is that the cultures of Africa are neither separate from our own nor equal in power to control their own destinies.

The "equal, just different" understanding of African cultures attempts to put us in the same time as those cultures, but without acknowledging the common history and space we share with them.

# An African Dialogue

Today, it is still difficult for Americans not to stereotype Africa in one way or another. Our most dominant stereotype is that Africa is culturally behind us, but the Wise Africa and "equal, just different" myths also have significant followings. Even those who consciously attempt to see Africa in more accurate terms find it difficult to locate everyday sources of information not already imbued with these stereotypes. What we know comes from teachers, newspapers, television programs, movies, magazine articles, and books that frequently tell us about an Africa that substantiates our myths, positive or negative. It usually takes a great deal of conscious effort to find material with which to construct whole pictures of Africa and Africans.

Africa is also vulnerable to stereotypical interpretations. It has no powerful group of advocates to challenge our myths. Moreover, events in Africa frequently lend themselves to stereotypical interpretation, and of all the continents, sub-Saharan Africa may seem the most culturally distant from us. This is true for both its rural and urban populations. Africa's diseases, famines, poverty, wars, corruption, weak governments, and other problems can be easily mistaken as indications of African backwardness rather than as evidence of the continent's complex history, in which we ourselves participated. In contrast, Africa's hospitality, communality, and other positive features can easily be construed as the true soul of Africa if one ignores the more problematic aspects of African cultures.

It is true that Africans are generally different from us. But African cultures are not remnants of primitive cultures that survived into the present, and they are not some version of our culture at a different stage of development. Neither are they "equal, just different."

Africans share the same biology, era, and planet as us. Rather than using Africa's difference as a tool to separate and control Africans, we can use their difference as an opportunity to deepen our understanding of what difference and sameness mean. Africa clearly represents for us the fundamental fact that *all* people are different and the same. We all share essentially the same DNA and occupy essentially the same time and space, yet we see the world in separate ways. Even *within* our own culture or family, there are distinct perceptions of reality.

Africa's difference is important to us because it helps to define ourselves and the world we live in. It is worth taking seriously. We should not try to minimize the difference by assuming that Africans are just like us. Nor should we exaggerate it by believing Africans are different *kinds* of humans. And we should not try to evaluate or dominate African difference by assuming that Africans would be better off if only they were more like us. Finally, we should not search for the admirable or negative qualities of Africans in isolation from their other qualities.

The first step to understanding African difference is to "listen" to African cultures and attempt to discover Africa in its own words and in its own context. We should work at understanding how Africans conceive of reality and how that reality has been shaped by their environments and histories. In other words, we must allow Africans to be our teachers. We need to learn African languages, find African friends, read African novels, eat African food, listen to African music, and live in African cities and villages.

Such attempts to understand Africa will be difficult. It is not easy to venture beyond our own comfortable corners of the world. Moreover, such attempts will be limited. I know of no one, not myself or any African, whom I would trust to define what Africa represents, because sub-Saharan Africa is a huge region with nearly forty countries, an enormous variety of cultures, and hundreds of millions of people. One person can only begin to understand a small corner of the continent.

Americans need both detail and context for Africa. When I tell people I am interested in Africa, they frequently inform me that they know someone who has lived in Africa, but cannot name the country or even the region where the person lived or lives. Others have asked me what the capital of Africa is, or whether I know their friend who went to Africa. Learning to distinguish among Africans and African countries and societies would help us to see Africans as real people, people who share our time and place, and paradoxically, such knowledge will make it more difficult to imagine that we have found the Real Africa. In fact, we will ultimately conclude that there *is* no one real Africa, just as there is no one real America.

Although Americans may never completely succeed in understanding Africa's difference or, for that matter, anyone's difference, we can learn to take our differences seriously through continuing dialogue. Dialogue with others implies both self-respect and respect for others, both listening and talking. It is the essence of life with others and, not coincidentally, of education. Through dialogue we can exchange ideas about the meaning and use of our common time and place. Dialogue implies *answer*-ability and *response*-ability. In a sense, dialogue puts people under mutual control. It recognizes that we have a claim on each other's actions, because we share our time and place.

Dialogue can help us avoid two significant dangers: universalism and isolationism. *Universalism* claims that we know the truth and that all true and good people should live according to that truth. Universalism leads to a hierarchical construction of the world and promotes control over others. Evolutionism is one form of universalism. At the other end of the spectrum, *isolationism* claims that everyone should be able to live however they choose, which is an impossibility on our shrinking planet and which will lead to wars over cultural differences and dwindling resources. Dialogue, in contrast, promotes *transversality*, the recognition that truth, so far as it exists for humans, lies somewhere between universalism and isolationism, between absolutism and relativism. Transversality affirms that we share the same time and place, that we are equal *and* different, and that we are interdependent.[7]

Living in a world of engagement with Africans and African difference complicates our lives and challenges many of our cherished values. It necessitates the added effort of learning about others and the difficulty of sharing decision making and resources. But the potential benefits are great. Africans may escape from their damaging mistaken identities, both primitive and wise. They may find the tools they need to accomplish *their* goals rather than ours. And together we may begin to develop the skills and attitudes needed to live peacefully in our ever-smaller neighborhood.

# Appendix

## *Learning More*

### *Learning More About*
### *American Ideas About Africa*

This book is mostly about what sub-Saharan Africa is *not* rather than what it *is*. Those who want to pursue the ideas discussed in this book will find many sources in the notes. However, these sources represent only the surface of the ways Africa has been treated in American popular culture. I have prepared a bibliography, "The Image of Africa," that includes books and articles that analyze Western images of Africa from antiquity to the present.[1] Those interested will find many more ways Americans mistake Africa.

The Internet is a good place to look for examples. Searches using terms such as *cannibalism, tribe, race,* and *primitive* turn up instances of obvious ways we stereotype Africa. Other interesting sources can be found by searching the web archives of newspapers and magazines or the online periodical indexes found in most public libraries (as distinct from academic libraries). Likewise, clear-cut examples of misuses of Africa turn up frequently in amusement parks, movies, documentaries, television programs, advertisements, and church literature.

Here's an interesting project for students living in Wisconsin and northern Ohio. What about Kalahari Resorts? This company builds and maintains Africa-themed convention centers that raise consciousness about premodern African cultural achievements, but also promote romantic views of Wise Africa and African wildness. Hundreds of guest rooms contain furniture made in Africa, African fixtures, and African pictures on the wall. In the lobby of the Ohio site, a huge wall map of Africa has wild animals and "natives" with masks and spears. But on a visit (close to Detroit and Cleveland), I found no Africans or African specialists on staff. What can we make of this effort? Someone who likes Africa started the company and often travels there to buy expensive contemporary art for the resorts. Is this an exploitation of African culture? Is it more of an exploitation than, say, an Africa-themed restaurant (which I, for one, would enjoy eating in)? Similar convention centers are planned for Fredericksburg, Virginia, and Tobyhanna, Pennsylvania.

I like to think about the subtlest stereotypes about Africa. Why, we should ask, did the Clinton administration's favorite examples of excellent African leaders mostly take power in coups and wars? Or how is my local newspaper reporting Africa, if at all? And how do churches, which obviously mean well, interact with Africans? I especially like to investigate the more subtle aspects of our cultural views of Africa, because such a pursuit will more likely challenge my own tendencies to mistake Africa. I am, after all, a part of this culture, and I also have to work to escape its stereotypes.

## Guidelines for Learning More About Africa

Those who want to learn more about Africa itself will find many resources. But before we look at sources of information, let me share some guiding principles that can help us think about what we should be looking for. For those who learn about Africa, and especially for those who teach about the continent, here are four principles I find useful. I'd be interested in knowing what principles others find most helpful.

1. The most accurate descriptions of Africa take into account its complexity. Treatments of Africa that focus narrowly tend to perpetuate exoticism and recommend mistaken solutions to problems. For example, *all* of today's Africa is conditioned by *both* urban and rural culture and experiences. Thus to treat rural Africa as if it has no urban connections through modern education, commerce, travel, and politics is almost always mistaken. It is also mistaken to treat most African problems as though only Africans have caused them. All of Africa is conditioned by historical and contemporary influences from *both* Africans and non-Africans.

2. African cultures are constantly changing and have always been changing. It is almost always inaccurate to say "as they have done for hundreds of years." While it is possible to see influences of the past in much of African culture, African culture is not static and never has been. This implies that most Africans are willing to change when reasonable options present themselves.

3. When we see something strange in Africa, a useful response is to ask why it turned out this way and what function it serves. Starting with the assumption that others are biologically the same as we are, we can try to imagine how we might have come to do and think the same things as Africans. This exercise in imagination can help us understand ourselves as well as Africans.

4. One way to help avoid objectifying or essentializing Africans is to think of learning about Africa as participating in a conversation about Africa. In conversations we assume we can never know everything our conversational partners know, think, and feel. We also assume that our partners don't know everything about a subject. On practically every subject related to Africa there are multiple perspectives, and we can all benefit from learning about and considering these perspectives.

## *Learning More About Africa*

The point of what follows is to help those interested in joining the conversation about Africa. Many readers of this book may also be taking a course in African studies, whether in African anthropology, art, economics, environment, history, literature, music, philosophy, politics, or sociology. In these courses, teachers may assign further readings and can answer questions about the best sources on a subject. For those who want to pursue a wide variety of subjects and for those who don't have an expert to guide them, I include pathways that lead to helpful materials.

On the Internet, the two outstanding metasites on African studies are those of Columbia and Stanford Universities at http://www.columbia.edu/cu/lweb /indiv/africa/cuvl/ and http://www-sul.stanford.edu/depts/ssrg/africa/guide .html. You can search these rich sites by topic and country, and they lead to many trustworthy resources. Other universities also sponsor useful sites that are less comprehensive but contain different links.

One interesting way to learn about Africa is to read African newspapers or listen to African radio. African newspapers are available through http://www .world-newspapers.com/africa.html. Try reading Nigeria's *Daily Independent* or *Guardian,* or the tabloid *Daily Champion.* Or try Kenya's *Daily Nation* or Uganda's *Daily Monitor,* all in English. (Try searching at http://www.onlinenewspapers .com/africa-newspapers.htm.) African radio can be accessed through http://www -sul.stanford.edu/depts/ssrg/africa/radio.html.

For current news about Africa the BBC is excellent, especially for English-speaking countries in Africa. Text and audio news are available at http://www.bbc .co.uk/news/world/africa/. Some other popular sites devoted to news and features about Africa include *Africa Focus Bulletin* at http://www.africafocus.org, *allAfrica.com* at http://allafrica.com, and *Africa News* at http://www.africanews.com. Print newsmagazines devoted to Africa include *Africa Today* (http://www .africatoday.com) and *New African* (http://www.newafricanmagazine.com/). In addition, check on the annual May issue of *Current History* (http://www.current history.com/), which contains excellent articles accessible to the nonspecialist.

For books on Africa, a good place to begin reading is April A. Gordon and Donald L. Gordon, eds., *Understanding Contemporary Africa*, 5th edition (Boulder, CO: Lynne Rienner, 2013). Readers who want to pursue specific areas such as art, literature, history, economics, or biology can find helpful suggestions by searching the Internet for the syllabi of courses on these topics.

Most disciplines produce scholarly journals that deal with Africa. In literature, for example, one major journal is *Research in African Literatures*; in art, *African Arts*. In history the choices include the *International Journal of African Historical Studies* and the *Journal of African History*. Some of these journals, including *African Arts*, are quite accessible to the nonspecialist. Most librarians can help locate specialist journals in an area of interest. Another scholarly resource is H-Africa, a Listserv for Africanist scholars. Although members are scholars, the archived discussion threads are available at http://www.h-net.org/~africa. Stanford University provides an excellent list of films, movies, and videos (http:// www-sul.stanford.edu/depts/ssrg/africa/film.html).

## *Teaching About Africa*

Teachers can help students join the conversation about Africa. Younger students can learn about African food or the African arts, but they can also learn about the language of the conversation. They can begin to understand how to use terms such as *rural* and *urban* or *traditional* and *modern*. Of course, that means that teachers must also join the conversation so they understand how these terms are used and misused.

Even very young children can begin to learn about Africa's complexity. For example, a variety of simple examples of one category of things (foods, art, or languages) from different cultures and parts of the continent can help students understand that Africa is not one thing.

Older students can study more complex forms of diversity and connectedness. It is especially important that older students begin to understand the deep historical and contemporary connections between Africa, the West, and the rest of the world. It is tempting to teach about Africa as though it is something one can isolate through "African music," "African art," or "African customs." But Africa is a huge continent, and, except for a very few generalizations, attempts to capture its imagined essence do Africa a great disservice. Many students want facts and generalizations. Help them instead to join the conversation by helping them see variety and relationships.

Many large American universities have African studies outreach centers to make knowledge about Africa available, especially for teachers. These centers serve especially K–12 teachers, community colleges, businesses, and educational organizations. Among others, for example, the University of Pennsylvania (http://www.africa.upenn.edu/K-12/AFR_GIDE.html) and Michigan State University (http://exploringafrica.matrix.msu.edu) provide K–12 teaching materials.

# Notes

## Chapter 1: Changing Our Mind About Africa

1. Julian Nundy, "France Haunted by Rwanda Genocide," *Telegraph Group Limited* (April 14, 1998), accessed October 23, 2012, http://www.hartford-hwp.com/archives/61/120.html.

2. Gary Althen, *American Ways* (Yarmouth, ME: Intercultural Press, 2003), 136–137.

3. Carol Beckwith and Angela Fisher, "Royal Gold of the Asante Empire," *National Geographic* (October 1996): 36–47. Beckwith and Fisher are known for their photographs of "vanishing Africa." They serve Africa, but they and *National Geographic* both have an obligation to put their work into context.

## Chapter 2: How We Learn

1. Astair Zekiros, with Marylee Wiley, *Africa in Social Studies Textbooks*, Bulletin no. 9550 (Madison: Wisconsin Department of Public Instruction, 1978), 4. An article by Wiley contains most of the same ideas and is easier to locate: "Africa in Social Studies Textbooks," *Social Education* (November–December 1982): 492–497, 548–552.

2. Bradley Rink (CIEE Study Center, Stellenbosch University), "From (Mis)Perceptions to Teachable Moments: Learning Opportunities On-site," presentation made at NAFSA Annual Conference workshop in Minneapolis, MN, "Rethinking Africa: (Mis)Perceptions and Realities," May 28, 2007.

3. The Travel Channel, "Bizarre Foods with Andrew Zimmern: Madagascar," Season 5 Episode 11 (2010), aired June 18, 2012.

4. The Travel Channel, "Bizarre Foods with Andrew Zimmern: Madagascar," accessed June 20, 2012, http://www.travelchannel.com/tv-shows/bizarre-foods /episodes/madagascar.

5. United Nations Children's Fund (UNICEF), "Madagascar: Statistics," accessed July 5, 2012, http://www.unicef.org/infobycountry/madagascar_statistics .html.

6. Charlayne Hunter-Gault, *New News Out of Africa: Uncovering Africa's Renaissance* (New York: Oxford University Press, 2006), 109.

7. Karen Rothmyer, "Hiding the Real Africa: Why NGOs Prefer Bad News," *Columbia Journalism Review* 49, no. 6 (March–April 2011): 18–19.

8. Charles Onyango-Obbo, "Seeking Balance in a Continent Portrayed by Its Extremes," *Nieman Reports* (Fall 2004): 6–8.

9. David Colker, "Cuddly Puppy Just a Figment of Scamster's Imagination," *Morning Call* (Allentown, PA) (May 30, 2007): A1, A3.

10. Bernard Block, "Romance and High Purpose: *The National Geographic*," *Wilson Library Bulletin* (January 1994): 333–337.

11. Tom O'Neill, "Curse of the Black Gold—Hope and Betrayal in the Niger Delta," *National Geographic* (May 2007): 88–117.

12. Peter Goodwin, "Johannesburg: City of Hope and Fear," *National Geographic* (April 2004): 58–77.

13. Hamilton Wende, "Brash and Brilliant," *National Geographic Traveler* (March 2005): S9.

14. Charlayne Hunter-Gault, "Changing the Rules in Africa," OUP Blog, posted July 20, 2006.

15. Neil Shea, "Africa's Last Frontier," *National Geographic* (March 2010): 96–123.

16. Ibid., 104.

17. Survival International, "The Omo Valley Tribes," accessed July 5, 2012, http://www.survivalinternational.org/tribes/omovalley. Also see a recently aired episode of Joseph Rosendo's Travelscope: "Southern Ethiopia: Tribal Lands and Primeval People," PBS-Create TV (December 15, 2012). In Rosendo's 2008 visit he was disappointed that tourists (like himself?) had overrun the region and that local people wanted to be left alone.

18. Busch Gardens Tampa Bay, accessed October 16, 2007, http://www.trade windsresort.com/busch-gardens-tampa-bay.html.

19. Sean Rouse, "Jungle Cruise Jokes," accessed October 4, 2007, http://www.csua.berkeley.edu/~yoda/disneyland/jungle.htm. For more on the Jungle River Cruise, see "Jungle Cruise," *Wikipedia*, accessed October 4, 2012, http://en.wikipedia.org/wiki/Jungle_Cruise and "The Disney Jungle Cruise

Narration," *Themed Attraction*, accessed October 4, 2012, http://www.themed attraction.com/jungle.htm.

20. "Animal Kingdom Lodge," The Walt Disney Company, accessed July 5, 2012, http://disneyworld.disney.go.com/resorts/animal-kingdom-lodge/.

21. Donnarae MacCann and Olga Richard, "Through African Eyes: An Interview About Recent Picture Books with Yulisa Amadu Maddy," *Wilson Library Bulletin* (June 1995): 41; Pete Watson and Mary Watson, *The Market Lady and the Mango Tree* (New York: Tambourine Books, 1994).

22. MacCann and Richard, "Through African Eyes," 41.

23. Yulisa Amadu Maddy and Donnarae MacCann, *Neo-Imperialism in Children's Literature About Africa: A Study of Contemporary Fiction* (London: Routledge, 2009).

24. Scott Wesley Brown, "Please Don't Send Me to Africa," *Out of Africa* (Costa Mesa, CA: Maranatha, 1998), lyrics at "Please Don't Send Me to Africa Lyrics," Leo's Lyrics, accessed July 7, 2012, http://www.leoslyrics.com/listlyrics.php; jsessionid=ECCC22B075A6208BD9C6CB0B40EFD120?hid=%2Bsz%2BZUX iHpY%3D.

25. See, for example, Timon Bengtson, "Silly Games Christians Play—Please Don't Send Me to Africa," *Exhalting and Enjoying Christ*, accessed February 16, 2012, http://pastortimonbengtson.wordpress.com/2012/02/16/silly-games-christians-play-please-dont-send-me-to-africa/. Also see "Please don't send me to Africa—Scott Wesley (1995)." YouTube, accessed July 7, 2012, http://www.youtube .com/watch?v=yyEDrwLIzC4.

## Chapter 3: The Origins of "Darkest Africa"

1. Djibril Tamsir Niane, *Sundiata: An Epic of Old Mali*, trans. G. D. Pickett (London: Longman, 1965), 1–2.

2. Frank M. Snowden Jr., *Blacks in Antiquity: Ethiopians in the Greco-Roman Experience* (Cambridge, MA: Belknap, 1970), 176.

3. Ibid., 217.

4. Ibid., 105–107.

5. Edwin M. Yamauchi, *Africa and the Bible* (Grand Rapids, MI: Baker Academic, 2004), 19–33; Gerhard von Rad, *Genesis: A Commentary* (Philadelphia: Westminster Press, 1959), 131–135; Walter Brueggemann, *Genesis: A Bible Commentary for Teaching and Preaching* (Atlanta, GA: John Knox, 1982), 89–91.

6. Yamauchi, *Africa and the Bible*, 25.

7. Acts 8: 26–40. See, for example, Gerhard Krodel, *Acts* (Philadelphia: Fortress, 1981), 37–38; and Johannes Munck, *The Acts of the Apostles*, rev. William F. Albright and C. S. Mann (Garden City, NY: Doubleday, 1967), 77–79.

8. Snowden, *Blacks in Antiquity*, 196–205.

9. Maghan Keita, "Africa Backwards and Forwards: Interpreting Africa and Africans in Pre- and Post-Modern Space," paper presented at the Sixth Annual African Studies Consortium Workshop, University of Pennsylvania, Philadelphia, October 2, 1998. Keita also notes that our modern lack of awareness of this favorable treatment of Africans during the medieval period parallels our lack of knowledge about the ancient Greek debt to black Egypt. That is, our ignorance is due to late-eighteenth- and nineteenth-century considerations of Africans in terms of racial inferiority.

10. Michael Adas, *Machines as the Measure of Men: Science, Technology, and Ideologies of Western Dominance* (Ithaca, NY: Cornell University Press, 1989), 22.

11. Philip D. Curtin, *The Image of Africa: British Ideas and Action, 1780–1850* (Madison: University of Wisconsin Press, 1964), 10.

12. A. Bulunda Itandala, "European Images of Africa from Earliest Times to the Eighteenth Century," in *Images of Africa: Stereotypes and Realities*, ed. Daniel M. Mengara (Trenton, NJ: Africa World Press, 2001), 67–74.

13. Curtin, *Image of Africa*, 35. Ivan Hannaford offers a comprehensive history of the idea of race in *Race: The History of an Idea in the West* (Washington, DC: Woodrow Wilson Center Press, 1996). For selected readings by Enlightenment thinkers, see Emmanuel Chukwudi Eze, ed., *Race and the Enlightenment: A Reader* (Oxford: Blackwell, 1997).

14. Curtin, *Image of Africa*, 123–139; David Jenkins, *Black Zion: Africa, Imagined and Real, as Seen by Today's Blacks* (New York: Harcourt Brace Jovanovich, 1975), 69. See also Christopher Fyfe, *A History of Sierra Leone* (London: Oxford University Press, 1962).

15. Jenkins, *Black Zion*, 73–88.

16. See, for example, J. Gus Liebenow, *Liberia: The Evolution of Privilege* (Ithaca, NY: Cornell University Press, 1969); and Tom W. Shick, *Behold the Promised Land: A History of Afro-American Settler Society in Nineteenth-Century Liberia* (Baltimore: Johns Hopkins University Press, 1977).

17. See, for example, Curtin, *Image of Africa*, 138, 239.

18. Adas, *Machines as the Measure*, 22.

19. Ibid., 71, 79–95.

20. For an extended discussion of this subject, see William Stanton, *The Leopard's Spots: Scientific Attitudes Toward Race in America, 1815–1859* (Chicago: University of Chicago Press, 1960).

21. Curtin, *Image of Africa*, 364.

22. Ibid., 479–480. The various European colonizers exhibited somewhat different theoretical patterns. The French, for example, seemed less racist and began to talk about *association* with Africans rather than conversion or trusteeship. They

also permitted the African *évolués* of the four communes of Senegal (small areas the government in Paris had declared part of France) to retain their French citizenship. Nonetheless, on the whole, all European colonizers thought of Africans as racial inferiors and excluded Africans from power.

23. Mungo Park, *Travels into the Interior Districts of Africa* (New York: Hippocrene Books, 1983).

24. Patrick Brantlinger, "Victorians and Africans: The Genealogy of the Myth of the Dark Continent," in *"Race," Writing, and Difference*, ed. Henry Louis Gates Jr. (Chicago: University of Chicago Press, 1985), 217.

25. Rudyard Kipling, "The White Man's Burden," in *Collected Verse* (New York: Doubleday, 1907), 215–217. The complete poem has seven verses. In the Philippines, Americans tended to conceptualize themselves as older siblings rather than as parents, but the effect was similar; Leon Wolff, *Little Brown Brother: How the United States Purchased and Pacified the Philippine Islands at the Century's Turn* (Garden City, NY: Doubleday, 1961).

26. Henry Morton Stanley, *Through the Dark Continent* (New York: Harper, 1878).

27. For a discussion of the recent historical literature on Stanley, see A. G. Hopkins, "Explorers' Tales: Stanley Presumes—Again," *Journal of Imperial & Commonwealth History* 36, no. 4 (December 2008): 669–684.

28. Theodore Roosevelt, *African Game Trails: An Account of the African Wanderings of an American Hunter-Naturalist* (New York: Syndicate Publishing Company, 1910), 94.

## Chapter 4: *"Our Living Ancestors"*: *Twentieth-Century Evolutionism*

1. Joseph Conrad, *Heart of Darkness: Authoritative Text, Backgrounds and Contexts, Criticism*, ed. Paul B. Armstrong, 4th Norton Critical Edition (New York: Norton, 2006), 33, 35.

2. Chinua Achebe, "An Image of Africa: Racism in Conrad's *Heart of Darkness*," in *Heart of Darkness: Authoritative Text*, 336–349.

3. Robert Caputo, "Zaire River," *National Geographic* (November 1990): 30.

4. Ibid.

5. Roosevelt, *African Game Trails*, 2.

6. Lewis Henry Morgan, *Ancient Society* (New York: Henry Holt, 1878; reprint, Cambridge, MA: Belknap Press of Harvard University Press, 1964).

7. Gaetano Casati, *Ten Years in Equatoria and the Return with Emin Pasha*, 2 vols. (London: Frederick Warne, 1891), 2: 114.

8. Roosevelt, *African Game Trails*, x.

9. Ibid., 2.

10. Enid Schildkrout and Curtis A. Keim, *African Reflections: Art from Northeastern Zaire* (Seattle: University of Washington Press, 1990).

11. Ibid., 143–147; Curtis A. Keim, "*Artes Africanae*: The Western Discovery of 'Art' in Northeastern Congo," in *The Scramble for Art in Central Africa*, eds. Enid Schildkrout and Curtis A. Keim (Cambridge: Cambridge University Press, 1998), 109–132.

12. Georg Schweinfurth, *Artes Africanae: Illustrations and Descriptions of Productions of the Industrial Arts of Central African Tribes* (Leipzig: F. A. Brockhaus, 1875), vii.

13. Georg Schweinfurth, *The Heart of Africa: Three Years' Travels and Adventures in the Unexplored Regions of Central Africa from 1868 to 1871*, trans. Ellen E. Frewer, 2 vols. (New York: Harper, 1874), 2: 46.

14. Sigmund Freud, "The Savage's Dread of Incest," in *The Basic Writings of Sigmund Freud*, trans. and ed. A. A. Brill (New York: Modern Library, 1939), 807.

15. Ibid.

16. See, for example, Octave Mannoni, *Prospero and Caliban: The Psychology of Colonization* (London: Methuen, 1956).

17. See, for example, Adas, *Machines as the Measure*.

18. For an extended discussion of the relationship between evolutionary science and social theory in the twentieth century, see Carl N. Degler, *In Search of Human Nature: The Decline and Revival of Darwinism in American Social Thought* (New York: Oxford University Press, 1991).

19. Lewis Thomas, "On the Uncertainty of Science," *Harvard Magazine*, September–October 1980.

20. Dennis Hickey and Kenneth C. Wylie, *An Enchanting Darkness: The American Vision of Africa in the Twentieth Century* (East Lansing: Michigan State University Press, 1993), 20–21.

21. Stanley Burnham, *America's Bimodal Crisis: Black Intelligence in White Society*, 3rd ed. (Athens, GA: Foundation for Human Understanding, 1993), 49–56. (The first edition was published in 1985.)

22. Ibid., 57–63.

## Chapter 5: Where Is the Real Africa?

1. Kathryn Mathers, *Travel, Humanitarianism, and Becoming American in Africa* (New York: Palgrave Macmillan, 2010), 181–195.

2. Uzodinma Iweala, "Stop Trying to 'Save' Africa," *Washington Post*, July 15, 2007, B7.

3. Michael Holman, "Africa: Celebrity and Salvation," *openDemocracy*, October 22, 2006, accessed February 21, 2013, http://www.opendemocracy.net/democracy -africa_democracy/africa_celebrity_4024.jsp.

4. Anonymous, interview by author, Bethlehem, PA, May 20, 1998.

5. Gerardine Lum, interview by Christina Townsend, August 1, 2007.

6. Carol Magee, *Africa in the American Imagination. Popular Culture, Racialized Identities, and African Visual Culture* (Jackson: University Press of Mississippi, 2012), 171.

7. See, for example, Christopher Steiner, *African Art in Transit* (New York: Cambridge University Press, 1994).

8. Mountain Travel Sobek, "Ghana, Togo, Benin: Golden Kingdoms of West Africa," accessed October 3, 2007, http://www.mtsobek.com/mts/agk.

9. ElderTreks, Small Group Exotic Adventures for Travelers 50 Plus, "Voodoo and Spirits of West Africa," accessed October 8, 2012, http://www.eldertreks .com/tour/ETTD000405. The trip was on sale for $7,995.

10. Ray Sahelian, "Yohimbe: Experience the Orgiastic Mating Rituals of the African Bantu. Yohimbe Bark Information and Yohimbe Side Effects," accessed July 9, 2012, http://www.raysahelian.com/yohimbe.html.

11. Ray Sahelian, *Natural Sex Boosters. Supplements that Enhance Stamina, Sensation, and Sexuality for Men and Women* (New York: Square One Publishers, 2004), 94.

12. Walter Chin, "Kenya: The Maasai," *Sports Illustrated*, special issue (Winter 1998): 66.

13. Magee, *Africa in the American Imagination*, 36–40,

14. Dodai Stewart, "Sex and Stereotypes: *Sports Illustrated* Swimsuit Issue Goes to 7 Continents, Finds Exotic People to Use as Props," *Jezebel* (February 12, 2013), accessed February 20, 2013, http://jezebel.com/5983737/sports-illustrated -swimsuit-issue-goes-to-7-continents-finds-exotic-people-to-use-as-props?post =57329185.

15. Tanya Rivero, "Sports Illustrated Swimsuit Issue Photo Shoot: Racy or Racist?" *ABC News* (February 17, 2013), accessed February 20, 2013, http:// abcnews.go.com/blogs/entertainment/2013/02/sports-illustrated-swimsuit-issue -photo-shoot-racy-or-racist/.

16. Ibid.

17. This missionary image persists. I have heard rural Africans referred to as "innocent" by a well-intentioned Christian pastor.

18. Malidoma Patrice Somé, *Of Water and the Spirit: Ritual, Magic, and Initiation in the Life of an African Shaman* (New York: Putnam, 1994). Also see the article by Somé, "Rights of Passage: If Adolescence Is a Disease, Initiation Is a Cure,"

*Utne Reader* (July–August 1994): 67–68 (adapted from an article in *In Context* [Winter 1993]).

19. Malidoma Patrice Somé, "About Malidoma," accessed August 12, 2012, http://malidoma.com/main/about.

20. Useful general studies on African American attitudes toward Africa up to the 1960s and 1970s include Tunde Adeleke, *UnAfrican Americans: Nineteenth-Century Black Nationalists and the Civilizing Mission* (Lexington: University Press of Kentucky, 1998); Harold R. Isaacs, *The New World of Negro Americans* (New York: John Day, 1963); Jenkins, *Black Zion*; Bernard Makhosezwe Magubane, *The Ties That Bind: African-American Consciousness of Africa* (Trenton, NJ: Africa World Press, 1987); and Okon Edet Uya, ed., *Black Brotherhood: Afro-Americans and Africa* (Lexington, MA: Heath, 1971). Sam Roberts, in a 2005 *New York Times* cover story, reported that more than 50,000 Africans immigrate legally to the United States each year and perhaps three or four times that arrive illegally. The report also said that African immigrants achieve a higher level of education than immigrants from most other regions of the world. And they are beginning to have a significant impact on what it means to be African American, particularly with regard to African American self-consciousness, which is pushing away from race toward ethnicity. Sam Roberts, "More Africans Enter U.S. Than in Days of Slavery," *New York Times*, February 21, 2005, 1.

21. Isaacs, *New World*, 105–113. A number of African Americans traveled to Africa in the precolonial and colonial eras. In Central Africa, for example, the missionary William Sheppard worked among the Kuba in the late nineteenth century. See David A. Binkley and Patricia J. Darish, "'Enlightened but in Darkness': Interpretations of Kuba Art and Culture at the Turn of the Twentieth Century," in *The Scramble for Art in Central Africa*, eds. Enid Schildkrout and Curtis A. Keim (Cambridge: Cambridge University Press, 1998), 37–62. Another African American, George Washington Williams, made a tour of Congo in 1890 and wrote an open letter to King Leopold that outlined the atrocities being committed there. Williams's biographer, John Hope Franklin, notes that, "of all the 1890 observers and critics of Leopold's rule . . . only Williams saw fit to make his unfavorable views widely known immediately." John Hope Franklin, *George Washington Williams: A Biography* (Chicago: University of Chicago Press, 1985), 262–263.

In the era leading up to the American civil rights movement of the 1960s, several African American writers are known to have traveled to Africa. Perhaps the most famous is Richard Wright, whose book *Black Power: A Record of Reactions in a Land of Pathos* (New York: Harper, 1954) discusses his mixed reactions to being in Africa. Most Europeans resisted allowing African Americans into their colonies, because their presence implied too great a measure of black independence. See Sylvia M.

Jacobs, ed., *Black Americans and the Missionary Movement in Africa* (Westport, CT: Greenwood Press, 1982).

22. See, for example, Uya, *Black Brotherhood.*

23. John Hope Franklin, *From Slavery to Freedom: A History of Negro Americans,* 4th ed. (New York: Alfred A. Knopf, 1974), 367.

24. William R. Scott, *The Sons of Sheba's Race: African-Americans and the Italo-Ethiopian War, 1935–1941* (Bloomington: Indiana University Press, 1993), 2–22.

25. Ibid., 23.

26. Ibid., 21–22. See also James Meriwether, *Proudly We Can Be Africans: Black Americans and Africa, 1935–1961* (Chapel Hill: University of North Carolina Press, 2001).

27. Scott, *Sons of Sheba's Race,* 192–207.

28. Carter Godwin Woodson, *The Mis-education of the Negro* (Trenton, NJ: Africa World Press, 1998); *The Negro in Our History,* 11th ed. (Washington, DC: Associated Publishers, 1966).

29. In the last years of his long life, Du Bois became disillusioned with the American situation, and in 1961 he moved to newly independent Ghana. For a discussion of African Americans in Ghana during the late 1950s and 1960s, see Kevin K. Gaines, *American Africans in Ghana: Black Expatriots and the Civil Rights Era* (Chapel Hill: University of North Carolina Press, 2006).

30. There are exceptions. For example, during the Afropessimist era of the 1990s two African Americans portrayed the continent in a relatively negative light: Eddy Harris, *Native Stranger: A Black American's Journey into the Heart of Africa* (New York: Simon and Schuster, 1992); and Keith Richburg, *Out of America: A Black Man Confronts Africa* (New York: Basic Books, 1997).

31. There are many opinions, pro and con, on Afrocentrism. For discussions by the originator of the idea, see Molefi Kete Asante, *The Afrocentric Idea,* rev. ed. (Philadelphia: Temple University Press, 1998); and *Afrocentricity: Toward an African Renaissance* (Boston: Polity Press, 2007). For largely favorable assessments, see Dhyana Ziegler, ed., *Molefi Kete Asante and Afrocentricity: In Praise and in Criticism* (Nashville, TN: James C. Winston, 1995). Three discussions that are critical but useful in the context of general American stereotypes about Africa are Tunde Adeleke, *The Case against Afrocentrism* (Jackson: University Press of Mississippi, 2009); Hickey and Wylie, *An Enchanting Darkness,* 1–6, 308–318; and Gary B. Nash, Charlotte Crabtree, and Ross E. Dunn, *History on Trial: Culture Wars and the Teaching of the Past* (New York: Alfred A. Knopf, 1998), 117–122.

32. Bob Tortora and Magali Rheault, "Mobile Phone Access Varies Widely in Sub-Saharan Africa," *Gallup World* (September 16, 2011), accessed August 7, 2012,

http://www.gallup.com/poll/149519/mobile-phone-access-varies-widely
-sub-saharan-africa.aspx.

33. BBC News, "IBM to Open Kenya Research Lab to Tackle Traffic Jams," (August 14, 2012), accessed August 17, 2012, http://www.bbc.co.uk/news /technology-19258863.

34. World Bank, "GDP Growth in Sub-Saharan Africa is Back on Track," *Africa's Pulse* (April 2011), accessed August 7, 2012, http://siteresources.world bank.org/INTAFRICA/Resources/Africas-Pulse-brochure_Vol3.pdf.

## Chapter 6: We Should Help Them

1. I have not attempted to document this chapter completely because the various arguments as presented here are more or less commonplace, even if they are much more complex in fuller discussions. The potential sources for this chapter are more extensive than for any other chapter in this book, and new sources appear frequently. For those interested in further reading, a good overview of African economic policies can be found in Virginia DeLancey, "The Economies of Africa," in April A. Gordon and Donald L. Gordon, *Understanding Contemporary Africa*, 5th ed. (Boulder, CO: Lynne Rienner, 2013), 115–165. A longer general discussion of development policies is available in Todd J. Moss, *African Development. Making Sense of the Issues and Actors*, 2nd ed. (Boulder, CO: Lynne Rienner, 2011). Claude Ake's *Democracy and Development in Africa* (Washington, DC: Brookings Institution, 1996) contributes a thoughtful African political perspective. The modernizing perspectives of the International Monetary Fund and the World Bank are reflected in analyses by the World Bank, which are available on the Internet at http://www.worldbank.org. For historical and cultural approaches see, for example, Martin Meredith, *The Fate of Africa: From the Hopes of Freedom to the Heart of Despair. A History of Fifty Years of Independence* (New York: PublicAffairs, 2005) and Ambe Njoh, *Tradition, Culture and Development in Africa. Historical Lessons for Modern Development Planning* (Burlington, VT: Ashgate, 2006). Collections of perspectives are available in Ernest Aryeetey, Shantayanan Devarajan, Ravi Kanbur, and Louis Kasekende, eds., *The Oxford Companion to the Economics of Africa* (New York: Oxford University Press, 2012) and in Vandana Desai and Robert B. Potter, *The Companion to Development Studies*, 2nd ed. (New York: Routledge, 2008). Many recent documents on African development policy are available from African Action, an Africa advocacy organization with an Internet site at http://www.africaaction.org/.

2. James Perry, *Living Africa: A Village Experience* (Bloomington: Indiana University Television, 1983), 35-min. videotape.

3. For a discussion of the civilizing mission in the first half of the twentieth century, see Adas, *Machines as the Measure*, 199–270.

4. Ake, *Democracy and Development*, 118–119.

5. See, for example, World Bank, *Economic Growth in the 1990s: Learning from a Decade of Reform* (Washington, DC: World Bank, 2005).

6. Regina Jere-Malanda, "Profiting from Poverty: How Western Companies and Consultants Exploit Africa," *New African* (November 2007): 16.

7. Marcela Rondon and Elmasoeur Ashitey, "Ghana: Poultry and Products Brief Annual," *US Foreign Agricultural Service Gain Report* (October 7, 2011), accessed September 9, 2012, http://gain.fas.usda.gov/Recent%20GAIN%20Publications /Poultry%20and%20Products%20Brief%20Annual_Accra_Ghana_10-7-2011.pdf.

8. Baby Milk Action, accessed October, 2, 2012, http://info.babymilkaction .org/nestlefree. A list of Nestlé brands can be found at Infant Feeding Action Coalition (INFACT) Canada, accessed October 2, 2012, http://www.InFact Canada.ca/nestle_boycott_product.htm.

9. Ali Mazrui, "A Clash of Cultures," Episode 8 of *The Africans: A Triple Heritage* (Boston: WETA; London: British Broadcasting Corporation, 1986), 58-min. videotape.

10. Organisation for Economic Co-operation and Development, "Final ODA data for 2011," accessed October 2, 2012, http://www.oecd.org/dataoecd/44 /13/50060310.pdf.

11. See, for example, Robert Calderisi, *The Trouble with Africa: Why Foreign Aid Isn't Working* (New York: Palgrave Macmillan, 2006); Jessica Cohen and William Easterly, *What Works in Development?: Thinking Big and Thinking Small* (Washington, DC: Brookings Institution, 2009); Paul Collier, *The Bottom Billion: Why the Poorest Countries Are Failing and What Can Be Done About It* (New York: Oxford University Press, 2007); William Easterly, *The White Man's Burden: Why the West's Efforts to Aid the Rest Have Done So Much Ill and So Little Good* (New York: Penguin, 2006); Dambisa Moyo and Niall Ferguson, *Dead Aid: Why Aid Is Not Working and How There Is a Better Way for Africa* (Vancouver, BC: Douglas & Mcintyre, 2010); and Jeffrey D. Sachs, *The End of Poverty: Economic Possibilities for Our Time* (New York: Penguin, 2005).

12. For an introductory discussion of women in African development efforts, see April A. Gordon, "Women and Development," in *Understanding Contemporary Africa*, eds. April A. Gordon and Donald L. Gordon, 5th ed. (Boulder, CO: Lynne Rienner, 2013), 305–333.

13. Linda McAvan and Fiona Hall, press statement, Practical Action (November 2006), accessed October 2, 2012, http://practicalaction.org/?id= pressrelease_mep112006.

14. Veronica Torrejón, "Moravians Confront AIDS as their Battle," *Morning Call* (Bethlehem, PA), July 26, 2007: 1, 8, accessed October 2, 2012, http://www .mcall.com/news/local/all-africamainstoryday4,0,7032269.story?page=1&coll=all _news_specials_util.

15. The Global Fund to Fight AIDS, Tuberculosis and Malaria, accessed October 2, 2012, http://www.theglobalfund.org.

16. The Clinton Foundation, accessed October 8, 2012, http://www.clinton foundation.org/buildingabetterworld/projects.php?initiative=CHAI; UNITAID, World Health Organization, accessed October 8, 2012, http://www.unitaid.eu; and Susan Dentzer, "Aids in Africa: Rwanda and Tanzania," *The NewsHour with Jim Lehrer*, Public Broadcasting Service, broadcast November 7, 2007, http://www.pbs.org/newshour/bb/africa/july-dec07/aids_11-07.html.

17. Benn Eifert and Alan Gelb, "Coping with Aid Volatility," *Finance and Development. A Quarterly Magazine of the IMF* (September 2005), accessed October 2, 2012, http://www.imf.org/external/pubs/ft/fandd/2005/09/eifert.htm.

18. DeLancey, "The Economies of Africa," 131–132.

19. Among the sources on participatory development is Stan Burkey's *People First: A Guide to Self-Reliant, Participatory Rural Development* (Atlantic Highlands, NJ: Zed Books, 1993); Karen Brock and Jethro Petit, eds., *Springs of Participation: Creating and Evolving Methods for Participatory Development* (Bourton-on-Dunsmore, UK: Practical Action, 2007); and Thomas Tufte and Paolo Mefalopulos, *Participatory Communication a Practical Guide* (Washington, DC: World Bank, 2009). Practitioners, who tend to see grassroots efforts as the only real solution to development, have written most of the works on participatory development. A large number of organizations are working to promote participatory development efforts. For example, InterAction—American Council for Voluntary International Action "is the largest coalition of U.S.-based international nongovernmental organizations (NGOs) focused on the world's poor and most vulnerable people" (InterAction website, accessed October 2, 2012, http://www.interaction.org). Also see the Institute for Food and Development Policy website, accessed October 2, 2012, http://www.foodfirst.org.

20. Ian Askew, *Community Participation in Family Planning* (Exeter, UK: University of Exeter, Institute of Population Studies, 1984), quoted in Burkey, *People First*, 205.

21. Mennonite Central Committee website, accessed October 17, 2012, http://www.mcc.org; Heifer International website, accessed October 17, 2012, http://www.heifer.org.

22. There are many books and articles describing and/or teaching social entrepreneurship. One of the best known is David Bornstein, *How to Change the World: Social Entrepreneurs and the Power of New Ideas* (New York: Oxford University Press, 2004).

23. Schwab Foundation for Social Entrepreneurship, news release, May 12, 2012, accessed October 9, 2012, http://www.schwabfound.org/pdf/schwabfound /seoy/SEOY2012_NewsRelease_Africa.pdf.

24. John A. Byrne, "Social Entrepreneurship: The Best Schools & Programs," *Poets and Quants* (2012), accessed October 9, 2012, http://poetsandquants.com /2010/08/13/social-entrepreneurship-the-best-schools-programs/.

25. United Press International, "U.S. Expands Secret War in Africa," September 24, 2012, accessed November 1, 2012, http://www.upi.com/Top_ News/Special/2012/09/24/US-expands-its-secret-war-in-Africa/UPI-76751348 504322/.

26. John B. Alexander, "Irregular Warfare on the Dark Continent," *Joint Special Operations University* (Hurlburt Field, FL: JSOU Press, May 2009), accessed July 7, 2012, http://www.globalsecurity.org/military/library/report/2009/0905_ jsou-report-09-5.pdf.

27. Andrea Cornwall and Rachel Jewkes, "What Is Participatory Research?" *Social Science Medicine* 41, no. 12 (1995): 1669.

28. Thierry G. Verhelst, *No Life Without Roots: Culture and Development*, trans. Bob Cumming (Atlantic Highlands, NJ: Zed Books, 1990), 62–63.

29. Ibid., 63.

30. Tatyana P. Soubbotina, *Beyond Economic Growth: Meeting the Challenges of Global Development* (Washington, DC: International Bank for Reconstruction and Development/World Bank, 2000). For more information, see "About This Book," accessed October 2, 2012, http://www.worldbank.org/depweb/beyond/global /about.html.

31. United Nations, Millennium Development Goals web page, accessed October 9, 2012, http://www.un.org/millenniumgoals. See also the United Nations "Millennium Declaration" web page, accessed October 9, 2012, http://www .un.org/millennium/declaration/ares552e.htm.

32. Pierre Pradervand, *Listening to Africa: Developing Africa from the Grassroots* (New York: Praeger, 1989), 204.

33. Information on many charities is available from the American Institute of Philanthropy website, accessed October 12, 2012, http://www.charitywatch.org, and from the Better Business Bureau Wise Giving Alliance website, accessed October 12, 2012, http://www.give.org/reports/index.asp. Both organizations provide guidelines for wise giving.

## Chapter 7: Cannibalism: No Accounting for Taste

1. Egerton O. Osunde, Josiah Tlou, and Neil L. Brown, "Persisting and Common Stereotypes in U.S. Students' Knowledge of Africa: A Study of Preservice Social Studies Teachers," *The Social Studies* 87, no. 3 (May–June 1996): 120.

2. Peter Forbath, *The River Congo* (New York: Harper and Row, 1977), 368.

3. David Levering Lewis, *The Race to Fashoda: European Colonialism and African Resistance in the Scramble for Africa* (New York: Weidenfeld and Nicolson, 1987), 32.

4. Ibid.

5. Caught in a snowstorm while crossing the Sierra Nevada in the winter of 1846–1847, a party of more than eighty migrants to California became stranded, and nearly half starved to death. Some who survived did so by eating the dead.

6. William W. Arens, *The Man-Eating Myth: Anthropology and Anthropophagy* (New York: Oxford University Press, 1979).

7. Philip Boucher, *Cannibal Encounters: Europeans and Island Caribs, 1492–1763* (Baltimore: Johns Hopkins University Press, 1992).

8. Marvin Harris, *Cannibals and Kings: The Origins of Cultures* (New York: Random House, 1977), 147–166.

9. Schweinfurth, *Heart of Africa*, 2: 92–93.

10. Schildkrout and Keim, *African Reflections*, 33–36.

11. Schweinfurth, *Heart of Africa*, 2: 55.

12. Bob Thaves, *Frank and Ernest*, Newspaper Enterprise Association, April 27, 1979.

13. Ibid., February 27, 1979.

## Chapter 8: Africans Live in Tribes, Don't They?

1. *Africa News* prepared a special issue in 1990 on the meaning of *tribe* in Africa. The Africa Policy Information Center also published a background paper on the meaning of the word. See Chris Lowe, "Tribe," *Africa Policy Information Center Background Paper*, no. 10 (New York: Africa Policy Information Center, 1997), accessed October 20, 2012, http://www.africafocus.org/docs08/ethn0801.php.

2. Barbara Miller, *Cultural Anthropology*, 4th ed. (New York: Pearson Education, 2007), 262–263. Many, though not all, introductory anthropology textbooks treat *tribe* in a similar way. Some avoid the term, and some warn students that it is a contested category. Frequently, anthropologists also specify that a tribe traces its ancestry to a single common ancestor. Sometimes, definitions include chiefdoms and tribes in a single category. Marshall Sahlins, for example, calls the chiefdom the "most developed expression" of the tribe. Marshall Sahlins, *Tribesmen* (Englewood Cliffs, NJ: Prentice-Hall, 1968), 20–21.

3. For a discussion of the tribal organization of ancient Israel, see Norman K. Gottwald, *The Tribes of Yahweh: A Sociology of the Religion of Liberated Israel, 1250–1050 BCE* (Maryknoll, NY: Orbis, 1979).

4. John Iliffe, *A Modern History of Tanganyika* (Cambridge: Cambridge University Press, 1979), 324.

5. Ibid., 331–337.

6. For examples, see ibid., 321–322, 326–327.

7. See, for example, Morton H. Fried, "On the Concepts of 'Tribe' and 'Tribal Society,'" *Transactions of the New York Academy of Sciences* 28, no. 4 (Fall 1966): 527–540; and chapters in June Helm, ed., *Essays on the Problem of Tribe* (Seattle: University of Washington Press and American Ethnological Society, 1968).

8. See, for example, Morton H. Fried, "The Myth of Tribe," *Natural History* (April 1975): 12–20.

9. See, for example, Aidan Southall, "The Illusion of Tribe," in *The Passing of Tribal Man in Africa*, ed. Peter Gutkind (Leiden, The Netherlands: E. J. Brill, 1970), 28–50; and Immanuel Wallerstein, "Ethnicity and National Integration in West Africa," *Cahiers d'Études Africaines* 1, no. 1 (1960): 129–139.

10. John Paden and Edward Soja, *The African Experience*, 2 vols. (Evanston, IL: Northwestern University Press, 1970).

11. For an overview of English-language perspectives on the idea of tribe in Africa, see Carola Lentz, "'Tribalism' and Ethnicity in Africa: A Review of Four Decades of Anglophone Research," *Cahiers des Sciences Humaines* 31, no. 2 (1995): 303–328.

12. Fried, "The Myth of Tribe," 14.

13. "First Nations" and "First Peoples" are increasingly popular alternatives to "Native Americans," presumably because the word *native* does not carry sufficient dignity or force.

14. See, for example, Julie Hollar, "'Tribal' Label Distorts African Conflicts," *FAIR. Fairness and Accuracy in Reporting* (May/June 2008), accessed October 20, 2012, http://www.fair.org/index.php?page=3409.

15. Anthony Appiah, "African Identities," in *Constructions Identitaires: Questionnements Théoriques et Études de Cas*, eds. Jean-Loup Amselle et al., *Actes du Célat* no. 6 (Quebec: Célat, 1992), 58.

## Chapter 9: Safari: Beyond Our Wildest Dreams

1. Children's Television Workshop, *Sesame Street*, broadcast by WLVT, Bethlehem, PA, September 3, 1998.

2. Jeff Cooper, *To Ride, Shoot Straight, and Speak the Truth* (Paulden, AZ: Gunsite Press, 1990), 310.

3. José Ortega y Gasset, *Meditations on Hunting*, trans. Howard B. Wescott (New York: Scribner, 1972; originally published, 1943).

4. Roosevelt, *African Game Trails*, ix.

5. Ibid., 20–23.

6. Marshall Everett, *Roosevelt's Thrilling Experiences in the Wilds of Africa Hunting Big Game* (Chicago: J. T. Moss, 1909), 60–61.

7. Bartle Bull, *Safari: A Chronicle of Adventure* (London: Penguin, 1992), 179–180. For another account of Roosevelt's safari and of the safari experience in general, see Kenneth M. Cameron, *Into Africa: The Story of the East African Safari* (London: Constable, 1990).

8. Roosevelt, *African Game Trails*, 288–289.

9. Ibid., 195–196, 257.

10. For an interesting discussion of Tarzan, see Marianna Torgovnick, *Gone Primitive: Savage Intellects, Modern Lives* (Chicago: University of Chicago Press, 1990), 42–72.

11. Bull, *Safari*, 281.

12. Ibid., 318.

13. Ibid., 322.

14. Ibid., 162.

15. Public Broadcasting Service, "South Africa," *Going Places*, original broadcast, May 18, 1998.

16. For a critique of the Western management perspective in wildlife conservation and research, see Jonathan S. Adams and Thomas O. McShane, *The Myth of Wild Africa: Conservation Without Illusion* (New York: W. W. Norton, 1992).

## Chapter 10: *Africa in Images*

1. I am especially grateful to Charles Guthrie for his *Images of Africa in the U.S.* (Gainesville: University of Florida, 1980), a slide show and teaching guide that includes some of the images used here.

2. Josiah Clark Nott and G. R. Gliddon, *Indigenous Races of the Earth* (Philadelphia: Lippincott, 1868). This image is reproduced in Stephen Jay Gould, *The Mismeasure of Man* (New York: W.W. Norton, 1996), 65.

3. Ibid., 65.

4. James W. Buel, *Heroes of the Dark Continent and How Stanley Found Emin Pasha; A Complete History of All the Great Explorations and Discoveries in Africa from the Earliest Ages to the Present Time, Including a Full, Authentic and Thrilling Account of Stanley's Famous Relief of Emin Pasha. . . .* (Guelph, Ont.: J.W. Lyon, 1890), 207. Available at http://ebooks.library.ualberta.ca/local/cihm_32563 (accessed July 15, 2012).

5. Henry Morton Stanley, *How I Found Livingstone: Travels, Adventures and Discoveries in Central Africa* (New York: Scribner, Armstrong, 1872; New York: Arno Press, 1970), 85.

6. Hergé, *The Adventures of Tintin, Reporter for "Le Petit Vingtième" in the Congo*, Trans. Leslie Lonsdale-Cooper and Michael Turner (London: Casterman, 1991), unpaginated.

7. Pierre Assouline, *Hergé: The Man Who Created Tintin*, Trans. Charles Ruas (New York and Oxford: Oxford University Press, 2009), 27–29.

8. Vernon Quinn, *Picture Map Geography of Africa*, revised edition, Illus. Charles E. Pont (New York: Lippincott, 1964 [4th printing]), 79.

9. Ibid., 77–78.

10. DC Comics, "Tarzan: Moon Beast," *DC Comics* 26, no. 225 (November 1973): cover.

11. Time Inc., "Africa. A Political Jungle," *Time* (June 5, 1978): cover.

12. Citicorp, "Lose Citicorp Travelers Checks in Maputo . . . " *Newsweek* (June 30, 1980): 2.

13. Packard Bell, "Ankle-biting Pygmies," *Parenting* (December 1996–January 1997): 246–247. Packard Bell has had many owners and was owned by Israelis in 1996.

14. International Business Machines Corporation, "If Carlos Knows He's Half Irish, . . . " *National Geographic* (July 2007): v–vi.

15. National Geographic Society, The Genographic Project, accessed July 27, 2012, https://genographic.nationalgeographic.com/genographic/ibm.html.

16. Keep a Child Alive, "I am African," accessed October 30, 2007, http://www.keepachildalive.org/i_am_african/i_am_african.html. Paltrow and David Bowie were also featured in Keep a Child Alive ads in *Vanity Fair* in September 2007.

17. GAP Travel, "Experience Africa," *Vacations* (March/April 2007): 70. A reverse (right to left) version is available at http://www.gapadventures.com/destination_guide/overview/Africa (accessed October 30, 2007).

18. Marie Javins, *Stalking the Wild Dik-Dik: One Woman's Solo Misadventures Across Africa* (Emeryville, CA: Seal Press, 2006), 184.

19. ExxonMobil Corporation, "We Face Challenges All Over the World," *Vanity Fair* (July 2007): 121; *National Geographic* (July 2007): vii.

20. David J. Lynch, "Exxon Reports $10.5 Billion in Quarterly Profit," *USA Today* (October 26, 2006), accessed July 15, 2012, http://www.usatoday.com/money/companies/earnings/2006-10-26-exxonmobil_x.htm. Steven Mufson, "Exxon Mobil's Profit in 2007 Tops $40 Billion," *Washington Post* (February 2, 2008), accessed July 15, 2012, http://www.washingtonpost.com/wp-dyn/content/article/2007/02/01/AR2007020100714.html.

21. Daniel J. Weiss and Rebecca Leber, "2011 Was Very Good to ExxonMobil," Center for American Progress (January 31, 2012), accessed July 15, 2012, http://www.americanprogress.org/issues/2012/01/exxonmobil_profits.html.

22. ExxonMobil Corporation, Africa Health Initiative, accessed October 30, 2007, http://www.exxonmobil.com/Corporate/community_health_malaria_ahi .aspx.

23. CBS, "Kuwait of Africa?," *60 Minutes* (November 16, 2003).

24. Steve Coll, *Private Empire: ExxonMobil and American Power* (New York: Penguin Press HC, 2012).

25. Joyce Hackel, "ExxonMobil and Chad's Authoritarian Regime: An 'Unholy Bargain,'" Public Radio International, *The World* (June 5, 2012), accessed July 24, 2012, http://www.theworld.org/2012/06/exxonmobil-and-chads-authoritarian -regime-an-unholy-bargain/.

26. For example, see "The True Cost of Chevron: An Alternative Annual Report, May 2011." Available online at http://truecostofchevron.com/report.html (accessed August 3, 2012).

27. House of Adler, "Jewelry With a Global Flair," accessed September 21, 2012, http://www.verybest.com/ezine/78/503/0/adler—jewelry-with-a-global -flair/ and http://www.adler.ch/adler/history/background.php.

28. FINCA International, Village Banking Campaign "Elegant," *National Geographic* (July 2007): 157.

29. For more information on FINCA International's Village Banking Campaign, see http://www.finca.org/site/c.6fIGIXMFJnJ0H/b.6088437/k.3253 /Microfinance_and_Village_Banking.htm (accessed February 11, 2013). For a history of FINCA, see http:// www.finca.org and http://en.wikipedia.org/wiki /FINCA_International (accessed November 26, 2007).

## Chapter 11: Race and Culture: The Same and the Other

1. See, for example, Chris Stringer and Robin McKie, *African Exodus: The Origins of Modern Humanity* (New York: Henry Holt, 1997); and Chris Stringer and Peter Andrews, *The Complete World of Human Evolution* (London: Thames and Hudson, 2005).

2. For an extended discussion of the origins of race thinking in the Western world, see Hannaford, *Race*.

3. See, for example, Jared Diamond, "Race Without Color," *Discover* (November 1994): 83–89; and Stephen Jay Gould, "Why We Should Not Name Human Races: A Biological View," in *Ever Since Darwin: Reflections in Natural History* (New York: Norton, 1977), 231–236.

4. Paul Hoffman, "From the Editor: The Science of Race," *Discover* (November 1994): 4.

5. Desmond Morris, *The Naked Ape: A Zoologist's Study of the Human Animal* (New York: McGraw-Hill, 1967), 127–128. See also Morris's *The Human Animal: A Personal View of the Human Species* (New York: Crown, 1994).

6. Desmond Morris, *The Human Animal*, prod. Mike Beynon (Alexandria, VA: Time-Life Video, 1995), six 50-min. videotapes.

7. Stringer and McKie, *African Exodus*, 212.

8. Ibid.

9. Robin Dunbar, "The Chattering Classes: What Separates Us from the Animals," *The Times* (London), February 5, 1994, quoted in Stringer and McKie, *African Exodus*, 208–209.

## Chapter 12: From Imagination to Dialogue

1. Iode Mbunza, interview with author, Namagogole, Congo (Kinshasa), September 29, 1976.

2. Batsakpide-Mandeandroi, interview with author, Nyoala, Congo (Kinshasa), September 1, 1988.

3. Many authors discuss evolutionism and the way it creates both racial and cultural hierarchies. Readers who wish to pursue the subject should first consult Fabian's *Time and the Other*. Fabian discusses the evolutionary hierarchies of twentieth-century anthropologists in terms of concepts of time.

4. Bernard McGrane, *Beyond Anthropology: Society and the Other* (New York: Columbia University Press, 1989), 55–76, 129.

5. Ibid., 129.

6. Ibid.

7. The concept of *transversality* has been employed by a number of modern philosophers. Ideas about transversality and the responsibility of dialogue and care are explicated in the work of philosophers Hwa Yol Jung and Calvin O. Schrag. See Hwa Yol Jung, "Bakhtin's Dialogical Body Politics," in *Bakhtin and the Human Sciences: No Last Words*, eds. Michael Mayerfeld Bell and Michael Gardiner (Thousand Oaks, CA: Sage, 1998), 95–111; Hwa Yol Jung, "Review Essay: Calvin O. Schrag, *The Self After Postmodernity*," *Philosophy and Social Criticism* 24, no. 6 (1998): 133–140; Hwa Yol Jung, "The *Tao* of Transversality as a Global Approach to Truth: A Metacommentary on Calvin O. Schrag," *Man and the World* 28 (1995): 11–31; and Calvin O. Schrag, *The Resources of Rationality: A Response to the Postmodern Challenge* (Bloomington: Indiana University Press, 1992).

## *Appendix: Learning More*

1. Curtis A. Keim, "The Image of Africa," *Oxford Bibliographies in African History*, ed. Thomas Spear (New York: Oxford University Press, 2012). http://www.oxfordbibliographies.com/view/document/obo-9780199846733/obo-9780199846733-0026.xml?rskey=7xeSvV&result=17&q=. Access to this bibliography requires an Oxford Online Bibliography paid subscription, which many research university libraries have.

# Works Cited

Achebe, Chinua. "An Image of Africa: Racism in Conrad's *Heart of Darkness*." In Joseph Conrad, *Heart of Darkness*, edited by Paul B. Armstrong, 4th ed., 336–349. New York: W. W. Norton, 2006.

Adams, Jonathan S., and Thomas O. McShane. *The Myth of Wild Africa: Conservation Without Illusion.* New York: W. W. Norton, 1992.

Adas, Michael. *Machines as the Measure of Men: Science, Technology, and Ideologies of Western Dominance.* Ithaca, NY: Cornell University Press, 1989.

Adeleke, Tunde. *The Case Against Afrocentrism.* Jackson: University Press of Mississippi, 2009.

———. *UnAfrican Americans: Nineteenth-Century Black Nationalists and the Civilizing Mission.* Lexington: University Press of Kentucky, 1998.

Ake, Claude. *Democracy and Development in Africa.* Washington, DC: Brookings Institution, 1996.

Alexander, John B. "Irregular Warfare on the Dark Continent." JSOU Report 09-5, Joint Special Operations University, Hurlburt Field, FL, May 2009. http://www.globalsecurity.org/military/library/report/2009/0905_jsou-report-09-5.pdf.

Althen, Gary. *American Ways.* Yarmouth, ME: Intercultural Press, 2003.

American Institute of Philanthropy. Accessed November 7, 2007. http://www.charitywatch.org.

Appiah, Anthony. "African Identities." In *Constructions Identitaires: Questionnements Théoriques et Études de Cas*, edited by Bogumil Jewsiewicki and Jocelyn Létourneau, Actes du Célat, no. 6, 53–61. Quebec: Célat, 1992.

Arens, William W. *The Man-Eating Myth: Anthropology and Anthropophagy.* New York: Oxford University Press, 1979.

Aryeetey, Ernest, Shantayanan Devarajan, Ravi Kanbur, and Louis Kasekende, eds. *The Oxford Companion to the Economics of Africa.* New York: Oxford University Press, 2012.

Asante, Molefi Kete. *The Afrocentric Idea*. Philadelphia: Temple University Press, 1987.

———. *Afrocentricity: Toward an African Renaissance*. Boston: Polity Press, 2007.

Askew, Ian. *Community Participation in Family Planning*. Exeter, UK: University of Exeter, Institute of Population Studies, 1984.

Assouline, Pierre. *Hergé: The Man Who Created Tintin*. Translated by Charles Ruas. New York and Oxford: Oxford University Press, 2009.

Baby Milk Action. Accessed October 2, 2012. http://info.babymilkaction .org/nestlefree.

Batsakpide-Mandeandroi. Interview with author. Nyoala, Congo (Kinshasa), September 1, 1988.

BBC News. "IBM to Open Kenya Research Lab to Tackle Traffic Jams," August 14, 2012. http://www.bbc.co.uk/news/technology-19258863.

Beckwith, Carol, and Angela Fisher. "Royal Gold of the Asante Empire." *National Geographic* (October 1996): 36–47.

Bengtson, Timon. "Silly Games Christian's Play–Please Don't Send Me to Africa." Last updated February 16, 2012. http://pastortimonbengtson.wordpress .com/2012/02/16/silly-games-christians-play-please-dont-send-me-to-africa/.

Better Business Bureau Wise Giving Alliance. Accessed November 2, 2007. http://www.give.org/reports/index.asp.

Binkley, David A., and Patricia J. Darish. "'Enlightened But in Darkness': Interpretations of Kuba Art and Culture at the Turn of the Twentieth Century." In *The Scramble for Art in Central Africa*, edited by Enid Schildkrout and Curtis A. Keim, 37–62. Cambridge: Cambridge University Press, 1998.

Block, Bernard. "Romance and High Purpose: *The National Geographic*." *Wilson Library Bulletin* 68 (January 1994): 333–337.

Bornstein, David. *How to Change the World: Social Entrepreneurs and the Power of New Ideas*. New York: Oxford University Press, 2004.

Boucher, Philip. *Cannibal Encounters: Europeans and Island Caribs, 1492–1763*. Baltimore: Johns Hopkins University Press, 1992.

Brantlinger, Patrick. "Victorians and Africans: The Genealogy of the Myth of the Dark Continent." In *"Race," Writing, and Difference*, edited by Henry Louis Gates Jr., 185–222. Chicago: University of Chicago Press, 1985.

Brock, Karen, and Jethro Petit, eds. *Springs of Participation: Creating and Evolving Methods for Participatory Development*. Bourton-on-Dunsmore, UK: Practical Action, 2007.

Brown, Scott Wesley. "Please Don't Send Me to Africa." *Out of Africa*. Costa Mesa, CA, 1998. Lyrics at www.leoslyrics.com/listlyrics.php;jsessionid=ECCC22B0 75A6208BD9C6CB0B40EFD120?hid=%2Bsz%2BZUXiHpY%3D.

Brueggemann, Walter. *Genesis: A Bible Commentary for Teaching and Preaching*. Atlanta, GA: John Knox, 1982.

Buel, James W. *Heroes of the Dark Continent and How Stanley Found Emin Pasha; A Complete History of All the Great Explorations and Discoveries in Africa from the Earliest Ages to the Present Time, Including a Full, Authentic and Thrilling Account of Stanley's Famous Relief of Emin Pasha.* . . . Guelph, Ont.: J.W. Lyon, 1890. http://ebooks.library.ualberta.ca/local/cihm_32563.

Bull, Bartle. *Safari: A Chronicle of Adventure.* London: Penguin, 1992.

Burkey, Stan. *People First: A Guide to Self-Reliant, Participatory Rural Development.* Atlantic Highlands, NJ: Zed Books, 1993.

Burnham, Stanley. *America's Bimodal Crisis: Black Intelligence in White Society,* 3rd ed. Athens, GA: Foundation for Human Understanding, 1993.

Busch Gardens Tampa Bay. Accessed October 16, 2007. http://www.tradewindsresort.com/busch-gardens-tampa-bay.html.

Byrne, John A. "Social Entrepreneurship: The Best Schools & Programs." *Poets and Quants* (2012). http://poetsandquants.com/2010/08/13/social-entrepreneurship-the-best-schools-programs/.

Calderisi, Robert. *The Trouble with Africa: Why Foreign Aid Isn't Working.* New York: Palgrave Macmillan, 2006.

Cameron, Kenneth M. *Into Africa: The Story of the East African Safari.* London: Constable, 1990.

Caputo, Robert. "Zaire River." *National Geographic* (November 1990): 5–35.

Casati, Gaetano. *Ten Years in Equatoria and the Return with Emin Pasha.* 2 vols. London: Frederick Warne, 1891.

CBS. "Kuwait of Africa?" *60 Minutes.* Broadcast November 16, 2003.

Children's Television Workshop. *Sesame Street.* Broadcast by WLVT, Bethlehem, PA, September 3, 1998.

Chin, Walter. "Kenya: The Maasai." *Sports Illustrated* special issue (Winter 1998): 67–72, 74.

Citicorp. "Lose Citicorp Travelers Checks in Maputo. . . ." *Newsweek* (June 30, 1980): 2.

The Clinton Foundation. Accessed October 8, 2012. http://www.clintonfoundation.org/buildingabetterworld/projects.php?initiative=CHAI.

Cohen, Jessica, and William Easterly. *What Works in Development?: Thinking Big and Thinking Small.* Washington, DC: Brookings Institution, 2009.

Colker, David. "Cuddly Puppy Just a Figment of Scamster's Imagination." *Morning Call* (Allentown, PA), May 30, 2007.

Coll, Steve. *Private Empire: ExxonMobil and American Power.* New York: Penguin Press HC, 2012.

Collier, Paul. *The Bottom Billion: Why the Poorest Countries are Failing and What Can Be Done About It.* New York: Oxford University Press, 2007.

Conrad, Joseph. *Heart of Darkness.* Edited by Paul B. Armstrong, 4th ed. Norton Critical Editions. New York: W. W. Norton, 2006.

Cooper, Jeff. *To Ride, Shoot Straight, and Speak the Truth*. Paulden, AZ: Gunsite Press, 1990.

Cornwall, Andrea, and Rachel Jewkes. "What Is Participatory Research?" *Social Science Medicine* 41, no. 12 (1995): 1667–1676.

Curtin, Philip D. *The Image of Africa: British Ideas and Action, 1780–1850*. Madison: University of Wisconsin Press, 1964.

DC Comics. "Tarzan: Moon Beast." *DC Comics* 26, no. 225 (November 1973).

Degler, Carl N. *In Search of Human Nature: The Decline and Revival of Darwinism in American Social Thought*. New York: Oxford University Press, 1991.

DeLancey, Virginia. "The Economies of Africa." In *Understanding Contemporary Africa*, 5th ed., edited by April A. Gordon and Donald L. Gordon, 115–165. Boulder, CO: Lynne Rienner, 2013.

Dentzer, Susan. "Aids in Africa: Rwanda and Tanzania." *The NewsHour with Jim Lehrer*. Public Broadcasting Service, November 6, 2007. http://www.pbs.org/newshour/indepth_coverage/health/aids/africa/index.html.

Desai, Vandana, and Robert B. Potter. *The Companion to Development Studies*, 2nd ed. New York: Routledge, 2008.

Diamond, Jared. "Race Without Color." *Discover* (November 1994): 83–89.

Disney Animal Kingdom. Accessed October 8, 2012. http://www.disney-world-orlando.com/animal_kingdom.htm.

Dunbar, Robin. "The Chattering Classes: What Separates Us from the Animals." *The Times* (London), February 5, 1994.

Easterly, William. *The White Man's Burden: Why the West's Efforts to Aid the Rest Have Done So Much Ill and So Little Good*. New York: Penguin, 2006.

Eifert, Benn, and Alan Gelb. "Coping with Aid Volatility." *Finance and Development: A Quarterly Magazine of the IMF* (September 2005). http://www.imf.org/external/pubs/ft/fandd/2005/09/eifert.htm.

ElderTreks. "Voodoo and Spirits of West Africa." Small Group Exotic Adventures for Travelers 50 Plus. Accessed October 8, 2012. http://www.eldertreks.com/tour/ETTD000405.

Everett, Marshall. *Roosevelt's Thrilling Experiences in the Wilds of Africa Hunting Big Game*. Chicago: J. T. Moss, 1909.

ExxonMobil Corporation. Africa Health Initiative. Accessed October 30, 2007. http://www.exxonmobil.com/Corporate/community_health_malaria_ahi.aspx.

———. "We Face Challenges All Over the World." *National Geographic* (July 2007): vii.

———. "We Face Challenges All Over the World." *Vanity Fair* (July 2007): 121.

Eze, Emmanuel Chukwudi, ed. *Race and the Enlightenment: A Reader*. Oxford: Blackwell, 1997.

Fabian, Johannes. *Time and the Other: How Anthropology Makes Its Object*. New York: Columbia University Press, 1983.

FINCA International. Village Banking Campaign. "Elegant." *National Geographic* (July 2007): 157.

———. Village Banking Campaign. Accessed November 26, 2007. http://www.villagebanking.org/site/c.erKPI2PCIoE/b.2394109/k.BEA3Home.htm.

Forbath, Peter. *The River Congo.* New York: Harper and Row, 1977.

Franklin, John Hope. *From Slavery to Freedom: A History of Negro Americans,* 4th ed. New York: Alfred A. Knopf, 1974.

———. *George Washington Williams: A Biography.* Chicago: University of Chicago Press, 1985.

Freud, Sigmund. "The Savage's Dread of Incest." In *The Basic Writings of Sigmund Freud,* translated and edited, with an introduction, by Dr. A. A. Brill. New York: Modern Library, 1939.

Fried, Morton. "The Myth of Tribe." *Natural History* (April 1975): 12–20.

———. "On the Concepts of 'Tribe' and 'Tribal Society.'" *Transactions of the New York Academy of Sciences* 28, no. 4 (Fall 1966): 527–540.

Fyfe, Christopher. *A History of Sierra Leone.* London: Oxford University Press, 1962.

Gaines, Kevin K. *American Africans in Ghana: Black Expatriots and the Civil Rights Era.* Chapel Hill: University of North Carolina Press, 2006.

GAP Travel. "Experience Africa." *Vacations* (March–April 2007): 70.

———. "Experience Africa." Accessed October 30, 2007. http://www.gap adventures.com/destination_guide/overview/Africa.

The Global Fund to Fight AIDS, Tuberculosis and Malaria. Accessed October 2, 2012. http://www.theglobalfund.org.

Goodwin, Peter. "Johannesburg: City of Hope and Fear." *National Geographic* (April 2004): 58–77.

Gordon, April A. "Women and Development." In *Understanding Contemporary Africa,* 5th ed., edited by April A. Gordon and Donald L. Gordon, 305–333. Boulder, CO: Lynne Rienner, 2013.

Gordon, April A., and Donald L. Gordon, eds. *Understanding Contemporary Africa,* 5th ed. Boulder, CO: Lynne Rienner, 2013.

Gottwald, Norman K. *The Tribes of Yahweh: A Sociology of the Religion of Liberated Israel, 1250–1050 BCE.* Maryknoll, NY: Orbis, 1979.

Gould, Stephen Jay. *The Mismeasure of Man.* New York: W.W. Norton, 1996 (1981).

———. "Why We Should Not Name Human Races: A Biological View." *Ever Since Darwin: Reflections in Natural History.* New York: W. W. Norton, 1977.

Guthrie, Charles. *Images of Africa in the U.S.* Gainesville: University of Florida, 1980.

Hackel, Joyce. "ExxonMobil and Chad's Authoritarian Regime: An 'Unholy Bargain.'" Public Radio International. *The World*, June 5, 2012. http://www.theworld.org/2012/06/exxonmobil-and-chads-authoritarian-regime-an-unholy-bargain/.

Hannaford, Ivan. *Race: The History of an Idea in the West*. Washington, DC: Woodrow Wilson Center Press, 1996.

Harris, Eddy. *Native Stranger: A Black American's Journey into the Heart of Africa*. New York: Simon and Schuster, 1992.

Harris, Marvin. *Cannibals and Kings: The Origins of Cultures*. New York: Random House, 1977.

Heifer International. Accessed October 17, 2012. http://www.heifer.org.

Helm, June, ed. *Essays on the Problem of Tribe*. Seattle: University of Washington Press and American Ethnological Society, 1968.

Hergé. *The Adventures of Tintin, Reporter for "Le Petit Vingtième" in the Congo*. Translated by Leslie Lonsdale-Cooper and Michael Turner. London: Casterman, 1991.

Hickey, Dennis, and Kenneth C. Wylie. *An Enchanting Darkness: The American Vision of Africa in the Twentieth Century*. East Lansing: Michigan State University Press, 1993.

Hoffman, Paul. "From the Editor: The Science of Race." *Discover* (November 1994): 4.

Hollar, Julie. "'Tribal' Label Distorts African Conflicts." *FAIR. Fairness and Accuracy in Reporting* (May/June 2008). http://www.fair.org/index.php?page=3409.

Holman, Michael. "Africa: Celebrity and Salvation." *openDemocracy*, October 23, 2006. http://www.opendemocracy.net/democracy-africa_democracy/africa_celebrity_4024.jsp.

Hopkins, A. G. "Explorers' Tales: Stanley Presumes—Again." *Journal of Imperial & Commonwealth History* 36, no. 4 (December 2008): 669–684.

House of Adler, "Jewelry With a Global Flair." Accessed September 21, 2012. http://www.verybest.com/ezine/78/503/0/adler—jewelry-with-a-global-flair/ and http://www.adler.ch/adler/history/background.php.

Hunter-Gault, Charlayne. "Changing the Rules in Africa." OUP Blog. Posted July 20, 2006. http://blog.oup.com/2006/07/changing_the_ru.

———. *New News Out of Africa: Uncovering Africa's Renaissance*. New York: Oxford University Press, 2006.

Iliffe, John. *A Modern History of Tanganyika*. Cambridge: Cambridge University Press, 1979.

Institute for Food and Development Policy. Accessed September 17, 2007. http://www.foodfirst.org.

InterAction—American Council for Voluntary International Action. Accessed October 2, 2012. http://www.interaction.org/.

International Business Machines Corporation. "If Carlos Knows He's Half Irish . . . " *National Geographic* (July 2007): v–vi.

International Monetary Fund. Accessed October 2, 2012. http://imf.org.

Isaacs, Harold R. *The New World of Negro Americans.* New York: John Day, 1963.

Itandala, A Bulunda. "European Images of Africa from Earliest Times to the Eighteenth Century." In *Images of Africa: Stereotypes and Realities,* edited by Daniel M. Mengara, 67–74. Trenton, NJ: Africa World Press, 2001.

Iweala, Uzodinma. "Stop Trying to 'Save' Africa." *Washington Post,* July 15, 2007.

Jacobs, Sylvia M., ed. *Black Americans and the Missionary Movement in Africa.* Westport, CT: Greenwood Press, 1982.

Javins, Marie. *Stalking the Wild Dik-Dik: One Woman's Solo Misadventures Across Africa.* Emeryville, CA: Seal Press, 2006.

Jenkins, David. *Black Zion: Africa, Imagined and Real, as Seen by Today's Blacks.* New York: Harcourt Brace Jovanovich, 1975.

Jere-Malanda, Regina. "Profiting from Poverty: How Western Companies and Consultants Exploit Africa." *New African,* November 17, 2007.

Jung, Hwa Yol. "Bakhtin's Dialogical Body Politics." In *Bakhtin and the Human Sciences: No Last Words,* edited by Michael Mayerfeld Bell and Michael Gardiner, 95–111. Thousand Oaks, CA: Sage, 1998.

———. "Review Essay: Calvin O. Schrag, *The Self After Postmodernity.*" *Philosophy and Social Criticism* 24, no. 6 (1998): 133–140.

———. "The *Tao* of Transversality as a Global Approach to Truth: A Metacommentary on Calvin O. Schrag." *Man and the World* 28 (1995): 11–31.

Keep a Child Alive. "I am African." Accessed October 30, 2007. http://www.keepachildalive.org/i_am_african/i_am_african.html.

Keim, Curtis A. "*Artes Africanae*: The Western Discovery of 'Art' in Northeastern Congo." In *The Scramble for Art in Central Africa,* edited by Enid Schildkrout and Curtis A. Keim, 109–132. Cambridge: Cambridge University Press, 1998.

———. "The Image of Africa." In *Oxford Bibliographies in African History,* edited by Thomas Spear. New York: Oxford University Press, 2012. http://www.oxfordbibliographies.com/view/document/obo-9780199846733/obo-9780199846733-0026.xml?rskey=7xeSvV&result=17&q=.

Keita, Maghan. "Africa Backwards and Forwards: Interpreting Africa and Africans in Pre- and Post-Modern Space." Paper presented at the Sixth Annual African Studies Consortium Workshop, University of Pennsylvania, Philadelphia, October 2, 1998.

Kipling, Rudyard. "The White Man's Burden." In *Collected Verse,* 215–217. New York: Doubleday, 1907.

Krodel, Gerhard. *Acts.* Philadelphia: Fortress, 1981.

Kuserk, Frank. Interview with author. Bethlehem, PA, April 28, 1998.

Lentz, Carola. "'Tribalism' and Ethnicity in Africa: A Review of Four Decades of Anglophone Research." *Cahiers des Sciences Humaines* 31, no. 2 (1995): 303–328.

Lewis, David Levering. *The Race to Fashoda: European Colonialism and African Resistance in the Scramble for Africa.* New York: Weidenfeld and Nicolson, 1987.

Liebenow, J. Gus. *Liberia: The Evolution of Privilege.* Ithaca, NY: Cornell University Press, 1969.

Lowe, Chris. "Tribe." Africa Policy Information Center Background Paper No. 10. New York: Africa Policy Information Center, 1997. http://www.africafocus.org/docs08/ethn0801.php.

Lum, Gerardine. Interview with Christina Townsend. Bethlehem, PA, August 1, 2007.

Lynch, David J. "Exxon Reports $10.5 Billion in Quarterly Profit." *USA Today,* October 26, 2006. http://www.usatoday.com.

MacCann, Donnarae, and Olga Richard. "Through African Eyes: An Interview About Recent Picture Books with Yulisa Amadu Maddy." *Wilson Library Bulletin* (June 1995): 41–45, 141.

Maddy, Yulisa Amadu, and Donnarae MacCann. *Neo-Imperialism in Children's Literature about Africa: A Study of Contemporary Fiction.* London: Routledge, 2009.

Magee, Carol. *Africa in the American Imagination: Popular Culture, Racialized Identities, and African Visual Culture.* Jackson: University Press of Mississippi, 2012.

Magubane, Bernard Makhosezwe. *The Ties That Bind: African-American Consciousness of Africa.* Trenton, NJ: Africa World Press, 1987.

Mannoni, Octave. *Prospero and Caliban: The Psychology of Colonization.* London: Methuen, 1956.

Mathers, Kathryn. *Travel, Humanitarianism, and Becoming American in Africa.* New York: Palgrave Macmillan, 2010.

Mazrui, Ali. "A Clash of Cultures." *The Africans: A Triple Heritage.* Episode 8. Boston: WETA; London: British Broadcasting Corporation, 1986. 58-min. videotape.

Mbunza, Iode. Interview with author. Namagogole, Congo (Kinshasa), September 29, 1976.

McAvan, Linda, and Fiona Hall. Press statement. November 2006. http://practicalaction.org/?id=pressrelease_mep112006.

McGrane, Bernard. *Beyond Anthropology: Society and the Other.* New York: Columbia University Press, 1989.

Mennonite Central Committee. Accessed October 17, 2012. http://www.mcc.org.

Meredith, Martin. *The Fate of Africa: From the Hopes of Freedom to the Heart of Despair. A History of Fifty Years of Independence.* New York: PublicAffairs, 2005.

Meriwether, James. *Proudly We Can Be Africans: Black Americans and Africa, 1935–1961.* Chapel Hill: University of North Carolina Press, 2001.

Miller, Barbara. *Cultural Anthropology*, 4th ed. New York: Pearson Education, 2007.

Morgan, Lewis Henry. *Ancient Society.* New York: Henry Holt, 1878. Reprint, Cambridge, MA: Belknap Press of Harvard University Press, 1964.

Morris, Desmond. *The Human Animal: A Personal View of the Human Species.* New York: Crown, 1994.

———. *The Human Animal.* Produced by Mike Beynon. Alexandria, VA: Time-Life Video, 1995. Six 50-min. videotapes.

———. *The Naked Ape: A Zoologist's Study of the Human Animal.* New York: McGraw-Hill, 1967.

Moss, Todd J. *African Development. Making Sense of the Issues and Actors.* Boulder, CO: Lynne Rienner, 2007.

Mountain Travel Sobek. "Ghana, Togo, Benin: Golden Kingdoms of West Africa." Accessed October 3, 2007. http://www.mtsobek.com/mts/agk.

Moyo, Dambisa, and Niall Ferguson. *Dead Aid: Why Aid Is Not Working and How There Is a Better Way for Africa.* Vancouver, BC: Douglas & Mcintyre, 2010.

Mufson, Steven. "Exxon Mobil's Profit in 2007 Tops $40 Billion." *Washington Post,* February 2, 2008. http://www.washingtonpost.com/wp-dyn/content/article/2007/02/01/AR2007020100714.html.

Munck, Johannes. *The Acts of the Apostles.* Revised by William F. Albright and C. S. Mann. Garden City, NY: Doubleday, 1967.

Nash, Gary B., Charlotte Crabtree, and Ross E. Dunn. *History on Trial: Culture Wars and the Teaching of the Past.* New York: Alfred A. Knopf, 1998.

National Geographic Society. The Genographic Project. Accessed July 27, 2012. https://genographic.nationalgeographic.com/genographic/ibm.html.

Niane, Djibril Tamsir. *Sundiata: An Epic of Old Mali.* Translated by G. D. Pickett. London: Longman, 1965.

Njoh, Ambe. *Tradition, Culture and Development in Africa. Historical Lessons for Modern Development Planning.* Burlington, VT: Ashgate, 2006.

Nott, Josiah Clark, and G. R. Gliddon. *Indigenous Races of the Earth.* Philadelphia: Lippincott, 1868.

Nundy, Julian. "France Haunted by Rwanda Genocide." *Telegraph Group Limited,* April 14, 1998. http://www.hartford-hwp.com/archives/61/120.html.

O'Neill, Tom. "Curse of the Black Gold—Hope and Betrayal in the Niger Delta." *National Geographic* (May 2007): 88–117.

Onyango-Obbo, Charles. "Seeking Balance in a Continent Portrayed by Its Extremes." *Nieman Reports* (Fall 2004): 6–8.

Organisation for Economic Co-operation and Development. "Final ODA data for 2011." Accessed October 2, 2012. http://www.oecd.org/dataoecd/44/13/50060310.pdf .

Ortega y Gasset, José. *Meditations on Hunting.* Translated by Howard B. Wescott. New York: Scribner, 1972. Originally published, 1943.

Osunde, Egerton O., Josiah Tlou, and Neil L. Brown. "Persisting and Common Stereotypes in U.S. Students' Knowledge of Africa: A Study of Preservice Social Studies Teachers." *The Social Studies* 87, no. 3 (May–June 1996): 119–124.

Packard Bell. "Ankle-biting Pygmies." *Parenting* (December 1996–January 1997): 246–247.

Paden, John, and Edward Soja. *The African Experience.* 2 vols. Evanston, IL: Northwestern University Press, 1970.

Park, Mungo. *Travels into the Interior Districts of Africa.* New York: Hippocrene Books, 1983.

Perry, James. *Living Africa: A Village Experience.* Bloomington: Indiana University Television, 1983. 35-min. videotape.

"Please Don't Make Me Go to Africa." Accessed October 3, 2007. http://prayersofateenageboy.wordpress.com/2007/09/12/please-dont-make-me-go-to-africa.

Pradervand, Pierre. *Listening to Africa: Developing Africa from the Grassroots.* New York: Praeger, 1989.

Public Broadcasting Service. "South Africa." *Going Places.* Original broadcast, May 18, 1998.

Quinn, Vernon. *Picture Map Geography of Africa.* Revised Edition. Illustrated by Charles E. Pont. New York: Lippincott, 1964 (4th printing).

Richburg, Keith. *Out of America: A Black Man Confronts Africa.* New York: Basic Books, 1997.

Rink, Bradley (CIEE Study Center, Stellenbosch University). "From (Mis)Perceptions to Teachable Moments: Learning Opportunities On-site." Presentation made at NAFSA Annual Conference workshop "Rethinking Africa: (Mis)Perceptions and Realities," Minneapolis, MN, May 28, 2007.

Rivero, Tanya. "Sports Illustrated Swimsuit Issue Photo Shoot: Racy or Racist?" *ABC News* (February 17, 2013). Accessed February 20, 2013, http://abcnews.go.com/blogs/entertainment/2013/02/sports-illustrated-swimsuit-issue-photo-shoot-racy-or-racist/.

Roberts, David. "Mali's Dogon: Below the Cliff of Tombs." *National Geographic* (October 1990): 100–127.

Roberts, Sam. "More Africans Enter U.S. Than in Days of Slavery." *New York Times*, February 21, 2005.

Rondon, Marcela, and Elmasoeur Ashitey. "Ghana: Poultry and Products Brief Annual." *US Foreign Agricultural Service Gain Report*, October 7, 2011. http://gain.fas.usda.gov/Recent%20GAIN%20Publications/Poultry%20and%20Products%20Brief%20Annual_Accra_Ghana_10-7-2011.pdf.

Roosevelt, Theodore. *African Game Trails: An Account of the African Wanderings of an American Hunter-Naturalist*. New York: Syndicate Publishing Company, 1910.

Rothmyer, Karen. "Hiding the Real Africa: Why NGOs Prefer Bad News." *Columbia Journalism Review* 49, no. 6 (March–April 2011): 18–19.

Rouse, Sean. "Jungle Cruise Jokes." Accessed October 4, 2007. http://www.csua.berkeley.edu/~yoda/disneyland/jungle.htm.

Sachs, Jeffrey D. *The End of Poverty: Economic Possibilities for Our Time*. New York: Penguin, 2005.

Sahelian, Ray. *Natural Sex Boosters: Supplements that Enhance Stamina, Sensation, and Sexuality for Men and Women*. New York: Square One Publishers, 2004.

———. "Yohimbe: Experience the Orgiastic Mating Rituals of the African Bantu. Yohimbe Bark Information and Yohimbe Side Effects." Accessed July 19, 2012. http://www.raysahelian.com/yohimbe.html.

Sahlins, Marshall. *Tribesmen*. Englewood Cliffs, NJ: Prentice-Hall, 1968.

———. *The Use and Abuse of Biology: An Anthropological Critique of Sociobiology*. Ann Arbor: University of Michigan Press, 1976.

Schildkrout, Enid, and Curtis A. Keim. *African Reflections: Art from Northeastern Zaire*. Seattle: University of Washington Press, 1990.

Schildkrout, Enid, and Curtis A. Keim, eds. *The Scramble for Art in Central Africa*. Cambridge: Cambridge University Press, 1998.

Schrag, Calvin O. *The Resources of Rationality: A Response to the Postmodern Challenge*. Bloomington: Indiana University Press, 1992.

Schwab Foundation for Social Entrepreneurship. News release. May 12, 2012. http://www.schwabfound.org/pdf/schwabfound/seoy/SEOY2012_News Release_Africa.pdf.

Schweinfurth, Georg. *Artes Africanae: Illustrations and Descriptions of Productions of the Industrial Arts of Central African Tribes*. Leipzig: F. A. Brockhaus, 1875.

———. *The Heart of Africa: Three Years' Travels and Adventures in the Unexplored Regions of Central Africa from 1868 to 1871*. Vol. 2. Translated by Ellen E. Frewer. New York: Harper, 1874.

Scott, William R. *The Sons of Sheba's Race: African-Americans and the Italo-Ethiopian War, 1935–1941*. Bloomington: Indiana University Press, 1993.

Shea, Neil. "Africa's Last Frontier." *National Geographic* (March 2010): 96–123.

Shick, Tom W. *Behold the Promised Land: A History of Afro-American Settler Society in Nineteenth-Century Liberia.* Baltimore: Johns Hopkins University Press, 1977.

Snowden, Frank M., Jr. *Blacks in Antiquity: Ethiopians in the Greco-Roman Experience.* Cambridge, MA: Belknap, 1970.

Somé, Malidoma Patrice. "About Malidoma." Accessed August 12, 2012. http://malidoma.com/main/about.

———. *Of Water and the Spirit: Ritual, Magic, and Initiation in the Life of an African Shaman.* New York: Putnam, 1994.

———. "Rights of Passage: If Adolescence Is a Disease, Initiation Is a Cure." *Utne Reader* (July–August 1994), 67–68.

Soubbotina, Tatyana P. *Beyond Economic Growth: Meeting the Challenges of Global Development.* Washington, DC: International Bank for Reconstruction and Development/World Bank, 2000. http://www.worldbank.org/depweb /beyond/global/about.html.

Southall, Aidan. "The Illusion of Tribe." In *The Passing of Tribal Man in Africa,* edited by Peter Gutkind, 28–50. Leiden: E. J. Brill, 1970.

Soyinka, Wole. *The Open Sore of a Continent.* New York: Oxford University Press, 1996.

Stanley, Henry Morton. *How I Found Livingstone: Travels, Adventures and Discoveries in Central Africa.* New York: Scribner, Armstrong, 1872. Reprint, New York: Arno Press, 1970.

———. *Through the Dark Continent.* New York: Harper, 1878.

Stanton, William. *The Leopard's Spots: Scientific Attitudes Toward Race in America, 1815–1859.* Chicago: University of Chicago Press, 1960.

Steiner, Christopher. *African Art in Transit.* New York: Cambridge University Press, 1994.

Stewart, Dodai. "Sex and Stereotypes: *Sports Illustrated* Swimsuit Issue Goes to 7 Continents, Finds Exotic People to Use as Props," *Jezebel* (February 12, 2013). Accessed February 20, 2013, http://jezebel.com/5983737/sports -illustrated-swimsuit-issue-goes-to-7-continents-finds-exotic-people-to-use -as-props?post=57329185.

Stringer, Chris, and Peter Andrews. *The Complete World of Human Evolution.* London: Thames and Hudson, 2005.

Stringer, Chris, and Robin McKie. *African Exodus: The Origins of Modern Humanity.* New York: Henry Holt, 1997.

Survival International. "The Omo Valley Tribes." Accessed July 5, 2012. http://www.survivalinternational.org/tribes/omovalley.

Thaves, Bob. *Frank and Ernest.* Newspaper Enterprise Association, April 27, 1979.

Thomas, Lewis. "On the Uncertainty of Science." *Harvard Magazine,* September– October 1980.

Time, Inc. "Africa. A Political Jungle." *Time* (June 5, 1978): cover.

Torgovnick, Marianna. *Gone Primitive: Savage Intellects, Modern Lives*. Chicago: University of Chicago Press, 1990.

Torrejón, Veronica. "Moravians Confront AIDS as their Battle." *The Morning Call* (Bethlehem, PA), July 26, 2007. http://www.mcall.com/news/local/all -africamainstoryday4,0,7032269.story?page=1&coll=all_news_specials_util.

Tortora, Bob, and Magali Rheault. "Mobile Phone Access Varies Widely in Sub-Saharan Africa." *Gallup World* (September 16, 2011). http://www.gallup .com/poll/149519/mobile-phone-access-varies-widely-sub-saharan-africa.aspx.

The Travel Channel. "Bizarre Foods with Andrew Zimmern: Madagascar," Season 5, Episode 11 (2010). Broadcast June 18, 2012.

———. "Bizarre Foods with Andrew Zimmern: Madagascar." Accessed June 20, 2012. http://www.travelchannel.com/tv-shows/bizarre-foods/episodes /madagascar.

True Cost of Chevron. "The True Cost of Chevron: An Alternative Annual Report, May 2011." Accessed August 3, 2012. http://truecostofchevron .com/report.html.

Tufte, Thomas, and Paolo Mefalopulos. *Participatory Communication: A Practical Guide*. Washington, DC: World Bank, 2009.

United Nations. "Millennium Declaration." Accessed October 9, 2012. http:// www.un.org/millennium/declaration/ares552e.htm.

———. "Millennium Development Goals." Accessed October 9, 2012. http:// www.un.org/millenniumgoals.

United Nations Children's Fund (UNICEF). "Madagascar: Statistics." Accessed July 5, 2012. http://www.unicef.org/infobycountry/madagascar_statistics .html.

United Press International. "U.S. Expands Secret War in Africa," September 24, 2012. http://www.upi.com/Top_News/Special/2012/09/24/US-expands -its-secret-war-in-Africa/UPI-76751348504322/.

Uya, Okon Edet, ed. *Black Brotherhood: Afro-Americans and Africa*. Lexington, MA: Heath, 1971.

Verhelst, Thierry G. *No Life Without Roots: Culture and Development*. Translated by Bob Cumming. Atlantic Highlands, NJ: Zed Books, 1990.

von Rad, Gerhard. *Genesis: A Commentary*. Philadelphia: Westminster Press, 1959.

Wallerstein, Immanuel. "Ethnicity and National Integration in West Africa." *Cahiers d'Études Africaines* 1, no. 1 (1960): 129–139.

The Walt Disney Company. "Animal Kingdom Lodge." Accessed July 5, 2012. http://disneyworld.disney.go.com/resorts/animal-kingdom-lodge/.

Watson, Pete, and Mary Watson. *The Market Lady and the Mango Tree*. New York: Tambourine Books, 1994.

Weiss, Daniel J., and Rebecca Leber. "2011 Was Very Good to ExxonMobil." Center for American Progress, January 31, 2012. http://www.american progress.org/issues/2012/01/exxonmobil_profits.html.

Wende, Hamilton. "Brash and Brilliant." *National Geographic Traveler* (March 2005): S9.

Wiley, Marylee. "Africa in Social Studies Textbooks." *Social Education* 46 (November–December 1982).

Wolff, Leon. *Little Brown Brother: How the United States Purchased and Pacified the Philippine Islands at the Century's Turn.* Garden City, NY: Doubleday, 1961.

Woodson, Carter Godwin. *The Mis-education of the Negro.* Trenton, NJ: Africa World Press, 1998.

———. *The Negro in Our History*, 11th ed. Washington, DC: Associated Publishers, 1966.

World Bank. *Economic Growth in the 1990s: Learning from a Decade of Reform.* Washington, DC: World Bank, 2005.

World Bank. "GDP Growth in Sub-Saharan Africa is Back on Track." *Africa's Pulse* (April 2011). http://siteresources.worldbank.org/INTAFRICA/Resources/Africas -Pulse-brochure_Vol3.pdf.

Wright, Richard. *Black Power: A Record of Reactions in a Land of Pathos.* New York: Harper, 1954.

Yamauchi, Edwin M. *Africa and the Bible.* Grand Rapids, MI: Baker Academic, 2004.

Zekiros, Astair, with Marylee Wiley. *Africa in Social Studies Textbooks.* Bulletin no. 9550. Madison: Wisconsin Department of Public Instruction, 1978.

Ziegler, Dhyana, ed. *Molefi Kete Asante and Afrocentricity: In Praise and in Criticism.* Nashville, TN: James C. Winston, 1995.

# Index